Effective Strategies for Teaching Adults

Don F. Seaman
Texas A&M University

Robert A. Fellenz
Montana State University

Merrill Publishing Company
A Bell & Howell Information Company
Columbus Toronto London Melbourne

Published by Merrill Publishing Company
A Bell & Howell Information Company
Columbus, Ohio 43216

This book was set in Korinna and Helvetica.

Administrative Editor: David Faherty
Production Coordinator: Sharon Rudd
Art Coordinator: Gilda M. Edwards
Cover Designer: Brian Deep

Library of Congress Catalog Card Number: 88–63287
International Standard Book Number: 0-675-20632-4
Printed in the United States of America
1 2 3 4 5 6 7 8 9—92 91 90 89

PREFACE

Developing a book about teaching strategies in adult education is a formidable task. Many issues must be addressed, including "Who is the intended audience?", "What kind of classification scheme would be most useful?", and "How can we provide a useful book on a topic about which little research data exist?" Every book has its particular slant, or emphasis, and this one is no exception. We have developed our own perceptions of how to effectively teach adults based upon years of experience in a variety of classroom and nonclassroom teaching/training/facilitating activities. This is not intended to be *the* way to teach adults. The contents could be organized in a number of ways, additional content could be included, and certain concepts could be treated differently. These are an author's prerogative, and we hope the reader understands and appreciates that option.

Anyone writing a book on the teaching of adults faces several decisions. Perhaps the most important of these is from what stance should teaching be addressed? It is too complex to be examined from every possible perspective within one book. So, should it be examined from the viewpoint of the learner? This would demand a thorough examination of the ways in which adults learn most effectively in various teaching/learning interactions and require teacher actions to conform to research findings on adult learning. A second approach would be to examine the interaction from the viewpoint of the teacher. What must the teacher do to fulfill most ef-

fectively his or her role as leader of the instructional process? How is a teacher to begin an instructional series, relate to students, ask questions, grade assignments? This is somewhat different from the perspective of the programmer or manager of the instructional process. A book written from this third vantage point would emphasize curriculum development, program evaluation, and other administrative concerns.

However, there is still a fourth perspective that could be selected. The one we chose, that is, an examination of the strategies that are available for use in teaching adults. Such a perspective calls for a close analysis of a variety of strategies, an acknowledgment of their respective strengths and limitations, and some suggestions for their effective use in various situations. This is what we have attempted to do. We believe this book will be useful to those many individuals who are relatively new to teaching adults, and we feel that even those who have had much experience will find useful ideas and concepts herein.

We are grateful to many persons who helped in the development of this book. Dr. Gary Conti, University of Georgia, gave much assistance with the original proposal and in some early developmental activities. Pat de la Fuente, Yueh Quey Huang, and Jacque Denyer worked diligently with the organization and editing of this manuscript. We are also grateful to Rhonda Brinkmann and Peggy Sue Hyman for their patience and word processing skills.

In addition we would like to thank the following people for reviewing the manuscript: Gerrald W. Apps, University of Wisconsin–Madison; Bill Dowling, the Ohio State University; Phyllis Cunningham, Northern Illinois University; and Ron Cervero, University of Georgia–Athens.

Finally, we owe gratitude to two groups of people. First, we have drawn upon a number of writers whose materials span a period of about twenty-five years. Second, we are grateful to the various editors at Merrill Publishing Company for their patience and understanding in this longer-than-intended endeavor.

C O N T E N T S

INTRODUCTION

Karen Buckner fidgeted nervously in her seat as she anxiously awaited the end of the class session. "Will this class never end?" she asked herself. She had registered enthusiastically for this course, entitled "Effective Parenting Skills," hoping to learn some new ideas about raising her two young children. Her husband didn't mind keeping the kids for the two hours her class met one night each week. "Besides," she thought, "the kids need some time alone with their father, and the experience will be good for him." Karen reasoned that even if the teacher wasn't very good, she could always learn from the materials and the other students as she had in her previous class in "Family Budgeting." However, this was the fourth class of an eight-session course, and she had decided not to return, even though the course fee and her time would be lost.

What caused her to change her mind? How did enthusiasm change to boredom? Could it be the style of instruction? During each class, the instructor lectured virtually the entire time, leaving no chance for questions or interaction. While on the ten-minute break, there was little time to talk to the other class members, and the instructor seemed reluctant to mix with the students outside the classroom. A local high school teacher, Karen had the reputation of being a good instructor, but she couldn't seem to retain her interest in the course. "Maybe it's me," she thought. "Perhaps my expectations are too high." However, as she glanced around the room, she noticed more empty seats each week and wondered if there would be anyone left for the last class session. She also decided

that she would "think twice" before taking another adult education class. This was no different from high school.

Alvin Scott had a different kind of problem. He had decided to spend one night per week taking a class on group leadership. His wife had not been very positive about his being away from home another evening because his position as supervisor at a local industry often required him to work late. However, he had recently been appointed to chair a couple of committees in his service club, and he was also chairperson of a commission in the church. Therefore, he felt the need to improve his leadership skills, and this course appeared to be a good way to do it.

However, he was now very disappointed with what was happening during the class sessions. The teacher, or leader, as he called himself, spent most of the time conversing with the fourteen students about their opinions on how to lead a group. Whenever a student asked a question or expressed an opinion, the leader would poll other class members asking, "What do you think?" or "How do you feel about that?" Alvin was becoming discouraged and frustrated. After three weeks, he felt he had learned nothing. He directed these thoughts (silently) towards the leader:

I don't really care what I or the other class members think. I came to learn from you. What do some of the authorities on the subject have to say? What are some ways to get a new group started? How can I tell if the group is really making progress? Oh, heck! I'd be better off *staying home with my family and trying to read something on my own. If only I knew what to read! Whoever said adults could learn in these classes anyway? I'll never do this again!*

How many other Karens and Alvins are out there—individuals who have a need to learn, but who have been discouraged by a negative experience trying to acquire new knowledge? Adults need and want to learn. Research has shown that one out of every three adults was engaged in some kind of organized learning activity during the calendar year 1979 (Cross, 1982). There is no doubt that the number has increased over the past few years. What kinds of experiences will adult learners have? Will they be encouraged about future efforts to learn? What can be done to facilitate or promote a positive attitude toward learning by adults who are actively engaged in the learning process?

Some years ago, one of us (Seaman) was unexpectedly thrust into a situation of having to teach a group of adults preparing to take the General Educational Development (GED) examination. A few individuals in the group were superiors (military noncommissioned officers), and I definitely wanted to be successful in my teaching role! Never having taught adults before, I frantically searched for materials on how to approach the task. Few were available, and those that were described the process in such general terms that they were not at all helpful. Many years later, when I searched for the same kind of materials, the void still existed. Therefore, the following factors convinced us of the need for a practical text on teaching adults:

1. Over fifteen years of teaching graduate courses entitled "Methods of Teaching Adults" and finding few useful materials available

2. Years of experience in training professionals in various organizations about

how to teach effectively, again without satisfactory materials

3. An investigation of research concerning the teaching of adults that resulted in a publication illustrating the paucity of materials on the topic (Seaman, 1977)

An incident that contributed to the decision to develop this text occurred at a national adult education conference. After seeking information about available materials on teaching adults from colleagues and other professional adult educators, we were becoming discouraged when a colleague asked, "Why don't *you* write a good, useful text? I, for one, could surely use one if it were available." After receiving the same reaction from others at the conference, we deliberated and eventually decided to develop a practical book for teachers or learning facilitators in adult education.

Adults Are Different

"Different from whom?" you ask. "From those who are *not* adults," we reply. Much has been written about the unique characteristics of adults in learning situations, and we do not intend to renew such discussions. In describing an adult, we have selected the following definition as our guide in preparing this material:

> Adult: A person who has reached the maturity level where he or she has assumed responsibility for himself or herself and sometimes for others, and who typically is earning an income (Hiemstra, 1976, p. 15).

In learning situations, adults are definitely different from youth. As indicated in chapter 1, the teacher must be aware not only of the felt needs of the adult learner but must be able to use teaching strategies that will enable the adult to begin to meet those needs early in the instructional process. If not, there will be more and more people like Karen and Alvin.

Growth of Adult Education

The growth of adult education during the past twenty years has been phenomenal. One of the first meaningful documentations of the extent of adult education was the Johnstone and Rivera study (1965) sponsored by the National Opinion Research Center. Their findings indicated that one in every five adults in the U.S. was actively engaged in some kind of formal learning activity. Vocational and recreational topics were the most popular.

A more recent study of adult participation in learning was published by Cross, Valley, and associates in 1974. Their research shows that one in every three adults was actively participating in some form of adult education. U.S. Department of Education statistics indicate that in 1984 over 23 million people took part in more than 43 million adult education courses (U.S. Department of Education [U.S.D.E], 1986).

The research surveys mentioned were somewhat limited in scope because they accounted for adult participation in group, classroom, or other organized settings. A major research breakthrough occurred when Tough (1971) pointed out that much adult learning is self-directed, outside any formal group setting. "First, how many persons conduct at least one major learning effort during the year . . . ? The answer is probably 90%, though the range from one study to another is from 70% to 100%" (Tough, 1978a, p. 172).

This means the task of serving the needs of adult learners has grown immensely in recent years. Although a portion of the learning is self-directed, this does not diminish the fact that millions of adults seek knowledge in groups, whether in credential-seeking activities or in nonformal settings. In group-learning situations, a teacher, facilitator, or leader is needed. Increased competence for the individual seeking to provide effective learning experiences strengthens the chances that participants will be able to reach their goals or fulfill specific learning needs.

Available Literature

One of the earliest attempts to organize and synthesize information on teaching adults was *Methods in Adult Education,* by Morgan, Holmes, and Bundy (1960). They indicated that their purpose was to present fundamental principles and techniques for teaching adults in a useful way. However, the term *methods* was never clearly defined, and the content addressed mostly *types of meetings* in which adults participated for learning. In 1962, Verner published a book in which he described teaching activities as procedures and attempted to differentiate between *methods* and *techniques* in teaching adults.

The next year, Bergevin, Morris, and Smith (1963) published their handbook comparing the different participation patterns of adults in learning activities and emphasizing the influence of the physical structure on participation and the communication process. Morgan et al. (1960) updated their book with a second edition (1963) but still did not define or describe *method*. In 1967, Carpenter produced a revised and updated version of Verner's work, but he did not differentiate between methods and techniques. Another treatment of the topic by Snyder (1972) was primarily directed toward teaching in adult basic education where joint activities between teacher and learner were foremost.

A number of other publications have addressed, in one way or another, the problems involved in teaching adults. In 1972, Klevins produced an edited handbook for practitioners. Since approximately forty different people were involved in writing the book, the result was a series of general, helpful items of information. In addition, the Klevins book treated materials as well as methods. Two years later, the National Association for Public Continuing Adult Education (1974) published one of the more practical texts for teachers of adults, *You Can Be a Successful Teacher of Adults*. One article (Fellenz) offered useful suggestions for effective teaching in adult education. However, in all of these works, the assumption was that, in most cases, adults were learning in groups.

A few years later, I attempted to synthesize the research on effective techniques for teaching adults (Seaman, 1977). That publication is best summarized by the following statement from the "Synthesis" section: "The paucity of 'hard' research data on the subject of teaching techniques in adult education is somewhat frightening. . . . When relevant research studies were found, the quality of the experimental designs was difficult to evaluate" (Seaman, p. 31).

Other publications in adult education devote some space to teaching, methodology, techniques, or selected topics. Adult education handbooks by Knowles (1960) and Smith, Aker, and Kidd (1970) have chapters devoted to the topic, but they are general and do not offer anything new. During the late 1960s and early 1970s, books, handbooks, and monographs were produced by commercial publishers, state Department of Education personnel, staff members of special projects funded by the U.S. Office of Education, and similar entities. Most were directed toward adult basic education but usually included one or two chapters on teaching the disadvantaged or undereducated adult (Cass, N. D.; Friedman & Knight,

1970; Hensley, 1972; Mattran, 1976; Smith, E., 1970; Snyder, 1971; Ulmer, 1972). Although generalities pervaded the materials on teaching, when specifics were provided, they were often directed toward particular kinds of instruction, such as techniques for teaching reading, arithmetic, writing, or spelling. In most cases, even though the techniques were excellent for adult basic education, they were not always appropriate for adults in general.

Two more recent books about teaching adults were by Draves (1984), and Niemi and Gooler (1987). Draves included some of the major strategies in teaching adults in his discussion, but they were treated somewhat briefly and examples of their usefulness were omitted. However, his was one of the first attempts to synthesize the many strategies being used in adult education. Although the text by Niemi and Gooler focuses upon the use of technology and not upon separate teaching strategies, it does illustrate how technology can have an impact on various teaching/learning situations.

In essence, the materials available about teaching adults are, to a great extent, dated and too general in their approach. They describe how to teach specific learners, and their needs seem to be the main concern. As important as those needs are, they are not the only ones to be considered.

Conceptual Framework and Definitions

If any professional field has ever been plagued by developmental confusion, it is adult education. Recognized leaders often disagree about the major concepts and ideas important in the field, and two national associations compete to "speak" for the profession. This confusion is often compounded by a growing army of "instant" adult educators . . . who, as a result of participating in a workshop or one graduate class . . . now suddenly emerge as experts with most, if not all, the answers (Seaman, 1977, pp. 3–4).

This is still basically true, except that the two national associations have now merged into one. Although some clarity has evolved in the area of teaching adults, there is still confusion about words that describe the teaching process, such as *strategy, method, procedure, technique, device,* and related terms. Therefore, we have chosen the word *strategy* to define the process through which teaching/learning occurs. We used the following definition to guide us in the development of this book:

> Teaching Strategy: The activity through which the teacher or learning facilitator assists the adult student in acquiring new knowledge or skills. Of all the activities described in previous literature, the term *strategy* relates best to the term *technique* as described by Verner (1962). It is through specific strategies, selected by the facilitator, that the learner or participant becomes involved in the learning process. If the strategy is effective, the participant should be stimulated to continue learning in the future.

Much of the research in teaching adults indicates that *active participation by the learner* and *meaningfulness of the content* are two constant factors influencing the effectiveness of the teaching/learning process. Meaningfulness of the content is addressed primarily in chapter 1, which covers the topic from the general perspectives of learners, teachers, content, and situations. Chapter 2 shows how adults can be grouped for effective learning, that is, as individuals, in collaborative groups, or in institutionalized patterns. The ways adults are grouped greatly influences which teaching strategies are most effective. Specific teaching strategies and their effective uses are addressed in chapters 3, 4, and 5. The kinds of strategies used by the teacher greatly influence *how much* the learner can participate and, indirectly, the *quality* of that participation. The impact of these major concepts should never be underestimated by the individual who plans or develops adult learning group activities. Chapter 6 provides information on the reasons, purposes, and means for evaluating teaching. Positive approaches to evaluation are emphasized.

What This Book Discusses

This book discusses a variety of strategies for teaching adults in a way that a practitioner can utilize them effectively in adult learning situations. As one of the readers of the original manuscript indicated, the strength of this book is not in the presentation of *new* material, but in how the material is organized. All of the strategies discussed are divided into three categories that reflect how virtually all adult education is taught—presentation, interaction, and action. Short situational examples identify a variety of teaching/learning activities like those existing in the "real world." Some have come from our own experiences, others from our friends and colleagues.

All material is oriented toward practitioners, although graduate students (most of whom are also practitioners) and college professors should find much of this material useful. While there is not much "hard research" to build upon, these strategies have proven successful for many years and are used widely. Therefore, we have presented them in a unique format that we believe the reader will appreciate.

What This Book Does *Not* Discuss

Because there is sometimes confusion in discussing some of the more important concepts in education, for example, learning, education, teaching, facilitating, etc., we want the reader to understand what this book is about and what it is *not* about. This is a book about teaching adults. It is *not* about adult learning, participation in educational activities by adults, or community-based education. One of the readers who evaluated the original manuscript was critical because those topics had not been included and cited several references (all well written and published recently) that we should have incorporated into our work.

We decided not to follow that advice because:

1. Each of those topics, although related to teaching, must be treated separately as they have been in the past.

2. To incorporate every topic related to teaching adults would produce a book so voluminous nobody could afford to buy it or have the time to read it.

3. If those topics have already been previously covered, why repeat the same material?

Selected Factors Influencing How Adults Learn

Attempting to explain how adults engage in learning activities is a complex challenge. Adults themselves are not always certain how they prefer to learn. Cross (1982) indicated that, when asked, adults usually express a preference for one kind of learning situation but often select another when given the choice. She concluded that adults "are better at telling us what is than what might be" (p. 217). However, this difference may simply indicate that adults do not always want (prefer) what they need, and when a choice must be made, needs win out.

Research on the subject can also be confusing because of the categories used by different researchers in compiling their data. For example, different categories of learning used by Tough (1978) and Penland (1979) clearly indicate that the discrepancies between and among the findings of research studies dealing with how adults learn are often due to "differences in categorization"

(Cross, 1982, p. 191) developed and used by various authors.

We have, therefore, developed our own format to discuss this topic, based on four general categories: learners, teachers, organizations, and content. Each of these categories will be discussed within the context of the two major concepts found in most adult education publications in some form— needs and preferences (wants). As we indicated, these were also found to be important in the findings of Cross (1982). Figure 1.1 illustrates the relationship between the concepts and the categories. The remainder of this chapter discusses the influence of the relationships between the categories and concepts and how such relationships may influence the selection of strategies for teaching adults.

Learners and Teachers

One cannot discuss learning without considering the people involved and how their personal characteristics, that is, needs, background experiences, competencies, goals, learning styles, and attitudes, affect their learning. Virtually every book written about adult learning or teaching assigns high priority to learner traits and lists many reasons why adults seek learning (Carp, Peterson, & Roelfs, 1974; Knox, 1977; Tough, 1971). Therefore, the teacher or

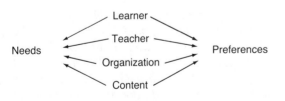

Figure 1.1
Factors Influencing the Selection of Teaching Strategies

learning facilitator in adult education "must understand both the characteristics and motivations of adult learners in order to select teaching techniques that suit the learner's needs" (Seaman, 1977, p. 3).

The Organization

In addition to the people, the situation in which learning activities occur can also influence how adults learn. Adult education can be seen as "practice or process without central organizational control yet organized within thousands of organizational structures, almost all of them autonomous" (McCullough, 1980, p. 161). Knowles (1980) was colorful in describing adult education organizations as "a band of wild horses, all going essentially the same direction but with many strays and much competition for leadership" (p. 160). With the organizational structure of the profession fragmented, such factors as public relations and recruitment, adequacy of facilities, attitudes of administrative staff toward adult education, and human and material resources available within a specific organization can determine whether the program succeeds or fails. Both adminstrators and teachers often cite organizational constraints as barriers to the growth and development of adult education.

The Content

The fourth concept, content, is often not given much importance in adult education literature. We feel this is a mistake. The content and the level of treatment dictate which teaching strategies will be most effective for the adult learner. For example, content can influence teaching style, classroom structure,

equipment, and furniture requirements. The level of treatment calls for a certain order in the presentation of material, practice, review, evaluation, and practice again during the learning activity. Because certain kinds of content demand the type of strategies that can be used effectively, content and its influence on teaching strategy must be included in any meaningful discussion of adult learning.

Needs

Much has been written about what the outcomes of adult education should be and how the teaching/learning process is affected by those outcomes. Although views differ, there seems to be universal agreement on one point: teaching (or for that matter, the entire educational program) should be based on the needs of the student or clientele. We disagree with that proposition as it is usually stated. This does not mean that we believe that adult education should *not* be based on the needs of the student. It definitely should. However, there are other important needs that have not been given sufficient attention. The first part of this chapter is devoted to a discussion of learners', teachers', situational, and content needs; their importance; and how they can affect the teaching of adults.

Needs of the Learner

Antonio Garcia quickened his pace as he neared the two-story brick building where he attended classes four nights a week. At first, he had attended only two nights per week, but his goal of obtaining a GED certificate had become even more important after the offer from Mr. Martin, his supervisor. "How life has changed! And the future looks even better," Tony mused. Only a few years ago, with little hope for the future, he had been a migrant, each year working his way across several states as the crops ripened. Although he was legally a U.S. citizen, having been born in south Texas, he had had little opportunity to go to any local school because his parents had always been on the move.

However, an uncle employed at a meat-packing plant in Kansas helped Tony get a job there and gave him a place to live. Although the work was hard, Tony adapted quickly. He politely declined when invited to attend an adult basic education class being taught on site in the evenings. He had better things to do than go to school at night. Being eighteen years old with money to spend, the only thing he wanted was a car!

Tony soon realized that he needed a license to drive a car, and he had to pass the driver's license examination in English. "Maybe those classes wouldn't be so bad after all," he thought.

They weren't bad; in fact, he enjoyed learning English, math, and the other subjects once he discovered he could learn. Since many of the other students were also employees in the plant, he found it easy to attend. Everyone seemed willing to help each other, and the teacher was really great. He treated everyone with courtesy and respect. What a change!

Yes, Tony recalled, from the driver's test to completing a job application and getting a job with the power company had been quite a jump. Now, after only two years, he had a chance to become an assistant supervisor—a promotion with better pay and increased responsibility. But the job required a high school diploma or its equivalent, and he hadn't kept up with his studying after changing jobs. Luckily, classes were being held at night in the local high school, but Mr. Martin had stated that he couldn't hold the job open for too long, and Tony didn't feel he was ready to pass the GED test and . . .

Does Tony have a need? You better believe it! And his need for education is not that different from that of millions of other adults engaged in all kinds of learning activities. Many people need a job or a better job. When millions of people became jobless in the United States in the early 1980s, many wanted a different kind of occupation, one that would be more recession-proof.

Regardless of what it may be, it is always the felt need or goal which motivates individuals to pursue their education in spite of the many obstacles that may loom in their way. As Udvari (1972) indicates, a learner's "test of reality is how immediate gratifications can satisfy his utilitarian need. The individual with special pressing needs cannot ignore his plight, or as in Alice in Wonderland, wish it away" (p. 113). Instead, people must do something about their situation if they expect to improve it, and they often see education or training as the means for achieving at least some of their goals. The national study conducted by Mezirow, Darkenwald, and Knox (1969) verifies this by concluding that "many of those who want to upgrade their jobs see the high school diploma equivalency as an essential vehicle for doing so. The experience of being unable to get a decent job without a diploma has led many to believe, with justification, that educational credentials are the main criteria in the competition for work" (p. 40).

Not all educational needs are related to credentials, however. Darkenwald and Merriam (1982) found that learning goals often reflect personal, religious, social, cultural, or escape needs, and that meeting new people or getting away from routine may be more important to some individuals than becoming better informed. In essence, as long as the learning one seeks is perceived as a movement toward meeting selected needs, the learning will be continued. When that perception is otherwise, the pursuit of *that* learning will cease.

The implications of this are many, but some of the more important are:

1. The teacher must know the learning goal(s) of the adult student, and they must be compatible with what the teacher intends as the learning outcomes for the student.

2. Adult learners must perceive that their learning activities will be helpful in attaining their desired goals. Whenever that perception does not exist, adults will stop participating. This means that the teacher must *continuously* provide learning activities that enable adults to move toward their learning goals even though the learners' perceptions of their needs sometimes change as they proceed through a learning activity. In other words, the *means* of instruction (strategies) must enable the learner to reach the *ends* of instruction (outcomes or desired learning).

3. Sometimes, the teacher or facilitator must be the one to help determine the learner's needs. This requires skills beyond the ability to design and implement learning programs and appropriate teaching strategies.

4. The adult education teacher must have considerable flexibility both in the use of various teaching strategies in different situations and in being able to accept that the learning goals of all individuals in the group will not be the same.

5. At times, the teacher may have to help students identify and clarify their learning needs. The student may have a goal, but not know how to reach it. As Fellenz (1974) indicates, "It is not

what the teacher believes is important, but what the adult student feels is relevant" (p. 96) that the teacher must deal with directly.

6. The perceived "pay-off" for the student's efforts should not remain too far in the future. The teacher may have to emphasize some intermediate goals to encourage adult students to keep trying, particularly when the need requires a long and sustained effort.

7. Obstacles to participation in learning activities emanate from family, job, personal, and community responsibilities. They must be considered and dealt with by the teacher or learning facilitator.

Needs of the Teacher

The auto mechanics class, scheduled one night a week for ten weeks, was in its eighth session. "Whew! Only two more weeks to go," thought the teacher, Josephine Owens, as she rested for a few minutes after checking the progress of the seven men and one woman who were working in pairs on the automobile. This had been a tougher assignment than she had anticipated, although she had been warned that teaching a "man's" subject to a class consisting mostly of men could be difficult.

Things had started out well enough. Fourteen people had registered for the class, including one husband-and-wife team. They were startled to discover that their teacher would be a woman, but when she told them her qualifications, including several years as a mechanic in a local car dealership, everyone seemed satisfied. They also realized that unless she taught the class, it would not be held, and they did want to learn some basic mechanical skills.

However, after a few weeks, some students began dropping out of the class. Although nothing was said directly, there were innuendos about the teacher being female. In addition, some of the others began trying to stay ahead of her in the class schedule each week, or they simply indicated that they only wanted to learn certain things from her then proceeded to go ahead on their own. When she offered to help with whatever they were doing, they never asked for assistance even though they sometimes needed it. Only four of those who were left actually seemed interested, but they couldn't always come to class because of other conflicts.

Jo was becoming discouraged. She had really wanted to do well and had planned a sequential schedule with enough flexibility to enable students to progress at their own rates of learning. She was competent, but that had not seemed to matter. "Why can't I be accepted for what I can do instead of what I am?" she asked nobody in particular. She also wondered why people enrolled in a class if they could not attend regularly. If this class was perceived as less than successful, what would become of her reputation as a teacher?

The main cause of Josephine's concerns is that the adult education teacher also has needs, and quite often those needs are neglected. If you disagree, think briefly about the literature in the field of adult education, or in most educational disciplines for that matter, and identify the times that the topic of teacher needs has been addressed. You won't run out of fingers while counting.

What kinds of needs could teachers possibly have? All kinds, the same as everyone else. Lorge (1947) identified categories of "Incentives for Adult Learning" (p. 25) in relation to why adults participate in educational programs as learners. But, some of these categories of needs also apply to why individuals teach. Among them:

1. *Popularity/Personal Prestige.* Almost everyone wants to be liked and respected by others. One way to achieve this is by teaching or leading others so they can reach their learning goals. The teacher may then achieve recognition as an authority on the subject being taught.

2. *Pride of Accomplishment.* The pride of having done something well, particularly when recognized by others, is difficult to exceed. Teachers enjoy being told they have taught well, and many feel this is their greatest reward. Enabling others to better their lives compensates for the time and effort devoted.

3. *Self-Confidence.* Everyone needs their self-confidence strengthened from time to time, and this can be achieved through successful teaching experiences. Josephine's self-confidence was shaken through her experiences, and that feeling may cause her to avoid involvement in any more adult education programs. "After all, who needs them?"

4. *Desire to Be Helpful.* Most people can remember how much a particularly good teacher helped them sometime in the past, and they would like a chance to do the same for somebody else.

5. *Expression of Personality.* Through teaching, we can share a part of ourselves with others, helping them to enjoy the things we enjoy and to appreciate other people regardless of how they perceive things.

6. *Self-Improvement.* A teacher can *always* learn. Adult education teachers benefit from the rich and varied experiences of their students.

7. *Financial Gain.* Although not high on the list of needs of most teachers, some receive financial gain for their efforts. This gets some teachers started in adult education but is usually not sufficient to keep them going. That is where dedication enters in. The fact that people need help and are willing to come to a class to get it is significant for many teachers.

Regardless of the teacher's role in the adult education process, their needs have serious implications that should be carefully considered:

1. The needs of adult education teachers should be taken into account by those who plan, direct, and implement adult education programs in any agency or organization.

2. Both administrators and teachers must be realistic about the possibility of meeting *all* of their needs in the teaching/learning situation. Unrealistic expectations can lead to unwarranted frustrations and disappointments.

3. Teachers should learn appropriate ways to communicate their needs to participants and administrators. Their needs are often omitted in the planning process because of the overconcern with and overemphasis on students' needs.

4. Needs of the teacher pervade all types of learning situations including group settings, tutorials, and facilitation of progress in learning centers.

5. Teachers also have barriers or problems that may interfere with their optimum performance in the adult learning situation. They need patience and understanding from students and administrators.

6. Different teachers have different leadership or teaching styles. Their styles are usually compatible with their perceptions of how learning occurs, and when these styles are unsuccessful, their own needs go unmet, their self-confidence is shaken, and they become frustrated as adult educators.

Needs of People Within an Organization

The class on genealogy had just concluded, and Henry Cargill was saying good night to the last of forty-seven students. After they had left, he picked up his materials and started home. On the way he went by the evening director's office and again said, "George, my class is simply too large. Can't we divide it and have two teachers? I cannot get any interaction with that many people in one group. It really cramps my style."

"I know, Henry, I know," replied George Wilson. "I'll see what I can do, but I can't make any promises." Henry left, and George thought to himself, "I know several classes are too large, but what can I do? I'm operating on a shoestring budget, barely making it, and cannot afford more teachers, at least not now." Two other teachers also felt like Henry, but so far, the others had not complained quite so much.

The continuing education program had begun three years before, and the president of the community college contributed a substantial part of the operating costs from his budget. The goal had been for the program to become self-sufficient in five years. Then came the institutional budget cuts nobody had expected, and the situation changed immediately. Now continuing education had to be entirely self-supporting. Although it had been growing each year, it wasn't ready for that. George was teaching two classes during the day for part of his salary just to keep the program going, and he needed more office staff, supplies, and other materials.

He had mentioned his dilemma to some of the teaching staff, including Henry, but they were not sympathetic. "Raise the fees," some had suggested. That was an alternative, but George knew that some of the participants, especially the retirees and others who had limited incomes, would be pinched a little tighter financially. They might stop enrolling, and the program would suffer. A bond election was being proposed which, if passed, would alleviate the present situation, but if people became upset because they could no longer attend classes, what would happen? If only folks would be patient and help him struggle to keep the program alive until things improved. "Our mission is to serve the community, so what else can I do?" he mused.

People often work in an agency or institution for years without ever knowing the institution's stated purpose or mission. However, every organization has its own needs to be fulfilled and these may often be reflected in the written goals, philosophies, or purposes that are available but seldom read. They can come from a variety of sources, but these are the most common:

1. *Authorized Legislation.* The purpose of an organization, if created by a legislative law or mandate, can usually be found in the wording of the act itself. Therefore, the organization needs to meet the requirements as stated or implied in that legislation. Political environment often affects the direction a program may take.

2. *Funding Source(s).* Although not all funding sources are equally demanding upon the organization's program, many are very demanding. People want certain returns for financial expenditures, whether they are legislators, philanthropic groups, bureaucrats, or taxpayers. The organization must fulfill those demands, especially if survival depends upon meeting them.

3. *Program Supporters.* These are the people who actively support the organization's educational program through participation. They may be students, teachers, volunteer workers, fund-raisers, or a combination of these or others. People who support an institution will stop doing so once that entity stops pursuing goals they think are important. Therefore, the community environment becomes crucial for program survival and growth, and the demands of supporters must be considered in educational program planning.

4. *Advisory Council.* One of the main functions of an advisory group is to help guide the organization toward appropriate goals. The organization's staff should listen to such advice and follow it as closely as possible. If this cannot be done, staff and council should discuss the issue and negotiate terms acceptable to both groups.

5. *Staff Goals.* The staff makes the institution function, and that function needs to reflect the ideas of the staff. While the programs offered should reflect the philosophy and purpose of the institution, the staff needs to agree that such purposes are important to them and to their own goals.

6. *External Factors*. Factors not directly associated with the educational program often influence the activities and perceptions of staff and participants. Enrollment can be affected by changes in the economy, new products requiring training for proper use (home computers), revised requirements for certification or licensing, or public perception of the purpose of educational programs or the organization's mission. The lack of qualified teachers may require undesirably large classes, which could affect the teaching/learning relationship negatively. Although these and other external factors may not disrupt the adult education program to any great extent, they must be anticipated and dealt with as effectively as possible by the program staff, especially the teacher.

7. *Administrative Philosophy*. Regardless of the stated philosophy of the organization, the administration can have a profound influence on the operation of the program. If the chief administrator feels comfortable with a particular style, that is the style which will be used. Scheduling, teaching assignments, facilities, and materials available for learning are all dependent on how the administration views program operations. Choices of teaching strategies may be limited because of administrative decisions.

Even though the needs of the target audience are the most important, administrative needs should not be underestimated or ignored by adult educators. People often do not understand why certain actions are taken or why selected programs are conducted instead of others. An understanding of administrative needs may provide the

answer. The fact that such needs exist and may influence decisions in adult education programs leads to the following implications:

1. Administrative needs could be perceived by teachers as being imposed from above. Programmers or administrators should seek to make clear to both staff and target clientele why those needs are important to the adult education program.

2. Even though we believe that an adult education program cannot survive unless the students' needs are met, the same can be said for administrative needs. Not only will the educational program fail, but the entire organization itself will fail if its needs are not met.

3. An agency or institution may decide not to offer an education program because it does not fit the administrative needs or goals. This may still be true even if the general public wants the program and if the probability of its success is somewhat high. However, flexibility in interpreting the institution's mission is a key to providing successful programs.

Content Needs

Tamisha Cook was driving home from the third session of her adult education class entitled "The Basics of a Good Home Garden." Vegetable gardening was her hobby. She was successful in her endeavors if judged by the food she put on the table and shared with friends and neighbors or by the ribbons and trophies she had won at fairs and similar exhibitions. However, she certainly would have to change her approach if she was to share her knowledge successfully with the adults in her class.

She was not a novice in adult education, having successfully taught evening courses for

GED students for four years. She taught the same subjects in high school and used similar teaching strategies for both groups, mostly lectures, group discussions, and question-answer periods near the end of each session.

However, the gardening classes simply weren't going smoothly with those same teaching strategies. The participants were constantly interrupting her "how-to" lectures with questions, seeking minute details from how to mix the plant food with the soil to how finely granulated the commercial fertilizer should be. Group discussions didn't work because the students did not possess sufficient knowledge to carry on a conversation. "I must change my tactics," she thought, "and find something that works better."

At the next class session, Tamisha began with a slide presentation that depicted sequential steps in preparing the soil for planting. She then displayed several pots, each containing soil of a different texture: clay, sand, and loam. She allowed the participants to add water to the containers and observe the effects with different soils. She then proceeded to ask group questions about what they had observed during the evening.

"What a difference," she mused as she drove home that evening. "Everyone, including me, came away tonight much more satisfied. Not only did the interest level rise, but some of the more enthusiastic students are going to bring in outlines of their proposed garden plots for the rest of us to critique and evaluate. It just illustrates that you can't teach everything the same way. I wish I had realized that sooner."

Tamisha is not alone in this discovery. Most of us who have struggled to develop effective learning experiences for adults have discovered the hard way that content needs must also be considered in adult education. Different kinds of content usually require different teaching strategies whether the learn-

ing activities are graduate credit courses, nonformal classes, or training workshops. Teachers who do not vary their strategies according to the content will fail to stimulate the participants sufficiently to achieve their learning goals.

Content needs often arise from the nature of the content itself. Regardless of whether the teacher or the learner feels a need for all of the content, a certain order of presentation is usually required for learning to occur. For example, learning basic concepts is always a prerequisite for learning more complicated materials whether in reading, mathematics, sports, or art. This means that content needs must be understood and considered equally with all other needs in adult education.

Although teachers should always be comfortable with whatever teaching strategies they use, comfort should not be an excuse for refusing to change approaches or to try something new. When content would be better taught with a strategy not used much in the past, the teacher should practice sufficiently to become comfortable in its use. One of the surest ways to guarantee failure in adult education is to make the participants nervous or ill at ease.

Several implications arise regarding content needs in adult learning activities:

1. Considering the variety of available teaching strategies, adult education teachers should constantly review their planning and preparation to ensure a high degree of compatibility between content needs and teaching techniques, particularly as the level of the content rises.

2. Teachers should be sensitive to the fact that as the content level changes, appropriate adjustments in teaching strategies are usually necessary.

3. Feedback from participants could be helpful in discovering the level at

which content should be treated and the need for a change in teaching strategies.

4. Trying something new occasionally may stimulate not only the students but also the teacher, particularly when the content is important for meeting a student's needs.

Needs: Summary

It would be incorrect to assume that content and the differing needs of learners, teachers, and organizations in adult education are unrelated. Despite their basic differences, elements of each overlap. For example, flexibility by students, teachers, and program administrators is crucial for effective learning activities. Although needs may change from time to time, and the same needs may vary in scope, intensity, and meaningfulness, all adults have learning needs. Helping each individual meet those needs is an important task for adult educators.

Preferences

Learners prefer to acquire certain kinds of knowledge or skills that require specific teaching strategies. Teachers prefer to use selected teaching strategies with which they feel most comfortable. The mission or purpose of the organization may not only influence the physical structure of the learning environment but may also determine which kinds of strategies are appropriate. Thus, preferences play a major role in the teaching/learning process in adult education.

Preferences of the Learner

The third session of the discussion series had just ended. Chiou Lee was delighted she had enrolled and was really looking forward to the

remaining five sessions. Not only was the content (nuclear energy) important and interesting, but the input from participants was fascinating. The format required each individual to read materials and react to a set of questions prepared for each weekly class session. The leader would encourage the group members to share their reactions about whatever aspect of nuclear energy was scheduled for discussion that evening. With a husband and two small children, Chiou had a definite concern about the future. This evening class, with the sharing of ideas from newscasts, periodicals, and research articles, was enlightening. "With all of this information, I can now make up my own mind," she thought. "I no longer will have to be dependent on others' opinions." She was also looking ahead and wondering if there were similar classes or seminars on other topics about which she had concerns, like water conservation and clean air.

The learning activity in which Chiou is participating reflects what Tough (1971) has written: "A person may look forward to a learning episode because it will help to satisfy his curiosity or puzzlement about something. In this case, he anticipates some psychological benefit from discovering part or all of the answer to a particular question. The psychological benefit may be the positive pleasure or satisfaction of finding the answer. Feelings of mystery, ignorance of the unknown, indecision, ambiguity, and the resulting doubt or unhappiness may be reduced" (p. 59). However, when individual preferences are not addressed, the adult learner can be "turned off" and may leave the learning experience with a negative attitude toward similar opportunities in the future.

Consider this incident:

Jacob Ciezobka was becoming more anxious and frustrated with each hour he spent in the community education class in "Practical Uses of the Home Computer." Jacob had initially enrolled in the class to learn how to use a personal computer to prepare his income tax returns. The course description indicated that students should already have some basic computer knowledge and that the course would focus on specific uses in the home. However, in the first two class meetings, it was evident that several students had virtually no knowledge about computers. Upon learning this, the teacher decided to spend a few class sessions reviewing basic computer concepts while working with more experienced students on their own special learning projects. This sounded acceptable to Jacob, but it hadn't worked. The teacher spent most of her time with the beginning students, and those who had enrolled for the "practical uses" got little attention.

Several "nonbeginners" soon began helping each other and decided they could do this in their own homes more easily than in the class. Jacob decided to join them. "I already know this stuff," he thought, "and I'll be more comfortable at home. I won't make this mistake again!"

Those who develop or facilitate learning activities for adults should definitely pay attention to the personal preferences of the students. As Hiemstra (1976) points out, "the concept of self, the wealth of experience, the variety of real problems, and the various reasons for learning that the adult brings to the educational setting must be reckoned with by the teacher" (p. 39).

The teacher's main task is to provide opportunities for the student to acquire the desired learning in a meaningful way. Chiou's teacher is using a strategy that encourages participation. When the adult is able to be an active part of the process, the learning becomes more meaningful. For example, a series of lectures with no opportunity for interaction or discussion could "turn off" adult learners who have serious questions about the material. Active participation enables

adults to compare their perceptions with those of others and either affirm what they already feel or know or change their ideas partially or completely.

Besides being able to participate actively in the learning process, adults also prefer practical learning. As Tough (1971) indicates, the reasons why adults engage in learning are many and varied, but in general they can be classified as follows:

1. To satisfy curiosity or puzzlement or to answer a question
2. To enjoy the content itself
3. To enjoy practicing a new skill
4. To enjoy the pleasure of learning
5. To complete unfinished learning
6. To enjoy associating with other learners who have similar learning interests
7. To benefit from a change in routine or from the escape that learning experiences provide (pp. 59–61)

The reasons adults participate were first investigated by Johnstone and Rivera (1965), who concluded that "It was quite clear from the results of our study that the major emphasis in adult learning is on the practical rather than the academic; on the applied rather than the theoretical; and on skills rather than on knowledge or information" (p. 3). As Cross (1982) has indicated, "nothing in the myriad of surveys since has changed that general conclusion" (p. 91). Therefore, the teacher must select strategies that enable adults to achieve preferences for learning that can be used immediately or in the near future. Only then will they be satisfied with the learning experience.

Preferences of the Teacher

As Sandra Taylor entered the Ace Computer store, she reflected about how far the learning group enrolled in her computer class had pro-

gressed. At first, the twelve students had been reluctant to participate in the discussions she tried to initiate. However, Sandra felt that adults always have experiences to contribute toward learning new knowledge or skills, and she persisted until they all began to interact comfortably. This afternoon, each individual would demonstrate and discuss some aspect of "learning by computers." Sandra believed the ultimate practical test was a demonstration of new learning, a hands-on experience that required active behavior by each individual. Past experiences indicated that students usually felt good about their demonstrations and often remarked that they were the best part of their class experiences. As usual, Sandra was looking forward to this particular afternoon in the computer store where the group always met. "I wonder what I'll learn today," she mused. "I always learn something new . . . "

There is usually more than one way to facilitate learning for adults. The teacher must know which strategies to choose and how to use them effectively. Although teachers should use different criteria for selecting one strategy over another, the old adage "We tend to teach the way we've been taught" does prevail. Those who have been lectured to in their learning experiences often use the lecture to teach because it may be the only strategy they know.

Another criterion for selecting a teaching strategy is teacher comfort; if the teacher is uncomfortable with a specific strategy, the learners will perceive this and usually be uncomfortable too. The main issue here may be how much control the teacher can share with the students. In the lecture, the teacher has almost total control, whereas in the discussion or seminar format, control of the situation is shared with the students.

In the previous example, Sandra knew exactly what she wanted the students to be able to do at the end of the learning experience. She selected teaching strategies to provide activities that previous students had indicated were most important in the overall learning experience. She had no hesitation in sharing control of the learning situation with the participants. In fact, she perceived that she could improve her own learning with the information presented by the adult learners in their demonstrations at the end of the class period. If someone suggested to Sandra that she change her teaching strategies, her reluctance to do so would be based upon (a) the learning goals she has established for the class, (b) the fact that she feels quite comfortable with the strategies she uses, and (c) the progress the students are making toward their learning goals.

Fellenz (1974) indicated that the effectiveness of the learning experiences provided by the teacher depends on the following circumstances:

1. The absence of threat to the learner
2. The meaningfulness of the experience to the learner
3. The supportive relationships evident to the learner
4. The amount of activity and participation by the learner
5. The degree to which responsibility for learning and change is accepted by the learner (p. 98)

The implications for learning preferences of students and teachers are these:

1. Even though a group of adults may have similar learning needs, individuals within the group may have different priorities for maintaining their interest and participation.

2. Teachers must use strategies with which they and the students are familiar and comfortable. This does not mean that they cannot try something new, but before doing so, teachers should practice and learn

how that new strategy can be effective.

3. When a teacher's expectations for student learning exceed those of the students themselves, the teacher must be careful to explain why such expectations are important and how they will benefit the learner.

Preferences of the Administration

Julio Valdez was somewhat chafed as he left the meeting of the curriculum committee of the State Technical Institute where he was head of the Department of Technology. Julio had proposed three new courses in technology, all of which were needed, he felt, to meet the institution's stated goal of training technicians to address present and future needs in the entire state. True, his proposal would require employing another staff member, and the equipment needed for instructional purposes would be costly. But, how do you teach the latest technical information without proper equipment and without personnel to use it for illustrating, demonstrating, stimulating, and providing "hands-on" experiences for the learners? Lectures, slides, discussions, and other activities may be effective in many classes, but they simply are not sufficient to teach technical skills for immediate employment. He had expected some resistance, but not to the magnitude that had occurred. "The other faculty simply do not understand or appreciate our teaching needs," he thought bitterly. "If we are to do what is expected of us by the people who support us, we must be able to teach the way the students can learn most effectively."

The mission of the organization can significantly influence how the content is taught. Julio's situation is an example of how the institution's purpose determines the content, which in turn requires the choice of certain kinds of strategies. Another example in-

volves organizations where the primary goal is to help people improve their speaking abilities. The emphasis is on speaking; the learning activities focus on listening and speaking skills such as knowing the various parts of speech, following an outline, practicing before a group, critiquing, and related activities. Instructors in such programs may use a variety of strategies, but they tend to select ones that will enable the participants to improve their speaking abilities most effectively. Strategies for improving writing ability may not be relevant beyond outlining or taking notes.

Organizations and institutions have different missions, and some may have more than one. When the mission is broad, such as, "To provide educational opportunities to help adult students meet their needs," the restrictions on selecting teaching strategies are usually determined by other factors, such as teacher preferences, content, and student background. However, when the mission is more specific, such as, "To enable adults to improve their skills in pulmonary resuscitation," the choice of strategies may be more limited. The teacher of adults must comprehend this and be able to work effectively within these imposed restrictions.

The mission of the organization provides the following implications for selecting teaching strategies:

1. The mission of the organization must be fully understood by both teacher and learner in order to appreciate the selected strategies. For learning to be most meaningful, the adult learner must perceive the relationship between students' needs, teaching strategies, and organizational mission.

2. Organizational mission can restrict strategies available for teachers, particularly if adequate resources are not provided as needed for instruction.

Students' Desired Level of Content

The fifth evening class session of "Essentials of Beekeeping" had ended, and David Owens was driving home. "Only one more class," he thought. "Although I've learned a lot, I still don't know exactly how to acquire and put into operation a beehive." The Owens's home was located on four acres of land, and David was trying to increase the financial return from those acres. The income from his horticultural pursuits was nice, not to mention the benefits for the family table, but a friend had recommended several hives of bees to provide additional income by selling the honey. Knowing nothing about bees, David read some bulletins from the county Cooperative Extension Service and then enrolled in a six-session course offered by the local extension agent. The agent used a number of resource people during the classes, including some successful honey producers, a bee specialist from the university, and a man who had raised and sold queen bees for many years before retiring. The resource people had significant knowledge to offer. David listened intently, took notes, and asked several questions. However, there seemed to be no continuity or sequence to the information presented. The county agent explained that he had to get the speakers whenever they were available, but David was simply having trouble putting all the pieces together. He wasn't certain whether to purchase the empty hives and then attempt to buy some queen bees, or whether to buy both together. When should he acquire an extractor: now, with the rest of the equipment, or later after the bees had settled? As he reviewed his class materials, he speculated that the answers to his questions may have been covered, but it certainly would have been more meaningful if each class session had built on the materials presented the previous week. "That way," he thought, "I could have developed some meaning from all

of this and decided if I really want to get into bees."

One of the earlier attempts to indicate how content can influence learning was by Bloom (1956), who wrote that cognitive learning occurs on six levels. A paraphrased description follows:

1. Knowledge: the ability to recall, or bring to mind, the appropriate material
2. Comprehension: the ability to make use of knowledge without relating it to other knowledge
3. Application: the ability to use knowledge, principles, and theories in practical situations
4. Analysis: the ability to break down knowledge into constituent parts to make organization of ideas clear
5. Synthesis: the ability to put together parts and elements into a unified organization or whole
6. Evaluation: the ability to judge the value of ideas or related entities using appropriate criteria

In some educational situations, the teacher and learner are operating on different levels, creating a barrier to learning. In the previous example, David needed to synthesize the information received from the various class meetings in order to make an important decision. However, the information was presented nonsequentially, in different segments, and at a comprehension level that did not enable David to achieve the synthesis he needed to assess and interrelate the knowledge of basic equipment, start-up and continuation costs, marketing strategies, labor requirements, and related information.

Therefore, not only the level, but the sequence of presentation were important to effective learning.

During the early class sessions on beekeeping, the county agent could have used resource persons to indicate what materials were needed to get started. Lectures, demonstrations, and illustrated talks could have been designed effectively. This might have been followed by field trips to see honey production operations of various sizes. Demonstrations of how to move bees, methods of reducing predators and disease, and proper procedures for taking honey would have enabled the learners to move their learning levels to the application, analysis, or even synthesis stage. The last classes could then have been devoted to interacting with someone who markets honey and learning the product quality requirements for selling the product. Practice in determining costs versus expected income under ideal or less-than-ideal conditions would also have been helpful. The learner could then evaluate the advantages of investing in this new venture using appropriate criteria and make the decision whether to invest in this enterprise.

The content of the learning material can therefore have a significant influence on the effectiveness of teaching strategies, particularly the level of learning in terms of the cognitive domain. Some content requires a step-by-step sequential presentation because each successive portion of material builds upon that previously presented. Other content may be presented without regard to sequence because a large amount of information must be comprehended before any further use can be made of it. Whatever the situation, the educator must be aware of the variety of teaching strategies that can be used and their relative effectiveness in different learning situations.

The level of content preferred is important to teaching strategies:

1. The teacher must know the level of content desired by the student if the latter's learning needs are to be satisfied. Providing only part of the learning preferred can only produce frustration or anger.

2. Various levels of learning require different teaching strategies. The teacher must, therefore, be able to use such strategies effectively whenever needed.

3. When uncertain, the teacher should provide activities that lead toward acquiring learning at the higher level of synthesis or evaluation. This should ensure that the learning is of benefit to the learner.

Preferences: Summary

Preferences of students and teachers, organizational mission, and level of content can influence adult learning. All learners may not fully understand their needs, but most come to the learning activity expecting to achieve a goal. The organizational mission may definitely determine what kinds of learning will be preferred by the students. Otherwise, adults would not attempt learning activities in that particular organizational setting. In addition, the learning content can be presented at different levels; the level desired by the student must be known and understood by the teacher. The teaching strategies selected must enable the adult learner to acquire knowledge at the desired level if the learning is to be meaningful, useful, and satisfactory.

In this chapter we have indicated that three general factors—people (learners and teachers), organization, and content—are unique but interdependent in the teaching/learning process.

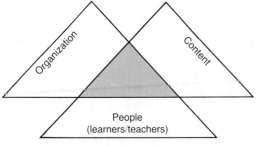

Figure 1.2
Interrelationship Among People,
Organization, and Content

The individual factors are important, but their interrelationships magnify their importance for adult learners, as indicated in Figure 1.2. The components should not be perceived as always having equal influence upon learning because it will vary with different situations. For example, administrative policies may be much more influential (restrictive) in one organization; in another, the adults' learning needs may dictate what is pursued regardless of preferences. Learning situations may also vary at different stages in a person's lifetime.

CHAPTER TWO

Ways to Organize Adult Learners

The first and frequently the most important decision to be made regarding strategies to use in teaching adults is a decision often not made by the instructional leader; it is surrendered to the institution or, more often, to tradition. This decision refers to the organization of the learners. Are they to be dealt with as individuals, brought together in small groups, or organized as a total community? Are they to be organized as human resources, as staff to be developed, or as self-directed individuals? Is priority to be given to specified objectives, to current applications, or to personal development? These, we would contend, are some of the most important decisions to be made as one begins to select effective strategies for teaching adults.

There is a tradition among adult educators to distinguish among methods, techniques, and devices. Methods are the ways of organizing people; for example, as individuals, in small clusters, or as a total group. Techniques refer to ways of organizing the interaction of learners and content. They range from lectures and panels to simulations and role playing. Devices are instruments such as audio or visual aids that support methods and techniques. This distinction, promoted by Verner as early as 1962, has been advocated, ignored, and misunderstood by educators. Our concern here is not with verbiage but with the important distinction between organizing learners and selecting teaching strategies.

The advantages of considering methods of organization can readily be identified by referring to the four elements upon which the instructional model of this book is based. Learners do differ in their abilities, interests, and preferred learning styles. Some will not only learn more effectively in small groups than they will in individual study but will also find more enjoyment (and thus persevere longer) in such learning efforts. Teachers likewise develop skills and preferences for certain methods. Some are excellent tutors but shy away from mass media approaches; some need specific content objectives while others are more concerned with the personal development of students. Emergency situations occasionally demand instruction not only in specific content but also through specific methodologies. For example, clientele needing training cannot always be brought together physically. Similarly, some organizations demand that all training endeavors be closely tied to organizational priorities, while others support broad educational approaches. Content objectives, too, call for different methods of organization. Entry-level objectives may be best met through an individualized, performance-based approach while mastery of a vocation may be best accomplished through small-group staff development practices. Haphazard choice of the method for organizing learners without considering advantages and disadvantages such as those mentioned above can make the instructional leader ineffective.

This chapter contains a brief examination of methods that have been used to organize learners according to traits of (a) learners, (b) teachers, (c) situations, and (d) content. Strategies traditionally used in structuring the interaction between teachers and learners are examined in depth.

Overview of Methods of Organization

Learning Approaches

People learn in three distinct organizational patterns, that is, as individuals, in collaborative groups, or in institutionalized patterns. R. M. Smith (1982) insists not only that each method is distinct but also that the choice of learning mode "obviously has implications for satisfaction and success in learning" (p. 90). When learning in the self-directed mode, the learner is both teacher and student. This can be frustrating, especially when the learner has not developed abilities in setting objectives, locating resources, and evaluating progress; yet, the advantages and satisfaction of learning in an individual mode have made it the most popular approach for adults (R. M. Smith, 1982; Tough, 1978). Learning through the collaborative mode has its own advantages. Members of the group provide support for one another in learning efforts. The development of interpersonal relationships, meaningful communication, and mutual motivation makes the small-group approach a secure and energizing environment for examining new ideas and attempting new behavior. However, the institutional mode is the approach most people visualize when they think of learning. We all have experienced schools and classes, lectures and credentialing. To a large extent, learning in

this way delegates the responsibility for planning activities, selecting resources, setting standards, and keeping records to the institution. Within such established parameters, learners are free to put their energy into learning.

Teaching Approaches

Teachers have used many ways to organize the individuals they teach. Much of our formal school system is based on homogeneous grouping according to age, interest, or achievement. However, in adult education, major attention has been given to the distinction between learners organized as individuals, as groups, or as a community. Houle (1972) listed eleven distinct groupings ranging from independent study to tutoring and various small groups to institutional formats and, finally, mass education. Boyd and Apps (1980) based their entire book on a model that identifies the individual, the group, and the community transactional modes. Such distinctions provide balance to the tremendous emphasis given to self-initiated and self-planned learning efforts by Tough (1978) and his followers. More attention will be given to Tough's approach later in this chapter.

Organizational Approaches

One broad approach for identifying ways in which learners are organized describes formal, informal, or nonformal organization. The term *formal* is applied to learning situations where an institution or educational agent has major decisional power over the objectives for learning and the methods by which those objectives are to be sought. Such approaches are usually thought of as a *school,* and in them the individual learner has little say regarding either the means or the ends. Nonformal approaches, on the other hand, give learners most of the decisional power over their learning objectives. A community learning center providing resources for the development of functional literacy skills is an example of a nonformal organizational approach. Informal approaches allow the learners to make most of the decisions about the means used to pursue the learning objectives, which have often been established by mutual agreement between the organizer and the learner.

From the perspective of individual organizations within a society and their philosophy of education, we could also distinguish among participants organized for (a) personal development, (b) staff development, and (c) organizational development. The first approach encourages members of the organization to use any learning opportunity available to grow as individuals. It presumes that their general development will ultimately be more beneficial than selected, specified training of personnel. At the opposite extreme are programs organized solely for development of the organization. Participants are viewed as resources to be molded through education into better instruments for the growth of the organization. Rigid control of objectives and strategies marks this approach. Between the two extremes is a broad array of staff development approaches. Learning programs are directed toward organizational needs, but they also take into consideration the needs and interests of the individual participants.

Content Approaches

Learner organization is affected in various ways by learning content. Some subjects have traditionally been taught through lectures, lab work, or on-the-job experience. Some skills are taught exclusively through formal programs while others are acquired informally. But the internal structuring of the content can also be important to learning.

For example, programs can be performance based, specialized for individual members (for example, leadership training), or content overviews or updates. The performance-based approach presumes that essential objectives can be identified and not only taught to all but taught so that the desired performance by participants is assured. Special group training usually attempts to instill higher-order skills in participants. It presumes that a combination of knowledge and problem-solving skills will enable the learner to transfer learned solutions to a variety of situations. On the other hand, the current issues approach identifies neither the essential elements of practice nor the specific skills needed to fill various roles. It looks at major trends or recent developments in the subject matter and presumes basic competence and special training on the part of learners.

Although all of the above methods can be useful when considering the important question of basic organization of the learning interaction, most attention has focused on the interaction of learners with the instructional agent. Houle (1972), Boyd and Apps (1980), and Brookfield (1984) based their books on a conceptual framework that distinguished between learners organized as individuals, as groups, and as community. The remainder of this chapter will examine specific methods for grouping individual learners into those three arrangements.

Organizing Learners as Individuals

Adults engage in many more learning efforts in an independent or individual mode than in group settings. This is not new; many early accounts of training programs for adults in our country were descriptions of apprenticeship programs. Directed individual study was a frequently used mode in the training of professionals, such as lawyers, and remains so today in much of higher education. Modern technology reemphasizes studying alone with improvements to programmed and computer-assisted instruction. But the work of Tough (1978) and his associates has made it clear that the overwhelming majority of adult-learning activities occur in a self-initiated, self-planned mode. In these cases the learner and the teacher are the same individual.

In examining the organization of learners in the individual mode, the following strategies will be considered: (a) self-directed study, (b) programmed or prepackaged instruction, (c) correspondence study, (d) apprenticeship or internship, and (e) tutoring or directed individual study. This will allow us to move from methods with a weak teacher/learner relationship to those with close relationships. The strengths and limitations of each method as well as suggestions for the effective use of the strategy with adults will be discussed.

Self-Directed Study

Often the terms *independent learning, self-directed learning,* and *self-teaching,* and sometimes even *individualized instruction* and *correspondence study,* are used in an interchangeable and confusing manner. In this section we use the term *self-directed study* to refer to adult-learning efforts that are initiated and directed by the individual. The resources used are frequently prepared by a professional educator or agency. However, the adult learner decides what resources will be used and how they will be used.

If the learner acts independently of the professional educator, why include this method in a book on teaching? There are two reasons. First, part of the educator's role is to teach students how to learn. If as many adults do engage in self-planned learning activities as Tough (1978) envisions, the impact

of teaching them how to learn could be tremendous. A second reason for considering this mode is that teachers frequently prepare learning materials for people with whom they will never interact personally. This is particularly true when teachers broadcast or disseminate their teaching efforts via radio, television, magazines or papers, computer-assisted instruction, or other mass media approaches. In this mode educators sometimes feel they are "teachers without learners," at least, without learners present.

Strengths and Limitations. Apparently 75 to 80 percent of all adult-learning projects are self-initiated and self-planned (Tough, 1978). The efficiency of learning in this individualized mode is obviously dependent upon the student's ability to direct the learning activities. The presumption that our days in school somehow automatically develop in us the ability to learn efficiently is being questioned more and more today. Efforts to teach adults how to learn are increasing, and results prove such efforts to be productive.

Many traditional principles of adult education support the notion of self-directed study. For example, the call to involve the student in planning and conducting adult-learning activities is met when the learner also becomes the teacher. Specific advantages of self-directed study include:

1. It contributes to what many maintain is the ultimate goal of all education, that is, the development of autonomous learners.

2. Successful direction of one's own learning often brings with it much satisfaction.

3. The learner frequently anticipates using the knowledge gained and plans the learning efforts to meet recognized needs.

4. The convenience and flexibility of choosing the time, place, and other incidentals of the learning experience make it more attractive.

A major concern with self-planned learning is the effectiveness of the average adult at planning learning activities. There are distinct limitations:

1. Directing one's own learning can be difficult and frustrating; moreover, one does not have the support of teacher or peer learners, which can easily lead to abandoning learning efforts.

2. Self-directed learners are seldom adept at evaluating learning experiences and thus rarely do it.

3. Many self-directed learners have little confidence in their learning outcomes (Brookfield, 1984).

Suggestions for Improvement. R. M. Smith (1982) identified four factors essential to learning how to learn:

1. There are the general understandings that provide the required positive attitude for learning. For example, mature learners need to know that adulthood is the prime-time for learning, that there are many opportunities for learning around us, and that we can take the responsibility for initiating and planning our own learning.

2. Basic literacy skills, especially listening and reading, are important learning tools.

3. Self-knowledge helps us recognize those things that serve as blocks to learning as well as the personal strengths and preferences we have for growth. These are crucial to our learning efforts.

4. Understanding the educational processes essential to each of the three modes of learning (self-directed, collaborative, and institutional) facilitates learning in each mode. In self-directed learning one needs to be able to plan learning activities, to set goals, to find and evaluate resources, to overcome blocks to learning, and to judge results. In the collaborative mode, group process and discussion skills are quite important while the institutional mode calls for knowing how to study, write reports, and do well on exams.

Another way of looking at self-initiated learning is by examining it according to the suggested steps for program development. Can the individual assess personal learning needs and set objectives that will satisfy those needs or desires? This examination of needs is the most important step in planning individual learning, but educators seldom offer independent learners help with this process. We have also found that adult learners use the most readily available resources rather than the most effective aids. This implies that many adults could use help in identifying and evaluating resources. Apps (1978) offers suggestions for sharpening study skills and suggests that adults start by rejecting attitudes that question their ability to learn effectively. Skills that can be improved by practice include reading, note taking, dealing with time constraints, expanding one's view to include the whole picture, and taking time to examine the theory upon which practice is based. Finally, a major aid in improving self-planned learning activities is developing evaluation skills. The adult who is serious about learning how to learn more efficiently should be encouraged to take time to evaluate learning efforts and should be helped in learning how to do so.

Adults can also be taught to develop their own learning contracts or plans. Traditionally we think of learning contracts as written agreements between a student and a teacher specifying learning objectives, resources to be consulted, activities to be completed, criteria by which to judge progress, and means of demonstrating and evaluating learning. Such contractual forms can be simplified to provide guidelines for self-planners that encourage them to proceed through the essential steps of a learning activity. When providing such aids, teachers should also include some guidance in their use; adults can be led to see such means as the ends of learning rather than as instruments to promote learning.

Communities or institutions engaged in educational brokering services can help learners trying to improve their self-teaching skills. The educational broker is often thought of as a provider of tutors or small-group learning activities for those interested in specific learning goals, but the idea of brokering can be expanded to include efforts to match resources with learners. Librarians do this when they make community members aware of resources, as do media specialists when they publicize effective learning instruments. Civic and social organizations occasionally promote or at least inform members of special opportunities for learning and growth. Observant adults can use all of these incidents as models for improving their own learning skills.

A final but important point is that all teachers of adults have many opportunities to help their students become more effective directors of their own learning. They themselves can model effective learning and discuss the process of learning as well as the content they are teaching. They can involve their students in a goal-setting process and guide them in selecting from the available resources. Teachers would also do well to encourage students to evaluate their learning efforts. A few words on how to deal with personal blocks to learning or how to improve learning efforts can have a lasting effect on adult learners and their attempts to be self-directed.

Prepackaged or Programmed Learning

Imagine studying auto mechanics while sitting in front of a TV monitor hooked to a computer and videodisc machine. The screen displays a close-up photo of a carburetor while the professional instructor gives a basic overview of its operation. As the instructor continues, an animated view of the workings of the carburetor is displayed. At its conclusion, you are invited to ask questions or to request a closer examination of any part of the function described. Once you feel in command of the process, the instructor invites you to turn to the model of the automobile engine next to you and to take the carburetor apart. The monitor provides audio and visual suggestions for proceeding and can be interrupted at any time for questions. When the task is completed, the instructor congratulates you on your progress and offers suggestions for learning events you might turn to next.

This packaged individualized instruction is not a view of learning in the future but is available today—or at least the technology for it is. Educators are being offered more and better vehicles for packaging instruction for adult learners every day. From the learner's point of view, such programmed instruction might be one aspect of self-directed study. However, in this instance the learner does not actually plan the learning. A teacher plans the learning even though there is no contact between the instructor and the learner.

Strengths and Limitations. The major advantage of prepackaged instruction is the unique opportunity it provides for teachers and learners to do their own thing at a time, place, and rate most convenient to each of them. The teacher can carefully prepare and present the instruction in the manner most appropriate for that content; the learner can choose which parts to review or how many times to review the material presented. Advantages of this approach are:

1. The time and effort necessary can be put into the preparation of the instructional material.

2. The learner is free to use the packaged material in the manner the learner judges to be most effective and most convenient.

3. The material can be presented through a variety of print, audio, and visual vehicles and in manners suited to a variety of learning styles.

4. The reinforcement of the learner as each step of the learning process is completed is given special attention.

5. Exact consistency of instruction is maintained through each repetition of the instructional process.

Nevertheless, prepackaged instruction has not always been popular with adult learners, who often label it as boring or irrelevant. The absence of a teacher for interaction and modification of learning activities is a basic problem. Other limitations include:

1. The programmer determines the learning goals for all learners.

2. Many forms of prepackaged instruction provide no flexibility in learning activities or procedures.

3. It is difficult for learners to raise ques-

tions or gain information relevant to their specific needs.

4. Relationships with teachers and peer learners are usually limited or nonexistent.

5. Good instructional packages are often expensive or difficult to locate.

6. Many forms of programmed instruction involve the use of supplemental equipment; learners may not be prepared to use or cope with machines when they break.

Suggestions for Improvement. The suggestions offered here will be directed toward those involved in preparing prepackaged learning activities for adults. The major question must be, How can you teach when you cannot tell who the learners will be?

One of the first decisions is the level at which the content will be presented. The assessment of the readiness level of the mature learner is a constant challenge in all forms of adult education, but it presents special problems when packaging learning for general use. Starting with the basics and proceeding step-by-step may be the logical procedure to follow, but it appeals to few adults. It is better to presume some experience with the content and build into the program ways of gaining remedial instruction for those who need it. Allowing adults some input into the manner and pace of proceeding through the lesson usually adds appeal to the package.

Allowing as much learner input and choice as possible is one way of keeping prepackaged instruction meaningful to a potential audience. This can be done in a variety of ways. For example, several learning strategies can be presented for reaching an objective. This allows learners to choose the instructional style that best fits their learning mode. Building variety into examples, illustrations, and applications increases the possibility of touching on topics to which the student can relate. Not all programmed instruction can be interrupted for questions or additional help, but providing some opportunity in a program makes it more meaningful.

Probably the most frequent excuse adults give for abandoning prepackaged instruction is that it is boring. This may mean that the content was not at their level or was not directed to their needs, but more frequently it indicates the designer has concentrated on what is being presented and has forgotten about what the adult learner is doing. Involvement of the learner is essential in programmed instruction.

Recent developments in computer software have reinforced the notion that materials prepared for adults are much better received when they are "user friendly." No one likes to feel threatened or stupid—by either a live instructor or a machine! A good orientation to the program, little reinforcements, progress indicators, and abundant reference or help sections are excellent ways of building in support for the concerned learner. Such additions should be included in a manner that does not interrupt the flow of the material.

Correspondence Study

Theoretically, correspondence study can be viewed as a compromise. It attempts to preserve the independent study of the learner and yet provide some personal relationship with a teacher. In delivering the prepared instructional materials to the student's home or office, it maintains many of the characteristics and advantages of independent and prepackaged study. By adding personalized feedback from the supervising "teacher" to the process, correspondence study also claims advantages of those methods that rely on the teacher/learner relationship to provide something extra to the learning experience.

Educators have not commonly accepted the correspondence approach as a proper vehicle for organizing adult learners. On the one hand, millions of adults enroll in correspondence courses each year, thus giving strong support to this method of providing highly structured learning activities together with at least limited availability of a resource person. Yet the correspondence industry has had to police its own ranks to prevent educational charlatans from discrediting the field by vigorous marketing of poorly designed and ineffective programs. Rumors have circulated regarding the high rate of adults who do not complete courses—often without comparison to the numbers that fail to complete other self-directed strategies.

Strengths and Limitations. Advancements in educational technology and increasing acceptance of individualized approaches to adult learning bode well for the future of correspondence study. Microcomputers and visual and audio communication add enormous potential for the improvement of this methodology. Some of its strengths include:

1. Programs can be organized and expertly prepared using modern technology and recent insight into the content for curriculum development.

2. This method has proven to be a fairly economical way of reaching large numbers of learners.

3. Correspondence study supports the independence of the adult learner while providing opportunities for positive support and individualized feedback from a professional educator.

4. The method has definite advantages to the program manager in the teaching,

testing, and administering of credits or credentials to individuals.

Whether the ineffectiveness of correspondence study is inherent in the methodology or caused by inadequate instructional design has not been determined. Perhaps the methodology is limited in that only certain types of learners—and teachers—seem to communicate well through written forms. In any event, specific limitations of correspondence study include:

1. Written communication is a limited and, for many adults, an unusual form of interpersonal communication.

2. Such study can move slowly on the part of the student or the teacher or through factors beyond the control of either.

3. The combination of incomplete control over the learning situation and lack of personal interaction with others can remove many of the motivating forces found in other methods.

4. Correspondence study tends to emphasize retention of factual information over application, synthesis, or evaluation of cognitive knowledge.

Suggestions for Improvement. Many of our suggestions for prepackaged learning are also applicable to correspondence study. The package that goes to the learner should be designed as expertly as feasible, but it should also be personalized. By adding some interaction between teacher and learner, the incorporation of traditionally advocated practices of adult education is achieved. For example, the student's needs and preferred learning style can be assessed. Applications of learning principles and processes can be directed to learner interests, and feedback can be given on learning process as well as content.

Certainly such interaction opens up potential forms of response to student questions. Attention to such traditional concerns of adult education could make correspondence study much more attractive.

Modern forms of communication add much to the traditional, all-print approach to correspondence study. The microcomputer, for example, makes it possible to package lessons in a variety of forms. It could also do much to personalize correspondence while reducing the time needed for the teacher's response. In fact, some courses could be completely automated and yet deliver to the student more specific feedback than formerly. Audio communication could be improved through increased use of tapes, phones, and slow-scan television for learners and content areas that benefit more from audio descriptions.

Feedback in correspondence lessons is particularly important for adult learners. Adults are used to having some control over their lives. Feedback that provides insightful information and points out options is more likely to be appreciated than the all-negative "Here's what you did wrong" style. It should also be relevant and appear to be personalized. To expect adults to struggle through reams of material to find information relevant to them is a clear invitation to learners to abandon correspondence study for some other method of learning.

Internship/Apprenticeship

The methodology involved in internships and apprenticeships is similar. Historically the term *intern* has been applied to one preparing for a profession; *apprentice,* to one attempting to master a craft. Both have long records of use in the training of adults in the United States and have even broader and more respectable use in other parts of the world. Because internship and apprenticeship are so similar in practice, they will be described here in common, and the two terms will be used interchangeably throughout this section.

The distinctive nature of this method of organizing individual learners is that instruction centers on the teacher as a model. Although many instruction techniques can be incorporated into the internship, learning depends primarily on close observation of the teacher-model, interaction and communication with that model, and opportunities to practice the newly developed skills under the supervision of the model or master. This close relationship to the teacher distinguishes the apprenticeship from the methods discussed earlier while the modeling nature of the relationship distinguishes it from the tutor or guide approach described later.

The modeling approach connotes a totally dependent relationship of the learner to the master. This could cause difficulties for both parties. Teachers, for example, may be younger and in some aspects less experienced or may have less prestigious titles than the learners. Training executives in computer usage is an area where such situations develop frequently today. The young master must accept a potentially uncomfortable relationship and the challenge to demonstrate ideal behavior in a specific area. The apprentice in turn must control feelings of resentment that may arise from the dependent relationship but do so without surrendering responsibility for learning.

Strengths and Limitations. Previously discussed methods of organizing learners as individuals contained only limited interaction between teacher and learner. In this approach the apprentice has a close working relationship with the teacher. The teacher or instructional leader is usually chosen for expertise in the skill under study. This arrangement has specific strengths:

1. The internship encourages attention to the complete learning cycle, that is, the assessment of student needs, setting of objectives, identification of various alternatives, selection and evaluation of at least one method of action, and practice of appropriate behaviors.

2. The practice orientation of this approach usually ensures the development of appropriate skills.

3. The modeling of the behavior of the master or professional usually results in the adoption and long-term retention of the learned skills.

The supervisor's inadequate understanding of the role of instructional leader often limits the effectiveness of the internship. Individuals chosen for this role may be selected for their content area expertise and have little or no training in education. Such an arrangement has limitations:

1. The apprenticeship can be limited in content to issues of the specific situation or to interests of the master.

2. The learner can be relegated to the role of an observer or performer of inconsequential tasks.

3. The intern can develop practical skills but be unable to transfer these skills to other situations because little attention was given to the theory upon which the skills were based.

4. The master/student role can threaten adults' self-concepts and weaken their sense of autonomy as learners.

Suggestions for Improvement. Most internships are effective learning strategies provided that adults are involved in tasks appropriate to their learning. Treating adults as partners rather than observers is a good way of accomplishing this. Learners are thus encouraged to bring their previous experience and knowledge to the situation and become actively involved in solving problems. Treating interns as partners leads to the formation of independent collaborators; treating them as observers leads to the development of dependent followers who need to keep calling on the master for guidance in practice.

Involving learners in the actual practice being studied promotes a sense of responsibility for the outcome of the project and confidence in their ability to carry out the task independently. Treating adult learners as adults is important at all levels of learning and practice.

This method is more effective when the leader is careful to attend to all aspects of the learning cycle. This means encouraging the learner to assess competencies and needs and to set appropriate learning objectives or priorities. It includes thinking through the various alternatives to action and evaluating possible outcomes. This decision-making process should include strategies for changing behavioral patterns when the situation calls for adaptation. The practice component should be extensive enough that the newly acquired skills become natural to the learner, not just imitations of the model.

Such an approach also enables learners to transfer learned skills to various situations. Thorough understanding and ability in basic competencies plus practice in a variety of similar situations are essential to such transfer. The teacher who not only models appropriate behavior but discusses with the learner the reasons for and the uncertainties about such action will be a better instructor.

It is much easier to learn from a model who is open, sharing, and human than from one who can only be observed from a distance.

Tutoring or Directed Individual Study

Tutoring is an individualized approach to instruction that emphasizes interaction between the teacher and learner. The history of its use is so broad and positive that Houle (1972) declared, "in some fashion or other it is universal to human experience. Most frequently it arises spontaneously as one person shows another how to do something, but it may be consciously fostered in institutions by the process which the English colloquially call 'sitting next to Nellie' " (p. 96). The institutionalized approach to tutoring is exemplified in the programs of English universities such as Oxford and Cambridge but has also become quite popular in many American schools with credit frequently assigned under a title such as Directed Individual Study. Recently it has been promoted as an effective way of involving volunteers in U.S. literacy efforts.

Much of the uniqueness—and the success—of the tutorial is because it matches the individual adult learner to a specific teacher who relates to the learner, as a total individual, while moving through a series of specially designed or selected learning experiences. This model has been extolled in the literature—from the Platonic image of the teacher (or lover) drawing the learner ever upward to new heights, to the Freirean insistence that true learning involves dialogue and learning on the part of both teacher and learner. However, it also fits well with modern principles of andragogy recommended by Knowles (1970). One-on-one teaching is an excellent way to direct instruction to the felt needs of the learner, to provide a supportive environment in which to experiment with new behavior, and to adapt teaching approaches to the background experience and readiness levels of the adult learner.

Strengths and Limitations. As noted earlier, tutoring combines organizing learners as individuals with establishing a close rapport between the teacher and learner. This is the ideal teaching/learning situation for most adults—provided that the instructional leader is competent both in the content area and in interpersonal relations. Specific advantages of directed individual study include:

1. The teaching can be easily adjusted to meet the learning needs and interests of the adult.

2. Physical facility requirements are usually minimal.

3. The immediate feedback that can be given to learning efforts and the personal support and encouragement that can be provided the learner are motivating factors for adults.

4. Alternatives can easily be provided for adults who do not respond readily to the more established or commonly used teaching methods or resources.

5. The individualized approach provides an excellent opportunity to teach not only content but also learning-how-to-learn skills.

6. At entry levels of skill development (for example, language learning), tutoring is frequently the best approach for supplying both the individualized attention and the strong support needed for adult learners who are uncertain of their ability to succeed.

Tutoring approaches do have some limitations. Most involve the tutor's lack of training or ability or the absence of peer learners; however, some are inherent in the process. Specific limitations include:

1. A good tutor may not be easy to find. Trained teachers tend to work in group-learning situations; volunteer tutors frequently have limited training in content or teaching strategies.

2. Tutoring can be very expensive.

3. Many tutors rely on verbal interaction with the learner; some learners make better progress using other modes of instruction.

4. Even adult learners can become dependent upon the tutor's guidance to the detriment of their self-direction as learners.

Suggestions for Improvement. Designing effective tutoring programs entails special consideration to the two major strengths of tutoring; namely, the supportive relationship between teacher and learner and the individualized approach to teaching. Houle (1972) identified four patterns most frequently followed in such directed study.

In the first model, the tutor is definitely the *teacher* proceeding through the process of preparing the student, presenting the material, evaluating the learning, and following up as needed. In the second model, the tutor follows more of a *programmer* role. The tutor specifies goals, assesses the learner's initial skills, presents and selects alternative learning strategies, monitors student progress, proceeds with instruction until predetermined levels of competence are reached, and uses feedback to improve the system.

A different pattern of tutoring uses the *coach* as a model. Here the student allows the tutor to provide guidance in new experiences, challenging and questioning assumptions, and ultimately encouraging self-directed behavior. A fourth is the *therapist* pattern, in which the facilitating tutor turns the learner's request for help back upon the learner, who is to find growth within the self. All models rely heavily either on the individualizing of instruction or on supportive interaction with the learner.

The individualized nature of tutoring can make adult learning more effective in a number of ways. For example, the tutor can discuss learning goals with the adult and probe for deeper needs and interests. The time saved in not covering unnecessary or irrelevant content can be devoted to a conscious, collaborative analysis of the learning process, that is, clarifying objectives, selecting resources, analyzing material, and evaluating progress. Careful balancing of traditional teacher roles, such as presenting information and recording progress, with process-oriented concerns, such as evaluation of resources or encouragement of deeper processing of information, makes tutoring a powerful strategy for promoting continued learning. Another example of tutoring effectiveness lies in teaching situations where the adult needs individualized assistance in learning. Literacy skills, complex psychomotor procedures, and advanced cognitive applications are often learned only through individualized guidance. Thus, taking full advantage of tutoring approaches demands customizing teaching according to learner needs.

The unique relationship of the tutor to the adult learner and the absence of other learners in the instructional transaction mean that the tutor's support must compensate for that supplied by both peer learners and the teacher in group learning situations. This implies that the tutor cannot be a mere presenter of information or a guide to resources. The tutor must also be a sharer of insights, an applier to practice, and a confidant of doubts and questions regarding the universal appropriateness of the information—for

these are some of the major inputs supplied by fellow learners.

In addition, the good tutor will realize that guiding the adult learner to ever greater independence as a learner is a major task. This can often be in direct opposition to a natural tendency to want to make the learners imitators or at least followers of self. In reality, learner self-directedness will be encouraged if the tutor responds primarily to learner needs rather than the needs of self or even the demands of the content. If this is done, the tutor becomes a true *educator* in the root meaning of the word, that is, one who draws out of the learner true knowledge or insight. The learner, then, is not passive but rather active in the dialogue that leads to wisdom. Houle (1972) quotes Anselm Strauss as concluding: "The best pupils, like the best children, get out from under the control and the vision of the best teachers, and the best teachers are pleased that this is so. At the outer limits of learning, the stages can no longer be as standardized as at the beginning; and the pupil discovers his own style, whether we are talking of religious conversion, musical composition, or anything else" (pp. 99–100).

Organizing Learners as Groups

In most adult-learning activities, students are organized into groups. In fact, we are so accustomed to grouping learners that we take this practice for granted and seldom consider organizing students as individuals or as a total community. Generally, it is the most economical approach because it allows one teacher to lead a group of students in their learning efforts. But it is not only the teacher who contributes to the effectiveness of the group-learning situation; the students interact, share, and enliven the learning environment. Thus, when the learners are experienced, skilled, and knowledgeable adults, the organization of individuals into groups can be a most productive strategy.

Dividing group approaches to learning into any logical order is difficult. Small-group approaches frequently differ dramatically from large-group strategies; yet, the degree of teacher directedness can make small groups function much the same as large groups. Some groups are learning groups only secondarily; they are organized primarily for other reasons. However, two general strategies for the interaction of the teacher and learners emerge. The teacher's role can emphasize either the promotion of action or the delivery of information. Based on this distinction, our treatment of the organization of learners as groups will begin with action methods, such as small action groups, clubs or groups with purposes beyond education, and workshops. It will then move to content-oriented approaches such as learning groups, courses, and presentations. Although not all strategies for organizing learning groups fit into these categories, this approach allows small- and large-group methods to be compared and contrasted.

Organizing Learners for Action

Adult learners are frequently organized in order to accomplish some objective besides learning. Many are problem-solving groups; they meet in order to study an issue and to uncover suitable options for resolving that issue. The mutual study and exchange of ideas is important, but the ultimate objective is to move the group to action. Some groups exist for other than educational purposes and only occasionally adopt learning activities to reach specific goals. Still others bring together members, sometimes in large numbers, to work on a task that involves learning. Once that task is accomplished, the group is disbanded. These types of learning

groups will be treated as (a) action groups, (b) clubs, and (c) workshops. We will list some of their strengths and limitations and offer suggestions for leading such groups.

Action Groups

Dozens of action groups organize in most every community. Churches, for example, form mission societies to study the problems of people in a certain area of the world and to decide if the local parish can or should do something to aid them. Communities bring together groups of citizens to study needed policy or to investigate civic improvements. Political parties form small cadres of followers to study certain issues and send them out to influence other potential voters. Recently, businesses have become intrigued with the idea of organizing their workers in *quality circles* or small groups that will study certain aspects of the business and offer suggestions for improvement to management.

Because such groups are designed for action, they are constantly involved in change and the effects of change. They incorporate some specific problem-solving strategy into their approach to learning. Usually this involves a fairly detailed study of the issue upon which they plan to take action. The more this study is open to all aspects of the problem and the more it involves all members (and even concerned nonmembers), the more effective the action is. Learners soon become adept not only at studying complex issues and selecting a plan of action but also at identifying effective strategies for putting their plan of action into effect. Because change takes time and is often accompanied by backlash or burnout, group members also develop methods of providing support to one another.

Action also gives rise to political and ethical questions. Some educators prefer not to be caught in the dilemma of choosing a stance on a controversial issue and believe that education can and should be neutral. Action groups are not for such teachers. But as Robinson (1980, p. 56) pointed out, the questions go well beyond simply debating whether learning should lead to action. Can an educator lead and yet remain neutral? Should public employees take a public stance on controversies? Can the group's values, or those of the teacher, not bias the learning activity? Or can an educator ethically confuse or disturb a group to the extent that members will be moved to seek change in their community?

Strengths and Limitations. The effectiveness of action groups is based on two factors: (a) the success of their strategy for bringing about change and (b) the enthusiasm they generate. Learning has a very special role to play in each of these factors. Unless the issue is well studied and unless the strategies for change are well planned, action groups are not likely to bring about the change they desire. Similarly, the enthusiasm of the group is largely caused by the mutual acknowledgment among members that they have learned to accomplish things and have grown as individuals. Specific strengths of action groups are:

1. The accomplishment of worthy tasks and the enthusiasm generated by success make the learning tasks appear more meaningful and worthwhile.
2. Problem-solving strategies and processes for implementing learning decisions are developed by the participants.
3. Group cohesiveness supplies support needed to face problems, to select among alternatives, and to act.
4. Group communication and interaction encourage growth in self-concept and ability to deal with change.

5. The broad experiences and diverse insights of a number of adult learners can be brought to bear on complex problems.

Although action groups can accomplish much, they do have limitations. Most are small or must be divided into subgroups if meaningful examination and discussion of an issue are to occur. Subdivision of groups implies the development and maintenance of some kind of structure to serve the total group, thus diverting much effort toward organization rather than instruction. Other limitations include:

1. The action goal can become more important than the learning and thus weaken both learning and action.
2. Controversy can readily erupt among members, and burnout can eliminate participants.
3. Actions proposed by groups can run counter to vested interests in the educational institution or in the community and lead to serious repercussions.

Suggestions for Effective Use. Two excellent models of the organization of learners into action groups are the League of Women Voters and the Christian Family Movement (CFM). Both groups have distinct approaches for recruiting concerned individuals into action groups and well-thought-out programs that help members to do intensive study of selected issues. However, the proposed outlines, the study materials, and the general support of the organization in no way take away the individual member's responsibility for discussion and action. Moreover, each group makes it clear that such study is to lead to action; CFM members are to influence parish, family, and community activities, while league members are to be a positive, nonpartisan influence in the political arena. A large part of the success of these groups can be attributed to the development of a national structure, which supports the small, local groups by providing educational materials, guidelines for operation, and support for action. Both have insisted on rigid ethical standards and have maintained a positive public image. Such factors are essential to effective action groups.

Action groups need some strategy that will lead members effectively through the learning and decision-making process to action. Some groups have established a series of steps to guide participants through a process. However, most problem-solving strategies will work well as long as there is someone to moderate the process. This is the major role of the educator: to make sure that the problem is defined, that potential options for the resolution of the problem are examined, that decisions are made, and that effective action is proposed. This simplified problem-solving process (sometimes described as "look, think, and do") is definitely a learning process that can be improved by a process-oriented adult educator. Unguided learners are likely to skip over the problem clarification or the alternative examination steps and end up with weak decisions or ineffective actions.

Much of the small action group's effectiveness derives from the group cohesiveness and interpersonal communication developed through this strategy. It is easier to promote closeness among participants grouped homogeneously. However, differences among group members can add insight and potential—provided there is the time and guidance necessary to form a unified group.

Leadership must arise from the group. The teacher is not central to the problem solving or to the action. The teacher's role is that of facilitator or moderator of the process. This involves helping the group form into a unified force that can study, decide, and act together and making certain the group does not neglect good learning procedures. The teacher who tries to dominate the group will either be ineffective or rejected.

Clubs

Some groups are organized for purposes other than learning but frequently make learning an important part of their agenda. Rather than organizing learners into groups, this approach accepts already organized groups and turns their members into learners. In this situation, the educator may be a group member asked to assume a teaching role. Occasionally an outside consultant is invited to provide the instruction. Because education is not the primary purpose, the learning experiences must be designed so that they appear to help the group meet its primary purpose. This allows an educator not only to help members learn about an issue relevant to them but also to impress upon participants the value of learning and the principles of the learning process.

Strengths and Limitations. In most organized groups, the time and energy necessary to recruit participants and form them into supportive groups have already been expended. This has distinct advantages:

1. They are naturally formed groups used to working together and thus can be ideal settings for group learning.

2. Some adults who are reluctant to return to school settings can be reached only through this or some similar manner.

3. Most such groups have endured over a considerable period of time and will continue to do so, thus providing a stable setting for continuing learning and action.

But, because learning is not considered their primary purpose, using them for educational purposes has limitations:

1. Members may be concerned about the primary purposes of the organization and consider learning activities as interfering with those goals.

2. The regulations, requirements, and rituals of clubs or other groups may have a negative impact on learning.

3. The physical facilities for meetings may not be conducive to teaching or learning.

Suggestions for Effective Use. The approach taken when working with formed groups will depend on the degree to which the educational leader is accepted as a member of the group. If the teacher is not a member of the group, it is useful to have a host or club member establish some basis for rapport with the group. This can include need assessments and introductions to group members prior to the meeting. Usually the teacher will not be able to take the role of a formal, professional educator. To do so is to invite the standard reaction of club members to teachers: showing respect but attributing little relevance to the immediate situation.

Establishing a learning climate is also important. This part of the organization's activities is to be for an acknowledged, educational purpose and not for the usual purposes of group meetings. If this is not done, it may be difficult to move members onward to any consideration of action suggested by the learning activity.

Workshops

A workshop brings people together in groups in order to develop specific competencies in the participants or to use the members' talents to resolve some common problem. In some educational circles it has become a broadly used term to identify any gathering for training purposes. However, we are using it here in its more restrictive sense. If it is indeed a workshop, some action is to result from the gathering.

Workshops differ from action groups in that they are usually designed to serve larger numbers of participants. They may be as short as one or two hours but can also last for several weeks. One type is the residential workshop in which participants are removed from familiar settings to live and learn together. Workshop planners choose a location that either possesses special teaching/learning resources or removes participants from their usual support systems in order to make change more likely. Gatherings in luxury hotels or resort areas may attract participants but may not lead to the type of action intended by the organizers.

Strengths and Limitations. A well-organized workshop offers many of the benefits of small action groups, but it provides them for many participants simultaneously. Careful planning and the use of a variety of resources are essential if this is to occur. Some specific strengths of the workshop are:

1. Workshops can serve large numbers of people at one time.

2. A variety of methods and techniques can be incorporated into one workshop.

3. The gathering of many people makes it feasible to employ a large number of resources to serve the workshop's objectives.

4. Workshops can benefit from the rich, varied backgrounds of adult participants and from the potential power of their pursuit of some course of action together.

5. This method has great potential for bringing about change in people and in the way they do things.

Poor workshops are often the result of poor planning, misunderstanding of the purpose of a workshop, or faulty implementation procedures. Workshops are action strategies; they bring participants together for the purpose of doing something. Gatherings labelled workshops but which treat participants as passive recipients or which are not adequately planned for efficient working together result in ineffective learning experiences. Some limitations are:

1. It is difficult for the leader to be aware of everything going on within small clusters of the larger group.

2. Depending on size and composition of the group, time limitations may not allow for development of group cohesiveness.

3. Good workshops usually call for extensive planning and many resources.

4. Workshop participants may be subject to a variety of differing problems and outside influences.

Suggestions for Effective Use. The key to successful workshops is the degree to which participants actually work together to accomplish some meaningful goal. Information sharing and processing is needed, of course, but there is a dominating need for discussion and group decision making and for consequent examination and planning of action strategies. The choice of facilities and the timing of the schedule should facilitate communication and interaction among group members and allow adequate time for planning and work sessions. Careful thought should be given beforehand to directions that the discussion and action might take so that

potentially useful resources will be on hand in case participants need them.

Good workshops consider the total person of the learner. Many would maintain that this goes beyond the need for food, comfortable surroundings, and occasional periods of relaxation. Vital components of the workshop would include building a spirit of enthusiasm among participants and instilling confidence in the adult learners so that they can accomplish the task before them. Music, song, art, humor, and the sharing of experiences can be useful for this.

The potential for bringing about lasting change in the behavior of participants can be increased in various ways. Eliminating support for "the old way" by physically removing participants from their fellow workers, family, friends, or whoever and whatever may support the former way of doing things is one such strategy. Including enthusiastic recent converts to the new approach among the participants promotes adoption of change. However, if such change is to carry over to "back home on the job," some form of networking among participants or building of long-lasting support groups is important. Sometimes repeated practice of the new behavior at the workshop can do this. However, skills and ideas not adopted as one's own or not supported in actual practice seldom endure.

Organizing Learners for Content Delivery

Many traditional models of teaching/learning interaction presume that the major purpose of the activity is dispensing information. These models are less popular in adult education because (a) adults tend to have a broad base of knowledge and experience, (b) they usually exert some self-direction in their learning activities, and (c) they generally choose learning activities directed to application or problem solving in preference to information- or content-centered procedures. Nevertheless, traditional strategies for the delivery of information remain the most frequently used methods for organizing adult learners—regardless of the purpose of the gathering. True, many of these approaches have been adjusted to include interaction among participants and to aim at higher levels of cognitive processing than simple knowledge sharing. However, we will examine them basically as vehicles for the delivery of content.

Strategies for organizing adult learners for the purpose of content delivery can be grouped as follows:

☐ Learning teams or small groups of information gatherers

☐ Courses or intermediate-sized groups

☐ Presentations or meetings of large groups

We realize that this is a somewhat arbitrary and restrictive use of terms, but in our minds it reflects traditional usage of these methods.

Learning Teams

The use of the small group as a setting for content delivery is not as popular as the use of such groups for planning action strategies or for interaction and discussion. When used it is often labelled a seminar or simply a small class. Here the use of the word *learning team* is deliberate for it implies that group members are banded together for learning in a manner that is somewhat different from that of a group taking a course together. Members are to be the primary instruments of learning for one another in contradistinc-

tion to reliance on the teacher for leadership of the group.

Strengths and Limitations. The major advantage of organizing learners into small groups for knowledge acquisition lies in the potential for personalizing information and sharing responsibility for learning. Adult learners more easily retain information related to their own needs or previous experience—especially when they have some responsibility for the learning process. Strengths of the learning team approach are:

1. Participants not only learn the content but also practice process skills essential to information gathering.

2. Through the team approach participants can practice teaching or communicating skills.

3. Small groups are less likely to engage in the competitiveness characteristic of many formal learning situations and more likely to encourage collaboration.

4. Greater involvement and sense of personal responsibility for learning promote the growth of self-direction and the spirit of lifelong learning.

The limitations of small-group information-gathering teams depend on the resources available. Internally, they are limited by participants' dependence upon one another; externally, they are frequently allocated fewer resources than larger groups. Specific limitations are:

1. It takes more time and energy for members to dig out information than for them to receive it from an informed source.

2. Individual members of the learning team can exert undue pressure on the

group either by leading it in unproductive directions or by neglecting their responsibilities.

3. The parochial vision and the specific interests of a few members of the group can limit the extent of what is learned.

4. Interests and needs of group members may be too far apart to encourage collaborative efforts.

Suggestions for Effective Use. Malcolm Knowles, who organized his graduate students into learning teams, directed much attention to this approach and recommended its use in many situations. He described a six-phase process:

☐ Setting a climate and identifying resources

☐ Diagnosing needs for learning through a collaborative teacher-student process

☐ Setting learning objectives

☐ Planning and conducting learning experiences

☐ Presenting learning outcomes

☐ Evaluating the learning activities (Knowles, 1970)

This strategy for organizing learners hinges on the composition of the group and the role of the teacher in it. Too much diversity among learners could lead to individual rather than collaborative learning practices; too much similarity could restrict efforts. This is true particularly when the diversity among members is due to differing levels of knowledge and experience in the content under consideration. In addition, the teacher is in the paradoxical position of being the major resource in the group but not the major presenter. A collaborative approach to learning as well as skill in promoting learning processes is essential.

Courses

Courses organize a group of learners by meeting at specified times and places to study a specific content area under the direction of a teacher. Although credit is often attached to classes or courses, this is not always the case. Similarly, the length of a course is usually tied to some formal program schedule, for example, a semester or a quarter; however, short courses of a few days or weeks are also possible. Knowles (1970) maintains: "The course is still the most efficient and most acceptable unit for organizing most kinds of learning, and since it has become freed from the shackles of the traditional lecture-recitation-examination ritual, it has become a much more flexible and dynamic instrument for helping people learn" (p. 144). Certainly it is the most commonly used method to organize learners into groups for the purpose of studying content.

Strengths and Limitations. The long acceptance and frequent use of the course as a means of organization automatically lends strength to the approach. Students and teachers are used to it; administrators are prepared to deal with it. Other advantages:

1. Courses are readily quantifiable and therefore more easily accounted for and administered than most other approaches.

2. Courses are so broadly used and accepted that they are the expected approach for organizing learners.

3. The ongoing nature of courses and the regular schedule makes it possible for students to be selective in preparation for and attendance at sessions.

4. Many different learning strategies and resources can be used during a course.

5. Courses can be cost-effective approaches for disseminating information.

In spite of their popularity, courses do have limitations. Many drawbacks result from trying to systematize the learning process not only for an individual but for a whole group of learners. This is particularly true for groups of adults because the diversity among mature learners is much greater than among younger students. Some other limitations are:

1. Time limits for courses are usually set by someone extrinsic to the teaching/learning transaction, such as the accrediting agency or the registrar.

2. As traditionally taught, courses tend to encourage passivity among adult learners.

3. Courses tend to be directed according to the needs of the system rather than the needs of the individual learners.

4. As the number of participants increases, it becomes more difficult to direct the content or the process of learning to the needs or learning styles of the individuals who make up the group.

Suggestions for Effective Use. Decisions about what information to present in a course and how to present it should be based on a clear knowledge of the following:

☐ Needs and expectations of the participants

☐ Needs or characteristics of the subject matter

☐ Needs or requirements of the sponsoring agency

☐ Needs of the community in which the course is offered

This calls for careful planning before the course and constant adjustment during it. Consequently, formative evaluation, that is, gathering information to improve the course while it is ongoing, is important to course improvement. Adults who are turned off by one course are usually reluctant to enroll in another.

Both by tradition and by structure, courses tend to be teacher directed, thus increasing the impact that the teacher has on the success of the activity. When working with adult groups, the selection of teachers cannot be solely dependent upon expertise in subject matter. Successful teachers must have some insight into how adults learn and how to teach them.

Large-Group Presentations

When organizing learners for information delivery, audience size is often considered irrelevant. A good speaker can address five thousand people as readily and effectively as fifty. While there is some truth to this, increasing the number of participants does have an effect on the learning environment. As size increases, the possibility of involving learners decreases. Question-and-answer sessions, buzz groups, and even the sharing of handouts become less manageable. More and more consideration must be given to physical facilities that support the learning activity and less to the individual learner. Yet, presentations to large groups can be effective in communicating information whether such sessions are presented in series or separately.

Strengths and Limitations. Presentations as strategies for organizing large groups are often used because they appear to be effective in terms of cost and energy. They serve large numbers of learners, so it is easy to justify the allocation of large portions of resources to them. Strengths of the large-group approach include:

1. The same information can be presented to all, thus avoiding repeated sessions in which more or less data might be presented to different groups.

2. More effective presenters and presentation devices can be justified in view of the large audience served.

3. Large groups can generate in participants a feeling of being part of something important and successful.

4. Increased numbers seem to have little effect on the learning of the individual in this setting.

Large-group approaches for information delivery have fewer intrinsic limitations than do large-group approaches aimed primarily at planning for action or at encouraging discussion among participants. Experienced learners whose objectives match those of the presenter can learn effectively. Others may have a great deal of difficulty. Other limitations include:

1. Ordinarily little or no feedback is available to the presenter during the presentation.

2. Although the same information is presented to all, the same message is not received by all.

3. Most large-group presentations rely mainly or exclusively on verbal symbols. Even adding visual aids has limited impact on those who learn best through doing.

4. Unlike readings or other prepared information sources, most presentations cannot be reviewed over and over by the learner anxious to commit the information to memory.

Suggestions for Effective Use. Many strategies for improving presentations to groups are presented in the next section of this book. Using a variety of strategies can add dynamics and interest to presentations thus improving audience attentiveness. All too frequently little can be done to increase the involvement of learners in the process; however, the presenter's skill in posing questions and inviting application of the information being presented can induce some interaction with the content. Once again, content expertise is not the sole requirement of the teacher. Adeptness in the process of teaching adults is also vital.

Much recent research on information processing and on memory (Glass & Holyoak, 1986) supports the value of helping learners organize information being presented. Advanced organizers, outlines, and overviews can provide such aid. In the same manner, summaries or ways of reviewing major points presented can increase learning effectiveness.

Organizing Learners as Total Communities

More frequently than we may realize, learning activities are organized for the total community. Such approaches appeal especially to those who see the role of education as vital to the growth of society. What could be better than to turn our communities into *learning societies,* to promote development, to make education and learning a vital part of the community problem-solving process?

Community, as used in this context, must be defined rather broadly, that is, as "a collectivity of people differentiated from the total population by a common interest" (Wright, 1980, p. 101). As such, it could be a geographic or political community, a university or business community, or a community of scholars. The distinctive mark of this approach is that the educative efforts are directed toward all people of the collectivity.

Organizing learners as communities, in contradistinction to organizing them as individuals or groups, has been given very little attention in the literature on educational methods. Boyd and Apps (1980) devote five chapters to what they call learning in the community transactional mode. The term *transactional mode* is used "to characterize the nature of the learner's situation: are adults working independently and individually, in groups or classes, or as members of a community?" (p. 5). Brookfield (1984) devotes considerable attention to the influence the community has upon the adult learner but contends that it is difficult to analyze adult learning in the community with these modes. In fact, he describes it as "at present an area characterized by conceptual confusion and practical contradictions" (p. 89). These authors reflect a growing interest in the analysis of community approaches to education but neither gives much attention to methodologies for doing so.

The advantages of communitywide approaches are apparent. Efforts that affect the behavior of the total community attract the attention of the "powers that be" and justify the investment of considerable resources. Their effect can be multiplicative for communitywide development, which can engender positive attitudes toward continued development and lead to progress in many areas. For those who view their community or organization holistically, it has special appeal—the whole being something greater than the sum of the parts.

The difficulties of working with a total community of learners are challenging. For example, one cannot describe a program by attendees or participants but must constantly keep in mind the total population, which makes any description of strategies for organizing learners as a total community rather nebulous. How do you talk about your population or assess the needs of learners if they are not gathered together or if you are not even sure whether they will participate? How do you evaluate such strategies? In fact, how do you even give an educational aura to activities that most would describe in political or organizational terms? Wright (1980) accepts this as a worthy challenge saying: "Adult educators have the opportunity to help communities perceive civic activities as educational and learning experiences. . . . An awareness of the educational function of the meeting can prompt the principals to consider the staging, conduct, and content of the session" (p. 103).

In spite of Brookfield's (1984, pp. 88–89) caution mentioned earlier, the following sections will attempt to describe in summary form various approaches to organizing learners as total communities and suggest some of the strengths and limitations of such methods. Strategies will be divided thusly:

☐ Those directed toward the individuals who comprise the community

☐ Those that join members of the community into groups

☐ Those that attempt to reach all members of the community simultaneously

Organizing the Community as Individuals

Community resource centers are one example of an attempt to educate the total community, but they do so by offering learning opportunities to members as individuals. City libraries and museums, college and university libraries, and resource centers of all kinds are justified by the good they do for the total community through the provision of opportunities for growth to every individual within that community. The fact that not all members of the community avail themselves of the learning opportunities provided does not negate the fact that these are attempts to educate the community as a whole.

Learning exchanges or educational brokerage organizations use a different strategy to reach the total community through its members. These are basically efforts to match the learning needs of individuals in the community with the available teaching resources. The broker, or educator, establishes some way of helping members identify their learning needs or desires and solicits other members of the group to act as teachers. Funding for the services can be provided by the organization or by the participants either directly or through a bartering of services. It differs from the resource center in that it attempts to mesh learners with human rather than physical resources.

Fairs or exhibits, as attempts to display or demonstrate products or recent developments, can also be considered community education affairs. Often the educational objectives of such activities are overshadowed by money-making efforts of participants. Yet this can be an effective teaching strategy. The long history of the Cooperative Extension Service's success through result and method demonstrations bears witness to the effectiveness of such methods in changing general practices within a community.

Strengths and Limitations. Directing any resource toward the total community rather than selected segments of it lends attractiveness if not strength to community organization efforts. Specific advantages include:

1. Efforts to reach the total community justify the expense of resources that could not be devoted to the education of individuals as individuals.

2. Frequently a spirit or excitement about the use of such opportunities is generated among participants and encourages other members of the community to join the learning activities.

3. The development of the individual has a lasting effect on the total community.

Limitations of such approaches generally reflect insufficient use of the resource by all members of the community. Major efforts are put into organizing the learning resource rather than organizing the learners. Specific limitations are:

1. Much effort is frequently necessary to make members aware of the learning opportunity, to convince them to use the resources, and to teach them how to best profit from the activity.

2. In planning and organizing such efforts, it is difficult to reflect the total interests and needs of the population.

3. It is difficult to get all or even a majority of members of the community to participate in the learning activity.

Suggestions for Organizing. The educator who attempts to work with community or association members as individuals faces a challenging task indeed. There are few guidebooks for this approach to the organization of learners. One basic principle follows from the tendency of adults to do much of their learning in the self-directed mode. Thus, the community educator should try to maximize opportunities for learning that might appeal to the self-directed adult learner. This is not as simple as adding books to the community resource center or consultants to the company's training programs. We have discovered that the self-directed learner often grabs the most readily available resources instead of seeking out the more effective ones.

The provision of resources is not complete until the learners are sold on their use. This includes making them aware of the existence and location of the learning opportunities, getting them excited about their use, and perhaps even offering help in their effective use.

As Brookfield (1984) pointed out, one of the challenges of working through community approaches is the need to become concerned with individual and community goals. What are the pressing issues to be faced? Where are the resources to go? What are the goals of development? Coggins (1980) recognized the need for those working with individuals in community problem-solving situations to have a schema for personal growth of individuals and suggested four categories of individual growth: stance toward self, toward others, toward life, and toward knowledge and process (pp. 159–170). The comments of Freire (1970) are also applicable here. He emphasized that the learner in the community must become conscious of the forces at work in the environment and convinced that change is not only good but possible.

Organizing the Community as Groups

Advisory committees have been used as one form of organizing a community through groups. This is especially true when a number of committees are established to handle various issues concerning the community and when members of the committees are selected because they represent different segments of the population. Well-managed advisory committees reach out into the community both through solicitation of input from all segments of the population and through a tapping of all the resources available for community problem solving. Poorly managed advisory committees are characterized by one or both of the following: they represent only selected voices in the community and/or they are seldom heeded by community decision makers.

The town meetings of today generally represent attempts to organize the total community through groups of interested individuals. When communities were smaller and issues less complex, public meetings may have attracted all the adults in the community. Today, however, their conveners are satisfied if participants are representative of community interests, hoping that the community at large will be involved through reports on the meeting disseminated through mass media.

The Community Education movement might also be an example of organizing the total community through groups. Leaders of the movement might consider it an effort to reach out to the community as a whole, but to observers most such efforts revolve around neighborhood schools and that portion of the population which can be attracted to educational events. Community Education does effect change in communities through community need assessments, neighborhood committees, problem-solving sessions, and in general encouraging citizens to become lifelong learners.

Strengths and Limitations. Campbell (1980) argues that community problem-solving groups are an excellent way to build a vast adult education program and to teach participants how to make a democracy work. He sees such groups as motivated and easy to organize, as dealing with educational issues that are directly relevant to their lives, and as addressing the true needs of adults. Specific advantages of working through groups are:

1. Members tend to pick up organizational strategies, which they use to im-

prove the operation of other groups in which they are involved.

2. Organizing citizens through groups encourages the collaboration of other groups in the community, especially those in which participants hold membership.

3. Collaborative efforts tend to be more effective than individual efforts.

4. Most people enjoy working together with others; thus motivation is usually high in group activities.

Organization of a community through groups can cause resentment and dissatisfaction among those who are not involved or not involved in the manner they desire. In larger communities, this also challenges the ability of the educational facilitator to involve a significant percentage of the citizens and to organize an appropriate number of groups. Specific limitations include:

1. Serious conflict can arise when community decision makers or minority groups within the community do not accept the decisions or the actions of representative groups.

2. The most competent individuals in the community may not be involved in the groups or in leadership positions within them.

3. Group activities can engender competition among groups or between individuals and thus damage interpersonal relations.

4. Working with groups demands a great deal of time and insight into group dynamics.

Suggestions for Organizing. Organizing community groups calls for ability both in the facilitation of groups and in the development of the community. Most groups need facilita-

tion at least in their period of formation. If the educator provides training in problem-solving techniques, in group leadership, in communication skills, and in evaluation of progress during the first three or four meetings of the group, the group will usually prosper. But the ultimate goal is not group development but community growth. It is important that not only the educational leader but group members recognize that their efforts are promoting community progress. Bringing members from various community groups together on occasion can promote such awareness.

Organizing the Community as a Whole

Community development efforts often take a holistic approach toward community improvement. Although they may at times involve only selected members of the community in the planning and action phases of a project, there is usually one general goal intended for the good of all community members. The educator's role in community development can be conceived of narrowly or broadly, whether the community is a selective group, such as members of one firm, or a total nation. In the narrow sense, or perhaps as part of a professional team, the educator can give leadership to efforts to clarify problems, inform citizens, and evaluate progress, for these are process concerns at which educators of adults should be adept. However, in a broader sense the educator can facilitate the overall planning, decision, and action phases of a community development program by making use of the resources of the community. For as Wright (1980) suggests: "If planning is a process for determining appropriate future action through a sequence of choices, then it is clearly a learning task" (p. 123).

Frequently, mass media ventures are efforts to deliver an identical message to the total community. Whether it is an extension agent's column on lawn care or a carefully orchestrated television blitz by a political body, media are being used as teaching devices. Technology is constantly offering educators new means for reaching out to the community. The channel made available for community programming by television cable companies or information data banks that can be tapped into by home computer buffs are but two examples. The fact that not everyone in the community is personally reached by the media does not detract from this approach, for those who are affected by the message will often pass it on to others.

Community celebrations are occasions or activities that project an image: This is who we are; isn't it good! Such celebrations vary from the honoring of a local hero or victory in a sporting event to national holidays or local festivals. Even museums, civic centers, or historic sites can be sources of celebration. Such events or sites not only give a spirit of self-identity and worth to an organization but become occasions in which goals of the organization are clarified and commitment to them renewed. Celebrations can be an excellent opportunity for the adult educator to direct the delivery of affective domain messages that can be so difficult to teach through traditional methods.

Strengths and Limitations. The impact of the social environment on learning and behavior has been documented repeatedly. Once a significant percentage of a community group has accepted new insight or new procedures, it is much easier to convince the rest of the group to do likewise. Other advantages of approaching the community as a whole are:

1. Cultural and societal reinforcement is supplied to all the members of the community as the new knowledge or behavior is implemented.

2. Such approaches deliver the same message to all elements of the organization at the same time thus eliminating the discrepancies caused when different elements of a group possess different information during a period of change.

3. When effective, such approaches are powerful methods of education especially in the affective domain.

The difficulties of working with the total community are indeed challenging. Potential learners are usually not organized in readily reached units; they are not intent on learning; they are attuned to many other issues and duties. This leads to some limitations:

1. The nebulousness of the audience makes it difficult to plan, conduct, and evaluate both learning process and learning outcomes.

2. Such approaches are often not seen as education thus making it difficult for educators to take charge or to use educational methodologies.

3. Most communities and organizations have limited vehicles for reaching the total population with the same message.

4. Usually the planning and conducting of the learning activities are under the control of a small group and do not involve the majority of adult learners.

5. Little study has been given to such approaches; thus, there is little information available on strategies for implementing communitywide approaches to education.

Suggestions for Organizing. An educator working with an entire community needs expertise in politics, sociology, economics, communication, and education or the ability to integrate interdisciplinary or interagency efforts. Rather than poring through books for directions on how to work with communities, a director's time might be more effectively spent getting to know the community—its problems, its resources, its stage of development. "Getting a feel for the community" expresses accurately the value of a naturalistic or ethnographic approach to learning about the community in con-

tradistinction to an analytical approach. Boyle (1980) warns about too much planning by the educator or an advisory group and too little community involvement in the planning. The challenge to the educator is to help community members become aware of community problems and the issues involved. Boyle feels this includes insight into how similar communities are affected by the problem and the cultural, social, psychological, economic, political, and environmental elements involved.

C H A P T E R   T H R E E

Using Presentation Strategies

"B*etter than I had anticipated," reflected Carrie as she left the community center following a presentation on various ways to improve home energy efficiency. The presenter had used a few slides and had some samples of materials one could buy, and that had really helped Carrie keep her mind on the presentation. However, the talk had lasted more than an hour. After about forty minutes, Carrie had trouble keeping her mind on the subject. "I really need to know that information, and I took some good notes," she mused while driving home. "I want to share this with Bob [her husband] tomorrow and determine if we need to buy some more insulation or other materials. I just wish I could have kept my mind on that information about the cost-effectiveness of various materials near the end, but the speaker's voice was a constant monotone, the seats got hard, and I kept wondering how the kids were doing by themselves. Why did Bob have to work late tonight. . . ?"*

Presentations are still a commonly used teaching strategy even though the efforts of many adult educators have lessened that tendency. For a long time, *teaching* has been equated with *telling* even though presentation strategies, for the most part, appeal to a limited number of sensory organs. However, in some situations these strategies foster effective adult learning. The successful educator must simply know when and how to use them correctly. Carrie had a felt need and, to some extent, the presentation was meeting her needs. How much more effective could the experience have been had the

presenter been aware of some fundamental aspects of utilizing a presentation-type teacher strategy? As Mager (1968) indicates, "If telling were the same as teaching we'd all be so smart we could hardly stand it" (p. 7). However, telling can be effective when used properly.

Overview of Presentation Strategies

Presentation strategies are used when the major objective is to convey information, whether to an individual or to a group. They include demonstrations, dialogues, illustrated talks, debates, interviews, lectures, panels, and symposiums. Since the purpose is to convey information, the learner is usually passive, and control or responsibility for the learning remains primarily with the teacher or presenter. This in itself should caution the reader that care should be taken to make those presentations as effective as possible. Without active learner participation, the teacher must be very astute to motivate learning.

Adult Learners and Presentation Strategies

Although presentation strategies do not appeal to the full range of human senses, adults do prefer those teaching strategies at times. While research on learning styles indicates that one style is usually preferred, most

51

students can learn from several different styles if the need and motivation are sufficient (Bureau of Educational Research and Service, 1972). Kidd (1973) has identified several roles of the teacher in giving presentations:

1. Animating or inspiring commitment
2. Presenting information or demonstrating processes
3. Raising relevant questions
4. Clarifying difficulties or obscurities (p. 293).

Kidd also indicates that teachers prefer presentations in specific learning situations. Some reasons might be:

1. *Control.* The presenter usually controls the learning environment. This may be desirable or necessary when sensitive or volatile topics such as environmental issues, political debates, or zoning problems are involved. In getting needed information to the public, controlled symposiums, panel discussions, or debates may be necessary. However, if control is the only reason for using these strategies, they could be misused rather than used wisely.

2. *Flow of Information.* When it is important to communicate a considerable amount of information in a limited period of time, presentations are a good strategy to use. They enable the dispensing of information at a pace controlled by those in the teaching role. The quality of presenting should always be high, but sometimes there is little attempt to determine quality when presentations are used.

3. *Time Efficiency.* In some cases where available time is limited, presentations can be effective since they restrict the amount of interaction by the participants. This is particularly true when

a great amount of information must be acquired in a short time.

Learning Styles and Presentation Strategies

Adults differ in their preferred learning styles, and there are several reasons why some prefer presentation learning activities.

1. Some adults have never experienced other kinds of learning activities and prefer to stay with a known strategy rather than try something different.

2. Adults with certain learning styles prefer presentation strategies. Cohen (1969) indicated that analytic learners, being field-independent, can select relevant information from an overall presentation activity. Cawley, Miller, and Milligan (1976) indicate that "the analytic learner tends to be more sedentary, prefers formal learning situations, sees a teacher as a source of information, prefers complexity, is achievement oriented and competitive, and prefers social distance" (p. 104).

3. Certain presenters are able to convey positive messages such as enthusiasm for the topic, enjoyment of teaching, and overall support for the adult-learning environment. As Verduin, Miller, and Greer (1977) state, "Verbal expressions and nonverbal movements send messages to adult students. It is important that these messages convey support, acceptance, responsiveness, and positive regard" (p. 64). This, in turn, enables the adult learner to feel not only secure but also enthusiastic about learning itself.

4. Presentations serve certain teaching functions better than other strategies. For example, when explanation, clarification, summarization, and other

similar functions are needed, presentation of the information is most expedient. In addition, some data may need to be repeated, and some may only be available from the personal experiences of the speaker.

Teachers and Presentation Strategies

People who are successful in presentation strategies often exhibit a combination of liveliness, enthusiasm, and organization. They enjoy talking or telling and are able to do so in a way that appeals to the listener. These qualities are important because, in most of these strategies, the teacher is appealing to a limited number of the human senses, and for this reason many adult education writers caution the teacher about using presentations as the only teaching strategy (Hand & Puder, 1967; Knowles, 1970; Seaman, 1977; and Verduin et al., 1977).

In presentation strategies, control of the learning process is maintained by the teacher or leader, who can thus determine not only the content but also the pace of the learning activity. Even when the learners ask questions, the teacher controls the climate within which such questions are encouraged or discouraged, the length of the question-answer period, and the kind of response given (analysis, comparison, clarification, etc.). Although some adult educators feel uneasy about having that much control of the learning environment, others feel comfortable. In fact, teachers who feel uncomfortable without such control should maintain it. If they are uncomfortable, they will certainly make learners uncomfortable regardless of whether control is a critical issue.

Of course, with more control comes less risk. For example, less flexibility is needed in comparison to action strategies. This does not mean that presentations should not be revised or changed according to time or other constraints, but these strategies are relatively structured and do not vary much in how they are used in most learning situations.

The successful presenter keeps good eye contact with the audience, has a voice that varies in tone and intensity, and does not use behaviors or actions that distract the learner from the content. Such a presenter commands a vast amount of knowledge about the subject; organizes the content into a logical, meaningful pattern; and presents material positively and enthusiastically.

Learning Objectives and Presentation Strategies

Presentations are most effective when the purpose of the learning activity is the dissemination of information in a logical, summarized form. This is particularly true when the content must be organized and presented in a particular way to a specific group. For example, the demonstration strategy can be used to teach recent changes to a group of technicians studying the latest chemicals developed to destroy household insect pests. The effectiveness of each chemical can be shown as it is applied correctly.

Presentations are also effective when the learning includes material of a controversial nature. In order to present all sides of an issue fairly and objectively, some kind of control must be maintained or a shouting match may evolve.

Another effective use of presentations involves the need to arouse learner interest in a topic or to "sell" participants on a particular topic. This is most effective when the initial interest of some of the group participants grows until everyone becomes emotionally charged and ready for action. Motivational speakers at sales meetings and at volunteer training meetings are examples of this kind of presentation when retaining information for the long term is not as important as becoming emotionally committed to some issue, concept, or idea.

How to Use Presentation Strategies Effectively

When limited time must be a consideration for learning, presentations may be the best teaching strategy. More information can be shared with learners more rapidly than with other strategies. If time is really short, the lecture or demonstration should probably be used. If time is available for structured discussion, the dialogue or panel should be used. Presentations are time-efficient, and this may be an important consideration in the learning environment.

Presentations can also be effective if students are only interested in acquiring information they can analyze at a later time or if they are satisfied in a passive role with minimal interaction. However, one must be cautious in using presentations when the content includes detailed, complex, or highly technical information. There must be *some* assurance that the material is being assimilated and understood by the learner.

In general, resources are not an important consideration with presentations. Lectures, symposiums, and panels need only a good sound system, tables and chairs, and microphones. The exception is a demonstration that could require a number of props, including a projector, flip-chart, or other assorted materials, although even these may not represent much expense for the user.

When presentation strategies are used, retention of the content beyond the short term is usually not anticipated. So although arousing interest or selling an idea can be effectively treated by presentations, long-term retention requires activities where the participant is more active. When the teacher uses a brief outline that emphasizes the salient

points of the presentation and refers to those points repeatedly, the chances of the participant retaining the information are enhanced. As one sage indicates, "Tell 'em what you're going to tell 'em, tell 'em, then tell 'em what you told 'em." This comment comes from Verduin et al. (1977), who indicate that the content of presentations must be "organized in terms of steps, manipulations, and behaviors" (p. 128). Specificity also enables participants to retain more data longer than when generalities are used. Finally, "the presentation should be ended with a brief summary in the form of examples or a self-test" (Verduin et al., 1977, p. 128).

The teaching strategies in this chapter include the lecture, symposium, panel, demonstration, dialogue, debate, and interview. The order reflects the amount of control the leader or teacher has in the strategy, from total control in the lecture to minimal control over the responses of the learner in the interview. These strategies were selected because they fit the criteria described previously in this chapter and because they are commonly used where presentations best fit adult learning. The uses of technology in presentation strategies is treated at the end of the chapter.

The Lecture

A speech or lecture is a well-prepared oral presentation on a topic by a qualified person (Bergevin, Morris, & Smith, 1963). No teaching strategy has been maligned more than the lecture, yet it is the strategy with which many adults are familiar in learning situations. Why? Because, as Eble (1976) points out, "it is the easiest thing to do; it is the subject. For these reasons, professors are likely to go on lecturing" (p. 42). However, Eble also indicates that there are times when the teacher might as well be lecturing. "Mediocre discussion classes, poor individual student reports, and ineffectual panel presentations are no improvement upon a teacher's mediocre lecturing" (p. 43).

Strengths and Limitations. Several authors (Bergevin et al., 1963; Eble, 1976; Legge, 1974; Kahler, Morgan, Holmes, & Bundy, 1985; Verner & Dickenson, 1967) have identified the following strengths of the lecture:

1. A lecture is relatively easy to plan and can be more economical than other teaching strategies.

2. Facts and related information can be presented in an orderly and systematic manner.

3. A skillful lecturer can stimulate an audience to become more knowledgeable about a topic or issue through further inquiry or related activities.

4. Information and facts can be given to a large number of people in a relatively short time.

5. Some adults would rather listen than read or become involved in a discussion.

Those same authors indicate that, like all other teaching strategies, the lecture has its limitations:

1. Some teachers are unable to plan and organize a talk for an audience.

2. There is usually no convenient way to determine whether or to what extent learning has occurred.

3. A speaker can distort facts and dispense erroneous information.

4. Only one person's views and perceptions are presented.

5. The speaker may use terminology that confuses or irritates the audience.

6. The speaker's behavior may distract the listener from the actual talk (for example, fixed posture, monotone, reading from notes, no eye contact with the audience, repeated hesitations, and failure to respect the audience's expertise or interests).

7. In general, learning begins to diminish after about fifteen minutes of listening to a lecture.

8. Long-term retention of content presented in a lecture is not very likely.

Much of the negativism toward the lecture is expressed in the following passage:

> In America, we have resorted to the lecture entirely too much. . . . Irresponsible speakers often take advantage of this fact and use the meeting for their own vested interests, not hesitating to distort facts. Since there is no audience participation, the listeners need not listen, need not remain alert, or even awake. (Kahler, Morgan, Holmes, & Bundy, 1985, p. 79)

Designing a Lecture. At one time, many teachers felt that the lecture was easy to design and implement: Simply organize the material in some logical format, prepare whatever notes are necessary, then present the material to the learners. However, because research has indicated that adult listeners have a short attention span—fifteen minutes—some attitudes about preparing for lectures have changed.

For example, Frederick (1986) emphasizes the importance of variety in lecturing, including deciding which learning goal and activities are appropriate for each class. "The important point is not the final chalkboard creation but the process. The participatory lecture requires less recording—and more thinking—than the oral essay" (p. 45). Therefore, the lecturer actually attempts to determine how effective a lecture may be long before it occurs.

The topic should be of interest to the audience and enable participants to fill some educational need, or at least some part of a need. There should be some determination that the topic is relevant and will stimulate the interest of the adult student. If the topic is part of a course, it should relate directly to at least one of the learning objectives developed for the course, ideally one formulated by both the teacher and the students. If the lecture is a special event for some community organization, some prior needs assessment is mandatory to ensure audience attendance and interest.

In organizing the presentation, the lecturer, cognizant that interest will surely wane after fifteen to twenty minutes, should plan some activity to stimulate the audience. A combination of lecture and discussion, use of buzz groups with short reports to the entire group, listening panels, media activities, and other ministrategies can liven up the lecture with participation and response from the listeners. Frederick (1986) suggests shifting the energy from teacher to student and back again every ten to fifteen minutes so that interest and enthusiasm are not lost. If the lecture is part of a regular course, then virtually any class period can begin with discussion not concluded during the previous class period.

Lectures should be varied for different types of learners. Frederick (1986) has proposed several variations of a lecture from the "Exquisite Oral Essay," a polished work prepared for an intellectual audience and delivered in a fifty-minute period, to the "Participatory Lecture," which involves students in brainstorming activities to develop new insights about a topic before the teacher clarifies and summarizes the issues raised.

Whatever the type of lecture, the teacher must consider other factors in developing the strategy. The use of verbal illustrations and examples can enhance learning. Simple language, relatively short sentences, emphasizing no more than five or six points, and not rushing too fast when speaking will increase student comprehension and retention. With lower educated adults, the lecture has limited use and must be kept short and extremely relevant (Verner & Dickenson, 1967). It should be used in conjunction with learning objectives that are easily reached and understood by undereducated adults.

A lecture is easy to design and implement. When delivering a lecture, the speaker should be visible to the audience and adequately heard by everyone. If needed, an adequate sound system should be provided. If a podium is used, the moderator and speaker should sit to the side of it when not participating in the activity. If the speaker intends to use visuals, a table, projector(s), flip chart, chalkboard, and other needed items must be readily available.

At the beginning, the moderator introduces the speaker and presents the lecturer's qualifications. Once the lecture has ended, the chairperson or moderator may take audience questions, to which the speaker responds. At the end, the moderator summarizes the main points, thanks the speaker, and ends the activity.

Adapting the Lecture. Before the lecture or class is held, the learners should prepare themselves by acquiring any knowledge which would make the presentations more meaningful. However, they should come to the lecture with an open mind in case the speaker's views and perceptions are different from theirs.

During the presentation, the learners should listen carefully and take notes of salient points which enhance the learning. All unclear or confusing data should be clarified during the question-and-answer period following the lecture. An audience-reaction team could represent the participants and ask questions for clarification or for further information. Relevant handouts would also assist participant learning as would a summary of the presenter's salient points. Ultimately, the learners should seek further knowledge from other sources as a result of information received from the lecture.

As chairperson and planner, the teacher must arrange for the proper facilities, adequate publicity if necessary, and an appropriate guest speaker for the lecture. The teacher coordinates the entire event: introductions, summarizing, evaluations (if called for), and the ending. The most important aspect is acquiring a speaker who is knowledgeable about the topic and who can stimulate the audience.

If the teacher is also the speaker, the following tasks must be added to the general coordination of the event:

1. Preparing the content of the lecture, including appropriate vocabulary

2. Delivering a logical, orderly presentation

3. Observing the learners and making whatever adjustments necessary to make the talk more meaningful

4. Concluding within an appropriate time

While all teachers need to develop their individual styles, lecturers should:

1. Be certain they are audible to the listeners.

2. Practice speaking to friends or friendly critics to improve good speaking habits and vocal qualities that encourage others to listen.

3. Improve their ability to read an audience and react accordingly (Legge, 1974).

Lectures can accommodate a variety of topics but, in general, they are most suited to dispensing facts and related information or convincing an audience about an issue. They are a quick strategy for presenting material because the speaker may move through several related subtopics in a logical, sequential manner. However, Verner and Dickenson (1967) suggest no more than seven points be presented during any lecture.

Eble (1976) gives a succinct but interesting description of what a lecture should contain:

> Once begun, the lecture must have body. The human body will do as an analogy to describe its proper kind. It should have a variety of parts both independent of, and dependent upon, other parts; much substance; density and lightness; its own pulse and rhythm; warmth—all the parts and attributes constituting a distinctive whole. We can usefully expand the analogy beyond human forms, for some lectures should be shaggy monsters, spooks, and freaks. Above all, lectures must live, vigorously, engagingly, and surprisingly. (p. 48)

In preparing the lecture, the presenter should plan a few important points for emphasis. They should be made, then highlighted with interesting examples with which the audience can identify. Eliminate marginal material. It is essential to select and retain only the best and most important information. In the classroom, time should be planned for student responses and questions.

Eble (1976) indicates that most teachers enter into lecturing too lightly and pay too little attention to what good lectures might accomplish. They often decide to lecture and devote little time to preparation. After all, "It's only talking and anyone can do that." But how many can do it effectively?

Although several authors have given suggestions about how to deliver effective lectures, Eble (1976) and Mitchell and Corby (1984) have the best ideas:

1. Fit the content to the time available. Do not elaborate too much or introduce too many ideas.
2. Vary the mode of presentation. Use examples, physical movement, and visual materials whenever possible.
3. Follow a logical sequence and use illustrations that relate to the audience's background and experience.
4. Tell the listeners where you are going, how you will get there, and how long it will take.
5. Stimulate the audience as often as possible. Pay close attention to its reactions and be prepared to change and improvise accordingly.
6. In the classroom, provide students with opportunities to ask questions or present different perspectives on an issue.
7. Always provide an appropriate ending that follows from the material presented.

In short, avoid giving the kind of lecture defined by Legge (1974) as "the means whereby the contents of the lecturer's notebook are transferred to the notebooks of the students without passing through the minds of either" (p. 57).

Example of a Lecture

Background: In 1986, the United States Congress was debating a radical tax bill that would greatly reduce the kinds and amounts of interest paid on loans that could be deducted from income taxes.

Situation: On Thursday, May 19, 7:00 P.M., the monthly meeting of the Jefferson County Certified Public Accountants (CPA) Association will be held in the conference room of the First National Bank in Mankeim.

Chairperson: Lynda Grig, President, Jefferson County CPA Association

Speaker: Mr. Randolph Hines, Regional Vice President, National Association for Certified Public Accountants

Topic: "How the Proposed New Tax Bill Will Affect You and Your Business"

Subtopics: Provisions of Present Tax Laws to Remain Unchanged, Provisions of Present Tax Laws to Be Changed, Provisions of Present Tax Laws to Be Eliminated, Effects upon Present Tax Codes and Business, Activities of CPAs, Proposals Your Association Plans to Take to Congress

(A question-answer period follows the conclusion of the talk.)

The Symposium

The symposium is a series of short presentations by two to five persons qualified to speak on related topics or on various phases of the same topic (Seaman, 1977). In some cases, there may be more than five distinct aspects. The presentations are short and specific, usually five to twenty minutes in length depending on the number of speakers. Each speaker is an expert on some particular aspect of an overall issue enabling the listeners to hear the complete story instead of only part of it. The topics are assigned well in advance of the symposium so speakers can be prepared. A moderator controls the series of talks and assures that the proper sequence is maintained within the time limit, both individually and collectively.

Strengths and Limitations. The strengths of the symposium include:

1. The variety of presentations enables the audience to acquire a wide range of knowledge or opinions.
2. Short talks help prevent monotony and keep the listeners alert and stimulated.

3. Even though the presentations are short, comprehensive coverage of a topic is possible.

4. In contrast to the lecture, if one presenter is poor, the others can compensate for that weak performance.

5. Since the speakers have limited time, they tend to stay on the subject and make certain they present the most salient points.

The symposium also has the following limitations:

1. It appears formal to the audience.

2. The learners have no opportunity to interact with the speakers.

3. There is no discussion or interaction among the speakers.

4. Obtaining a number of speakers who are both technically and verbally competent may be difficult.

5. If the moderator is not competent, repetition of information or even general confusion may occur.

6. One or more speakers can neglect the assignment and change the content.

Designing a Symposium. Because many people are involved, the physical arrangements for a symposium may be demanding. These would include a stage or platform to accommodate all the participants and ample audio equipment to enable the learners to hear all the presenters adequately.

The key to a successful symposium is locating speakers who can address various aspects of an issue within the time limitations. The presenters must be technically competent. They must also be able to present factual information without personal biases and in a logical, orderly manner. The schedule, including the order in which the

presenters will appear, is also an important facet of the symposium.

Conducting or Leading a Symposium. The teacher, or moderator, must arrive early to make certain the physical arrangements are ready. As the speakers arrive, they should be introduced to each other and seated in the order they will be speaking. This may help the listeners associate a specific point or question with a particular speaker.

The moderator begins the symposium by introducing the topic, the speakers, and their subtopics and by announcing any ground rules such as time constraints for speakers, procedures for asking questions, etc. The moderator can sit at one end of the group or in the center. If all have microphones, there is no problem wherever he or she sits.

Each speaker is treated cordially and professionally but time restrictions are kept. At the end of all presentations, the moderator asks for questions from the audience, from a listening panel, or through whatever activity has been arranged. At the end of the questioning, the moderator repeats the purpose of the symposium, thanks the speakers and the audience for participating, and ends the activity.

Adapting the Symposium. As in all other presentation-type teaching strategies, the learners play a passive role. They must listen attentively and carefully to each speaker, noting the differences or similarities in the content of each presentation. They should relate this information to their own experiences and learning needs. After the symposium has ended, a listener may want to contact an individual presenter about any unclear points. As a follow-up activity, the learner should undertake additional inquiry to supplement the learning that occurs during the symposium. Chamberlain and Kelly (1981) indicate that occasionally, after the speakers finish, they may engage in discussion with the audience about the content of the presentations.

Teachers have an active role in the symposium. Therefore, they must be comfortable introducing and interacting with others in front of an audience. Most people can do this rather easily because their role, although active, is limited. Having acquired some information about the topic and the speakers helps the teacher perform these responsibilities.

During the symposium, a frequent smile and a profound interest in the entire activity are a must. The goal is to impart knowledge from a few individuals to the many in the audience, so the moderator must be completely supportive of the proceedings. The teacher is also interested in follow-up activities with the adult students in order to learn more about the issue or topic being addressed. Presumably the moderator can control the overall activity while allowing the speakers to present their ideas in their own way. That is what makes the symposium an effective teaching strategy.

The symposium is often used when a controversial topic is presented to an audience whose points of view differ. It can present a wide range of opinions or perceptions about an issue or provide a factual analysis of related aspects of a controversial topic. A common use of the symposium is allowing candidates to present their platforms and views at political rallies or meetings. These can be taped and presented through the media or at later meetings in conjunction with a question-and-answer session by telephone with the speakers.

In the classroom, a symposium helps listeners understand the relationships of various facets of an issue. Some issues can be more clearly defined by several symposium speakers, particularly if the topic is complex.

Kahler et al. (1985) indicate that since the purpose of a symposium is to present many points of view on a subject, this strategy does help present all the aspects of a topic to the listeners, thus broadening their knowledge. The symposium is often more acceptable than a lecture because of the variety in pace and style of the speakers. When differing ideas and opinions are desired but possible reactions from the audience should be controlled because of the controversial nature of the topics, the symposium can be used to present the information. The main point is that the symposium dispenses a variety of information and data in an organized way. The audience can be large or small as long as participants can hear the speakers.

Example of a Symposium

Topic: The Effects of Adult Illiteracy upon Development in the United States

Time: Thursday, June 12, 1986, 2:00 P.M.

Location: West Ballroom, Southern Hotel, St. Louis, Missouri. This will be the opening event of the annual regional meeting, Region II, Adult Basic Education Association.

Speakers:

1. Mr. William Scott, U.S. Department of Treasury. Mr. Scott will focus upon the economic effects of the problem.

2. Ms. Roosevelt Johnson, Training Director, ABC Corporation. Ms. Johnson will discuss the problems industry has in finding qualified employees because of illiteracy.

3. Dr. Grace Hully, Counseling Psychologist. Dr. Hully will present data about the effects of illiteracy upon an individual's self-concept and perceptions of self-worth.

4. Dr. Samuel Hutto, Director, Social Services Agency, City of St. Louis. Dr. Hutto will discuss the effect of illiteracy upon the family structure and related problems of crime and delinquency.

Moderator: Dr. Christina Martinez, Associate Professor, Adult Education, St. Louis University

Brief Description: Dr. Martinez will introduce the topic and the speakers in the order they will appear. Each speaker will have ten to twelve minutes to present information, after which Dr. Martinez will give a brief summary and conclude the meeting.

The Panel

"A small group of persons, usually about six, who sit around a table and discuss a topic in which they have special knowledge" is the way Kahler et al. (1985, p. 82) describe a typical panel discussion. In contrast to the lecture and symposium, the panel involves mostly discussion by the presenters, although in most cases each will begin with a three-minute statement on the chosen topic. Panel members are selected not only for their expertise but also for their ability to discuss the topic with other experts in front of an audience.

Strengths and Limitations. Panels do have some distinct strengths over other teaching strategies, namely:

1. Several experts can be used to present a variety of viewpoints on a particular subject.
2. Viewpoints can be explored and discussed more fully than through presentations alone.
3. The informality of discussion is usually well received by most audiences.
4. A skillful moderator can emphasize important points that will add to the knowledge of the listener.
5. Panels allow learners to choose presenters or points of view with which they agree.

6. Some learners prefer to explore various viewpoints rather than reach a single decision.

The panel has the following limitations:

1. Much of this strategy's success depends upon the moderator, who must be extremely skillful in leading a discussion.
2. Finding several panel members evenly matched in knowledge and ability to discuss their views may be difficult.
3. More planning and organization are required than for most presentation strategies.
4. Unless the audience is really interested in the issue, panels can be very dry events.
5. One or two panel members can dominate the discussion.

Designing a Panel. The panel requires much planning and organizing. The topic must strongly appeal to adult learners. An extensive search must be made for panel members who are knowledgeable and who can freely discuss the topic before an audience. Not only should all of the participants receive the same information in advance, but the moderator should meet with the panelists just prior to the activity to communicate the procedures and ground rules. The panel members should be balanced in knowledge and assertiveness.

The moderator and panel members should be on a raised platform in full view of the audience. Each member should have a separate microphone for discussion purposes. An adequate public-address system is essential. If the listeners will be asking questions after the panel discussion concludes, that must also be planned.

A moderator must be skillful in stimulating and coordinating a discussion with experts. The moderator should be seated in the middle of the panelists and should adhere to all agreed-upon procedures and time limitations.

Adapting the Panel. As in all other presentation strategies, the learners must listen intently to the discussion, analyze the points being made, and record those that are unclear or those that need follow-up study. In most panel presentations, the audience is to ask questions at the conclusion of the discussion, and learners should be ready to participate at that time. Learners should compare the panelists' different points of view and relate them to their own beliefs and experiences. Learners should not distract other listeners or the panel members by interrupting the discussion with applause or abuse.

Although many panels occur outside a classroom setting, the teacher may have to organize the panel and serve as moderator. This requires time to locate discussion experts for the panel, coordinate the schedules of several busy people, and arrange the physical facilities.

In the classroom, the teacher often assumes the role of moderator. The teacher makes certain that all panelists understand the procedures and then ensures that they are followed. All panelists must have an equal opportunity to participate. During the discussion, the moderator attempts to draw out comments from the participants that would make the learning more meaningful to the listeners. The teacher always remains neutral, summarizes occasionally, and guides the discussion toward the goals and purposes of the activity.

Panel discussions are frequently used during workshops and conferences when a number of divergent or opposing views about an important topic can be discussed in front of the participants. The topics are usually contemporary issues related to some impending change. They may even be controversial and require a moderator who can keep emotions down and rational discussion high. Sometimes, the discussion is focused on clarifying the advantages and disadvantages of a particular course of action being considered by the group. The content of a panel discussion can range from facts and knowledge to opinions and perceptions, or even to speculations about what might happen in the future. The main consideration is to have a subject that can be discussed and that will hold the interest of an audience. Topics can range from the theoretical to the practical, depending upon the needs of the learners.

Occasionally, the main purpose of a panel discussion may be to stimulate interest in an issue or to ascertain whether the audience or general public has any interest in a particular topic. City councils and school boards are often uncertain how citizens will react to a proposed course of action. A discussion by a panel of experts in an open hearing with audience reaction could provide the needed information. In other cases, the need may be to provide several points of view, clarify them with an in-depth panel discussion, and then ask the learners for feedback. All the likely results of a proposed action are discussed so that clarification is as thorough as possible. Panels present all sides and should not be expected to reach any conclusion or decision.

Example of a Panel

The community of Centerville is between two large, rapidly growing metropolitan centers. The city council members have discerned a need for stricter land and property use laws in order to channel some continuity and organization into the growth of Centerville. However, realizing that the issue of controlled land use is always controversial, the council has decided to hold an open public meeting at which time a panel of experts will discuss the possible effects of the proposed property use ordinances. The panelists will include:

1. Mr. Bernie Kappel, President, Centerville Builders' Association
2. Mrs. Atha Coutrill, Consultant, Tax Division, Office of the State Controller
3. Mr. Franklin Smith, Member, Volunteer Citizens' Council, Centerville/Henton County
4. Mr. Tom Ranier, President, Centerville Chamber of Commerce
5. Mrs. Leah Wong, Vice President, Centerville Chamber of Commerce

The moderator will be Dr. Gustavo Lopez, academic dean of Henton County Community College. Dr. Lopez's academic preparation is in urban and regional planning. His experience includes that of city planner, corporation trainer, and government consultant. He is an accomplished speaker and widely known for his planning and organizational skills. The meeting will be publicized widely and held at a time when conflict with other events will be minimal. The entire program will be taped and made available to community groups and other organizations.

The Dialogue

A dialogue is a discussion by two people competent in a subject area and capable of communicating effectively with each other. The dialogue is usually conducted in front of a group interested in the topic being discussed, but more recently the dialogue is used with videotapes. Although not found in some of the earlier literature about adult education strategies (Bergevin et al., 1963; H. L. Miller, 1964; Morgan et al., 1976; Ulmer, 1972), the dialogue is now becoming accepted as an effective form of presentation in certain situations. Examples include the American Medical Association's use of videotapes in the late 1960s to provide an opportunity for physicians to acquire the latest

technical information in their specialities. A series of videotapes was also developed at the University of Maryland in the early 1970s to provide adult basic education to staff members and to upgrade their competencies and skills. Each tape incorporated a dialogue between the moderator and the consultant featured in that particular lesson.

Strengths and Limitations. The dialogue offers the following advantages (Carpenter, 1967):

1. It is relatively simple and easy to plan. Only two people are required and a wide variety of material can be used.
2. The strategy provides for direct communication between the two participants regardless of their points of view on the content.
3. If the subject is controversial, the dialogue removes the audience from any emotional involvement since only two participants enter into the discussion. In this way, salient points may be debated in an atmosphere of objectivity.
4. Instead of debating, the participants may actually support each other's views and conduct a mutually supportive discussion.

However, as with all strategies, the dialogue is not without limitations:

1. Because they are usually more knowledgeable and well prepared about the subject than the audience, the participants may talk over the heads of the listeners and proceed too rapidly. This is especially true when the content is complex or technical. Audience preparation is crucial to this strategy's success.
2. If the participants become combative, the dialogue can become an argumen-

tive debate and lose much of its potential as a teaching strategy.

3. Participants can become so involved they forget that the purpose of the activity is to teach or communicate the content to others.

4. If one person is more vocal and aggressive, the two sides may not be presented equally when discussing opposing points of view.

Designing a Dialogue. The dialogue is not complicated in design and operation. While physical structure requirements are minimal, dialogue content is most important. The observers must be interested in the topics, or the dialogue loses all value. The nonparticipatory nature of the strategy demands content that is meaningful to the listeners, hence the previous suggestion of controversial materials as a base.

Once the subject has been determined, two knowledgeable persons must be selected to engage in the dialogue. They can use notes, if desired, but rather than making a series of short presentations, they should engage in free discussion with each other regardless of their views about the content. Through this interchange, the salient points about the subject should be discussed and emphasized.

The dialogue team is situated so that all observers and listeners can see the participants and hear the discussion. An audio sound system is usually required to ensure that all can hear well in large rooms or auditoriums. A moderator introduces the activity and, if time allows, receives questions from the audience once the dialogue team has finished its discussion. However, as Beal, Bohlen, and Raudabaugh (1962) indicate, the dialogue members must work as a team, share the leadership, summarize, and provide adequate transition and timing when necessary. Boyd (1984) supports that notion and cautions against letting the dialogue

become too mechanical, thus limiting the observers' interest and learning.

Adapting the Dialogue. As in other teaching strategies, the needs and interests of the dialogue participants and the observers must be known. The topic must be relevant and timely and lead toward some point even though no final conclusion is always reached. The participants must be able to interact freely with the teacher or leader and not be prone to argue or dominate the discussion. This can usually be accomplished by most adult students as long as the aforementioned conditions are met.

However, if the adult learner is hesitant or shy about participating in a dialogue, especially in front of a group, the leader should plan carefully with the learner before the dialogue occurs. The topic, direction of discussion, and intended outcome can be agreed upon, and the learner can have time to prepare for the activity.

Observers should be encouraged to listen intently and objectively as the dialogue progresses. If students express great concern about being active participants, they can be guided toward learning by being an observer. If time does not allow for everyone to be an active participant, a critique of the strategy by the observers can substitute to some extent for that experience.

In the dialogue, the teacher can assume either of two roles—moderator or dialogue participant. As moderator, the teacher introduces the topic and the participants and serves mostly as an observer until the question-and-answer period (if one is planned) at the end of the activity. As a participant, the teacher makes the introductions, initiates the discussion, and takes responsibility for concluding the teaching strategy. Control is maintained by the dialogue team or the moderator, who must keep the discussion within the content boundaries and the time limitation.

If comfortable as an active participant, the teacher should lead the dialogue discussion, being careful not to dominate. The teacher should know enough about the participating student(s) so that questions and comments will be relevant and meaningful. The teacher must also be responsible for keeping the discussion moving and avoiding periods of silence.

Teachers who are not comfortable participating in the dialogue can still moderate. Their participation will be limited, but they can still keep the discussion moving in the right direction by an occasional question or clarifying comment when needed.

The potential versatility of the content is an attractive feature of this teaching strategy. The purpose of the dialogue can range from simply extending the knowledge base of the listeners through presentation of factual information to providing the observers with data to aid in their own synthesis or evaluation. Therefore, regardless of the learning objective(s), the dialogue can easily be adapted to meet the learners' needs. Those utilizing the dialogue teaching strategy should carefully ascertain the learners' needs and develop the content accordingly.

Because of the versatility of the dialogue, a wide range of situations is available. Success depends on the selection of two persons who understand:

☐ The purpose of a dialogue

☐ The learning needs of the listeners

☐ Their role(s) within the structure of the dialogue as a teaching strategy

☐ How to carry out their roles accordingly (that is, not become too technical in their discussions, refrain from emotionalism, and adhere to time limitations)

Example of a Dialogue

Topic: The Need for More Surface Water Storage in Nevada.

Dialogue Team:

1. Dr. Fred Scott, Soil and Water Scientist, U.S. Department of Agriculture

2. Dr. Susan Allen, Land Use Management Specialist, Parks Department, State of Nevada

Moderator: Ms. Roberta Brown, Regional Vice President, U.S. Conservation Club

Time: Monday, July 8, 1986, 7:30-9:00 P.M.

Location: Westbury Community Center, 112 Lackland Street, Reno, Nevada

Brief Description: Dr. Scott and Dr. Allen will discuss the findings of a recent study indicating that Nevada could be facing a shortage of safe, usable water during the next decade unless new resources are developed. The dialogue team will also discuss the relative advantages and disadvantages of developing surface water storage in the state, including costs, time involved, and effects upon the environment. Time for questions from the audience will be provided.

The Debate

A debate is a structured discussion during which two sides of an issue are presented and argued by two or more individuals within a given time period. In many instances, teams of up to four people represent the two sides (Draves, 1984). Similar to the dialogue, the debate is conducted in front of an audience interested in the issue being debated or taped for later use by adult education groups. Little mention of the debate as a strategy for teaching adults is found in the early literature, but more recently it has been shown to be an effective means of presenting information to adults (Chamberlain & Kelly, 1981; Draves, 1984).

Strengths and Limitations. As a teaching strategy, the debate offers the following advantages:

1. It is usually a stimulating experience

for the listeners because of the argumentative nature of the strategy.

2. Since each side is trying to win the debate, only the most salient points will be made within the time allowed. No time will be wasted with useless or irrelevant information.

3. The combination of a variety of speakers and short presentations prevents the boredom potentially generated by some presentation strategies.

4. It is a convenient way to present controversial materials because the audience is removed from entering into the debate.

As with other strategies, the debate also has some limitations:

1. The moderator must be well trained in conducting a debate and make certain the participants adhere to the ground rules, including time limitations.

2. Learners who are uncomfortable with a competitive or argumentative atmosphere may find the debate an unpleasant teaching strategy.

3. The structure must be followed carefully to allow fairness, which leaves little room for flexibility.

4. The participants may become emotionally involved in trying to win the debate and forget the educational purpose of the activity.

5. In an effort to win the debate, some participants may withhold pertinent information or slant their facts instead of presenting them objectively.

Designing a Debate. The debate is more complicated to plan and conduct than the dialogue. Not only should the content be relevant to the learning needs of the listeners, but

the moderator and the participants must be more carefully selected. Maturity and objectivity are crucial characteristics for the moderator. Participants must also be able to prepare and present rebuttal statements within a few minutes.

The participants should be seated on a stage or raised platform where they can be seen by the audience. The debating teams should be seated at an angle on each side of the moderator so they can be seen by both their opponents and the audience. Each team should be seated behind a table provided for note taking or holding any necessary resource materials.

Before the debate begins, the moderator welcomes the audience, presents the topic for discussion, introduces the debate team members, and announces which side of the issue they are defending. The order of presentation, questioning, and ground rules are announced to the audience.

The debate begins with one member of the "pro" team giving reasons for favoring the issue; then a member of the "con" team presents reasons for being against it. "This procedure continues until each team member has had an opportunity to present evidence and supporting facts" (Chamberlain & Kelly, 1981, p. 95). Once the prepared material has been presented, team members have an opportunity to respond to their opponents. However, during these responses, new issues are usually prohibited.

At the end of the team presentations, the moderator briefly summarizes the main points of each side. If each team agrees, questions from the audience may be taken, but this must be carefully handled by the moderator to prevent one side from gaining any apparent advantage from the questions and subsequent responses.

Adapting the Debate. The audience must listen to a debate with their ears as well as with their hearts in order to learn. Therefore, the moderator should remind the audience to listen to the main points of both sides of the issue. If the material is presented objectively, the learners can then weigh the merits of both sides in pondering the issue. When time allows, questions from the audience can be helpful to the learners if the questions focus upon content and not upon emotional issues. In the classroom, some practice in critical listening and thinking before the debate also enhances learning.

The participating teams must thoroughly research the topic and present only the most important facts to support their position. In the classroom, teachers can help the teams organize their material in a logical sequence for presentation and the moderator attain a high level of objectivity in the leadership role. The teacher should assist the student-audience to differentiate between facts and speculation and to evaluate the relative importance of the facts to the topic. In some cases, the teacher may want to be the moderator in order to ensure objectivity in that role. Stephens and Roderick (1974) caution that teachers must prevent the "transformation of the staged performance into a personal argument which can severely damage relationships within the class and so impede learning" (p. 87).

In a debate, the participants are trying to persuade the audience, or each other, to perceive an issue in the way the debaters perceive it. Therefore, definite positions for and against the issue must be supported during the debate. This requires the participants to research the topic thoroughly so they can present only the most salient facts and be ready to respond to the facts presented by their opponents. Although the issues can range from relatively minor issues to more important topics, the main requirement is that the two sides are clear and can be argued logically and objectively. At the beginning of a debate, the topic is usually presented in the form of a positive or negative statement by the moderator (Chamberlain & Kelly, 1981).

The debate is well suited to topics and issues where the correct answer is not easily found or determined. This is why debates must be carefully planned and conducted only after the class or group has been together for some time and has developed some degree of friendliness and trust, particularly when the debaters are part of the learning group. By observing or participating in the debate, adults not only learn the content but the process as well, from researching the topics to presenting the final argument, or rebuttal. Learning occurs more easily from debates in which the topic is not so volatile because the presenters can be more objective and the observers can listen more readily for facts instead of becoming involved with their emotions. The debate is not for everyone, but when used properly, it can be an effective teaching strategy for adults.

Example of a Debate

Topic: Resolved—That every person, upon reaching the age of eighteen years, should devote one year of service to the national, state, or local community.

Debate Team A (Pro): Angela Coffey, Social Worker, Local Rehabilitation Center; Col. Winston Jones, U.S. Armed Forces; Lee Chin Wen, Administrator, State Volunteer Agency

Debate Team B (Con): Mason Matgba, American Civil Liberties Union; Manuel Trevino, Coalition of Local Business/Industry; Susan Blake, National Youth League

Moderator: Dr. Leah Laska, National Council of Churches

Time: Friday, October 12, 10:00-11:45 A.M.

Location: Auditorium, Westside High School, Malas, Massachusetts

Brief Description: Dr. Laska will introduce the topic and the debating teams to the audience. Team members can then make their six-minute presentation. Team A will make the first presentations, followed by Team B, then Team A again, etc., until all prepared talks have ended. Following a five-minute period for preparing rebuttal statements, each team can respond to the statements of the opposing team for five minutes. During the rebuttal period, no new issues can be raised, but new facts or other supporting information can be used whenever relevant. The moderator will then briefly summarize the most important points presented by each team. (If agreed to prior to the debate by each team, some questions may be received from the audience for responses from the members of either or both teams.)

The Demonstration

"A demonstration is a carefully prepared presentation that shows how to perform an act or use a procedure. It is accompanied by appropriate oral and visual explanations, illustrations and questions" (Bergevin et al., 1963, p. 63). According to many Cooperative Extension Service manuals and guidelines, a demonstration can be classified as either *result* or *method*. The result demonstration shows the results of some practice or procedure whereas the method demonstration illustrates how to do something in a successive, step-by-step manner. They have been used effectively for many years, particularly by county extensions agents, teachers, trainers, and others helping adults attain a new skill or ability. Effective demonstrations can be seen daily on television commercials, and their effect upon the buying habits of the general public can be great.

Strengths and Limitations. Kahler et al. (1985) present several advantages of demonstrations:

1. Demonstrations attract and hold attention. They are interesting.
2. Demonstrations present subject matter in a way that can be understood easily. They make clear what might otherwise be vague and meaningless.
3. They convince those who might otherwise doubt that a thing could be done, or that they themselves could do it.
4. Demonstrations are objective and concrete.
5. They show by example the practical applications of theory and knowledge.
6. Demonstrations usually yield a high rate of "takes" to "exposures." (pp. 139–140)

The same authors list the following limitations of demonstrations, whether result or method:

1. Good demonstrations are not easily developed. They require much time and skill to develop.
2. The "result" demonstration may require a long time to achieve and could be expensive.
3. Certain conditions are required for demonstrations and some teachers tend to use them too often at inappropriate times.
4. Equipment needed may limit the locations where demonstrations can be held. (p. 140)

Designing a Demonstration. Certain procedures are necessary before a demonstration can be an effective teaching strategy. The observers must be located so they can clearly view the demonstration and hear the explanations and directions. Before any actions occur, the audience must know precisely the purpose(s) or objective(s) of the activity. These are usually stated by the demonstrator(s) before the activity begins and repeated when it has been completed. Before starting, the demonstrator(s) should have all equipment and materials ready and should have a sequential, step-by-step plan for presentation outlined for referral purposes.

Once the demonstration begins, certain activities make it effective (Chamberlain & Kelly, 1981):

1. Be prepared so the activity will go fast and smoothly.

2. Work at a pace that will allow the students to follow all of the details without becoming confused.

3. Practice beforehand until all manipulation becomes automatic.

4. Work in full view of everyone so that the observers do not lose interest.

5. Keep the work surface neat and uncluttered. Keep equipment organized and in good condition.

6. Speak to the audience, not to the equipment whenever possible.

7. When the demonstration has been completed, ask for questions from the audience. Encourage questions unless you are certain everyone fully understands what has occurred (pp. 163–164).

Adapting the Demonstration. Demonstrations can maximize learning opportunities for adults. When an individual can both watch and listen, learning is enhanced over listening alone. Add to this a step-by-step presentation that is carefully sequenced so that each step builds upon the previous one, and learning is even more assured. However, the best use of the demonstration in teaching is to enable the observers to actually try the activity themselves. If this is not possible, then a representative of the observers should try it to ensure that the desired learning has indeed occurred. When skill development is the objective, demonstration and practice are essential. In general, adults like the demonstration strategy because it brings in-

to the learning situation the material the group is interested in learning (Draves, 1984).

Most learners are comfortable with the demonstration because it may allow handling materials used in the learning activity. Usually those who have never seen a demonstration easily adapt to this strategy because several of the sensory organs may be involved depending upon the kinds of materials used in the demonstration. Because of this, the knowledge gained is retained without much difficulty.

The teacher of adults should like the demonstration strategy because it allows movement, manipulation of materials, and other activities that help hold the observer's attention. The activity can (and should) be carefully planned and conducted without interruption because the presenter controls the pace and flow of the communication. However, this also places the responsibility upon the presenter to make certain the pace is conducive to learning. The teacher can get help from others in preparing the demonstration and can present it as a team if necessary. Teachers who have never given a demonstration can practice the activity until they feel ready to present it before a group. Since the process is similar regardless of the content, the teacher will gain confidence with each successive demonstration.

The content of the demonstration can vary widely. As Kahler et al. (1985) indicate, method demonstrations can include effective bidding in bridge and other card games, upholstering furniture, fly-tying, planting trees, or figuring cost analysis of various purchases. More recently, the videotape has been used for teaching guitar playing, flower and vegetable gardening, and exercise programs. Result demonstrations range from a simple activity completed in a few minutes to multiple activities requiring several weeks or even a few months, depending upon the learning goals.

Demonstrations are useful in a variety of adult-learning situations. They are used to promote new products, to create awareness and interest in a new procedure, to teach manipulative skills, or to promote confidence in new ideas and concepts by demonstrating possible outcomes of their acceptance. They are usually more effective than talks or discussions when materials must be presented in an orderly sequence. When time prevents the use of other strategies, the demonstration can present information that can be learned and applied in a short time. When psychomotor skills are to be acquired, the demonstration is the most effective strategy available. "Demonstrations occupy a favored place among the methods used in adult education" (Kahler et al., 1985, p. 139).

Example of a Demonstration

Situation: The Community Vegetable Garden Club is holding its monthly meeting at the home of one of the members. Fourteen members are present.

Topic: "The Importance of Soil Analysis in Successful Vegetable Gardening"

Leader: One of the members who regularly takes soil samples and delivers them to the county extension office for analysis

Procedure: After presenting information through an illustrated talk about the importance of soil analysis, the leader takes the group to a garden site where the equipment for taking soil samples is arranged for the demonstration. The leader then proceeds to take a soil sample from the garden site, carefully explaining each procedure as it is completed. When finished, the member asks for questions or comments from the group. After that, one or two members are asked to complete the demonstration. When they have finished, and the leader is satisfied that the

learning has been successful, the demonstration is completed.

The Interview

As a teaching strategy, an interview is a presentation in which an interviewer asks questions of one or possibly two resource persons before an audience. The resource persons are knowledgeable about a previously determined topic of interest to the audience and should have been informed about the kinds of questions that will be asked, especially those that will open the interview. Questions may be prepared in advance, improvised by the interviewer as the activity progresses, submitted to the interviewer on small cards by members of the audience, or a combination of the above.

Strengths and Limitations. According to Bergevin et al. (1963), the interview has many advantages:

1. The interview is relatively simple to plan and develop.

2. Because the audience is interested in the topic, boredom and apathy should not be a concern.

3. Many resource persons perform better during an interview than by other presentation strategies.

4. Points of interest can be clarified or discussed more in depth when necessary.

5. The audience can be indirectly involved in the questioning.

However, the interview also has limitations:

1. The interviewer must be skilled in asking questions and must not get personally involved during the interview process.

2. If the resource persons do not give relatively short responses, the interview can become a series of short speeches.

3. The resource persons might fail to answer the questions adequately, even after several efforts by the interviewer.

4. Some important details may be omitted if the right questions are not asked.

Designing the Interview. The interview is not difficult to design or conduct. The interviewer and the resource person(s) must be placed in full view of the audience, perhaps on a stage or raised podium, and an adequate sound system must be provided.

The main tasks must be done before the interview actually occurs. The topics selected must interest the expected audience. The interviewer must be skilled not only in phrasing questions, but also in setting a tone that will produce a relaxed, informal learning atmosphere. The resource persons must be apprised of the purpose of the activity and should be given any information that could enhance the quality of their responses, such as any special interests expected in the audience. If the audience is to submit questions before the activity begins, then the means of handling this procedure must be organized. Alternative procedures would be needed if questions are allowed during or after the interview.

When all participants are ready, a chairperson or leader introduces the topic, the interviewer, and the resource persons. All could be done by the interviewer if there is no chairperson. Questioning begins and the interview continues for the designated time limit. Questions from the audience, if allowed, may be solicited at the conclusion of the interview, at which time the chairperson

summarizes the interview and the activity is completed.

Adapting the Interview. Learners must listen intently and quietly and not react when a response pleases or displeases them. Audience members should take notes if a response is unclear or if they need more information about particular points. For the interview to be more meaningful, the learners should have previously acquired basic knowledge of the topic. When the interview is over, the learners should be willing to undertake any necessary follow-up study and interaction.

The teacher has the responsibility of arranging all of the components for a successful interview. Often, the teacher assumes the role of interviewer and performs all the introductions. The interviewer then asks questions in a conversational manner, allowing ample time for the resource persons to respond. The interviewer's responsibility includes trying to make the audience feel a part of the interview. This is made easier by the teacher's familiarity with both the resource persons and the audience. As interviewer, the teacher can direct the interview to address the learning needs of the student-audience and can encourage whatever follow-up study and activities are appropriate.

When the teacher feels uncomfortable using the interview strategy, practice with other teachers and counselors may be beneficial in acquiring skill and confidence with the interview. Learning to ask meaningful questions is crucial to conducting effective interviews. Observing good interviewers on television or with videotapes can also be helpful, especially toward helping the adult learner feel comfortable in the interview situation.

The interview accommodates a variety of content. When facts and related information are derived from experts on a topic, the interview is useful. This strategy can also be used to clarify issues and to develop interest in a topic through the knowledge and enthusiasm of the resource persons. In this case, the interview brings the resource persons and audience together for further learning or even possible action. Examples of varied content can be seen in the television programs "Meet the Press" and "Face the Nation."

As Draves (1984) and Bergevin et al. (1963) indicate, this strategy is best used in adult learning situations to:

1. Present information in a relaxed and informal manner.
2. Explore or analyze problems.
3. Stimulate interest in a topic.
4. Obtain the perception of an authority about a specific subject.
5. Use outside resources effectively without having to listen to speeches.
6. Encourage the audience to participate in asking questions about the topic.

Example of an Interview

The Junior League of Windover Community meets monthly to study current trends and issues affecting members' lives. At the March meeting, the program chair arranged an interview of two individuals:

1. Cindy Fisher, local social worker
2. Esteban Ruiz, detective, juvenile branch, city police

The topic selected by the program chair was "Child Abuse and What Can Be Done about It." During the interview, the members of the club learned the following information:

1. The extent of child abuse is much greater in Windover than club members had imagined.
2. Certain behavior by children can indicate that they are being abused.
3. Child abuse occurs in many forms and at all socioeconomic levels within a community.

4. There is a need to educate the public about the extent of child abuse and what can be done to prevent it.

At the conclusion of the interview, the members of the Junior League asked several questions of the resource persons. At the April meeting, the members voted to make child abuse their primary topic for study the following year and tentatively agreed to seek information in regard to establishing a hot line for child abuse in Windover in the near future.

Utilizing Technology in Presentation Strategies

As advances in technology influence our lives, we discover more and more choices in how to do things. Education is no exception. Technology has provided the adult educator with new opportunities for learning and the teacher of adults can also utilize these new opportunities to improve teaching strategies.

Various technologies have been used in teaching for many years, including slides, films, audio tape recorders, and related equipment. However, in the past two decades, the term *technology* has acquired new meaning. Not only has the quantity of new devices increased, but the sophistication level has risen correspondingly. Much time and effort could be devoted to describing how many technological devices can be utilized with presentation strategies. However, the format for this section follows that used by Buskey (1984) and consists of three areas of concern—audio technologies, video technologies, and computers. The information presented is concise; for more complete information about utilizing technology in adult education, the reader should consult the excellent book, *Technologies for Learning outside the Classroom,* edited by Niemi and Gooler (1987).

Selecting Technology

Technology should be viewed as something the adult education teacher utilizes to enhance the learners' ability to acquire the knowledge or skills desired. Therefore, whatever devices are chosen should fit into whatever activities have been planned to enable students to reach their learning objectives. Too often, teachers try to determine what technology is available (for use by themselves or by someone else) and then try to design the procedures around it. Buskey (1984) rejects this idea and indicates that only after the learning objectives have been established (by the learner and the teacher) should consideration be given to selecting the media and technology to be utilized. This is especially true in learning activities outside the regular classroom setting.

Buskey also suggests several criteria to consider in deciding which media or technology to use. These include the size of the group (if not individualized), nature of the content to be learned, instructional strategies, portability of equipment, the learners' experience with the technology, and the facilitator's ability to use it effectively. In addition, Niemi and Gooler (1987) indicate if technology is to be effective in adult education, the preparation of those who use it is of utmost importance. Because of adults' various learning styles, the technology must not only support a preferred learning style but must also be used in a way that helps the adult to maximize learning efficiency.

Audio Technologies

In using audio technologies, the teacher must recognize the difference between hearing and listening. Whereas hearing is a physiological process, listening is more of a psychological process. Audio equipment should be utilized not only to enhance listening but also to en-

courage it (Heinich, Molenda, & Russell, 1982). Breakdown in audio communications between the sender and the receiver can occur at many points, and faulty or improperly used equipment can easily contribute to such barriers.

Strengths and Weaknesses. Audio media and devices have many attractions, including:

1. They are relatively inexpensive when compared to other forms of media.
2. They are usually easy to use.
3. They can be utilized in learning activities for all adults.
4. Many of them are small and portable.

However, as with other media, audio equipment also has limitations:

1. Because only one of the senses (hearing) is involved, people may easily tune out the message or simply hear instead of listen.
2. Tapes and related devices can be erased, broken, or lost if not carefully monitored.

Using Recordings in Learning Activities. Prerecorded tapes and records have many uses in adult education. In the study of the Franklin Library series, Great Books of the Western World, recordings can bring alive the speech of someone from world history or one of the great philosophers. For undereducated adults, recordings can supplement worksheets or other study guides in literacy or English-as-a-second-language classes, particularly in pronunciation activities. Kemp and Dayton (1985) indicate that recordings have two main instructional formats. The audio notebook uses the recording to introduce the topic or explain the content and learning activities that will follow. After the student has completed a section in a study guide, the tape can be used again for questions or follow-up discussions. With the audio tutorial system, the recording actually directs the learner to or through all of the learning endeavors: reading, observations, worksheets, and related activities.

Heinich et al. (1982) suggest that business and industry have also capitalized upon learning opportunities with audio technology. For example, sales repesentatives often spend hundreds of hours each year either in their automobiles or in airplanes. Utilizing audio tapes, sometimes with earphones, employees listen to lectures about the proper approach in contacting new clients or to a symposium about the future marketability of the products they are trying to sell. In addition, "Many companies and individuals have found cassette tapes extremely useful for personnel development" (Heinich et al., 1982, p. 155). Major uses range from instruction in basic reading skills to problem-solving and decision-making strategies.

Adults with special needs, particularly the blind or visually impaired, can benefit from audio media. Interviews with important politicians, a speech from a prominent world figure, or a panel discussion about current environmental issues can help keep the visually handicapped person up-to-date. With the increasing emphasis on oral history, not only can visually impaired persons learn from the interviews, but they can also become involved in the process and contribute to the making of history themselves!

Using the Telephone in Learning Activities. Although available for many years, the telephone has only recently been utilized extensively in adult education. Buskey (1984) has stated that the real potency of telephone use in instruction is in networking. Through dedicated lines, speaker telephones, or amplifier-microphone systems, and careful arrangements, virtually the entire world could be available to the adult learner. The telelecture can enable an instructor on one continent to lecture to a group of adults on another or be interviewed by group members in place of or following a speech. With a larger telephone network, several groups of learners can benefit from the consultant's expertise at the same time or cooperatively interview the expert with a prearranged format. Candidates for public office or politicians already in elected offices could participate in a symposium or a panel discussion even though hundreds of miles may separate them. The telelecture can also be supplemented with visuals; this is discussed in the next section.

Using Radio in Learning Activities. Radio is probably used more for educational purposes in developing countries than in the more developed world. Publications of the United Nations Educational, Scientific, and Cultural Organization (UNESCO) report that radio has been one of the principal mediums for providing literacy education in several parts of the world. Cost-effectiveness is one of the main reasons for that extensive usage, especially when mass instruction is feasible (Takemoto, 1987).

However, the relatively fast-paced format can serve the adult clientele in any country. Timely lectures can be delivered, symposia held, and interviews conducted for the learner. In the 1960s, "Everybody's Farm Hour," a program popular with farmers in parts of Ohio, Indiana, and Kentucky, was broadcast daily over radio station WLW in Cincinnati. Panel discussions with leaders of farm organizations, talks by marketing specialists, and interviews with successful farmers were presented for the mostly rural listeners. National Public Radio also broadcasts several programs that use lectures, panel discussions, and other teaching strategies.

Takemoto (1987) indicates that radio is used extensively in many remote areas like Alaska to augment courses that are amenable to audio formats, especially foreign language instruction. Radio combined with telephone call-ins or related feedback is also available on a limited basis. Even though radio is viewed primarily as entertainment, its potential for teaching still exists. As Takemoto (1987) states, "Although often regarded as the missed opportunity and the forgotten medium, radio has played a relatively quiet but steady role in U.S. formal education" (p. 24).

Audio technology can be utilized effectively in teaching adults. As Heinich et al. (1982) point out, "The uses of audio media are limited only by the imagination of teachers and students" (p. 153).

Video Technologies

Before discussing video technologies, there must be a clear understanding of *video*. According to McInnes (1980), "Video is the use of electronic cameras, recorders, and display screens . . . every teacher should be aware of the whole range of media that are useful in the teaching/learning process—*video* is just one of them" (p. 9). He also emphasizes that video is not a new medium and that teachers need to begin using it properly to enhance their students' learning.

Unfortunately, too many educators feel that video or visual technologies should be left to professionals and therefore never acquire the knowledge to use visual media properly in learning activities. Heinich et al. (1982) insist we understand that the concept *visual literacy* is becoming as important as the original term *literacy,* meaning the ability to read and write. This importance is based upon the "quantum leap in the production and distribution of visual messages" (Heinich et al., 1982, p. 65). These messages not only

appear over television but on tapes, billboards, posters, newspapers, and lately even T-shirts. They also indicate that as teachers or facilitators of learning, we have some responsibility to teach our adult students the skills of visual literacy so they can read visual messages accurately and use them in their own learning endeavors (Heinich et al., 1982, p. 64).

Video technologies include several kinds of media, but for this chapter only three will be discussed: video and films, television, and computers.

Using Video and Films in Adult Education. Kemp and Dayton (1985) support discussing films and video together because "video recordings and motion pictures share a close relationship . . . both . . . can present information, describe a process, clarify complex concepts, teach a skill, condense and expand time, and affect an attitude" (p. 221). The advantages of both include:

1. They show process and motion.
2. They are particularly useful in teaching knowledge and skills.
3. They allow close-ups, image freezing, emphasis of key concepts, and related techniques which can be most useful in learning.
4. They can be used many times to study sensitive situations and hazardous materials (Heinich et al., 1982).

Even though video recordings and motion pictures are similar, the film used in motion pictures has a higher resolution, better color fidelity, and greater contrast range. However, video is less sensitive to light, does not need developing, is more easily edited, and can be duplicated at lower cost. Kemp and Dayton (1985) state, "As technology continues to improve the electronics of the video medium, and as greater standardization is realized, it is evident that video will increasingly become the major format" (p. 221). Therefore, major emphasis in the following pages will be given to video recording, both tape and disc.

Business and industry were the early users of video for the education and training of adults, and they still account for over 50 percent of such use (Bunyan, Crimmins, & Watson, 1978). Kinds of presentations that can be delivered on video include new employee orientation, safety instructions, preretirement planning, and current problems facing the corporation. In addition to lectures, a panel of experts from within or outside the company can deliver timely information, while demonstrations of technical skills or examples of how to solve management problems are distributed widely on both films and tapes.

Both turnover rates and growth have fostered the use of films and video tapes in government agencies at all levels. Employees of local government listen to presentations about new policies and procedures while city police employees view demonstrations of how and how not to invoke the law. Panels and symposia of international experts talk about the Acquired Immune Deficiency Syndrome (AIDS) virus, terrorism, nuclear war, the environment, and related issues at national conferences and workshops. With demonstrations and lectures from experts, employees learn how to apply insecticides, pesticides, and other chemicals and how to adhere to new legal standards.

Wide use of video can also be found in the medical field. The Center for Continuing Education at Hendrick Memorial Hospital, Abilene, Texas, produces videotaped lectures and seminars for physicians, nursing students, medical technicians, and operating room personnel (Bunyan et al., 1978). Continuing medical education uses tapes exten-

sively through lecture-based presentations and a wide range of demonstrations.

Because of their storage capacity videodiscs are destined to play an even greater role in adult education. In addition, the recent introduction of laser disc systems offers the potential for recording events at local levels instead of having to depend on using materials produced elsewhere for the education of adults.

Using Television in Adult-Learning Activities. Television is widely used today in adult education because of local cable access, channel availabilty via satellite, and microwave transmissions. Some trainers feel that television could almost replace a live teacher, but Wiesner (1987) notes that several authors caution against that attitude. Indeed, Harrington (1977) cites lack of personal contact as the nemesis of television for instructional purposes, and Wiesner (1987) states that "when it comes to documenting the experience of distance learners, the research on television falls short" (p. 13). But, he also feels that adult students will sacrifice personal contact and interaction for the convenience of not having to attend classes at a site requiring travel: "From an educator's point of view, the question is to what extent the convenience of telecourses justifies the lack of interaction and contact" (p. 13).

The advantages of utilizing television in adult education include:

1. Because it is an electronic rather than a mechanical process, its signals can be transmitted long distances, recorded, and played back instantly.

2. Large audiences can be reached at relatively low cost.

3. Viewers can be dispersed over long distances.

4. The "open learning" concept can be activated through television (Heinich et al., 1982).

Instructional television can provide learning experiences that would otherwise be unavailable to adults. Interviews with scientists, political figures, teachers, and business leaders can be broadcast to virtually any part of the world where a receiver exists. Applications are most notable in medical education (live demonstrations of surgical procedures or videotaped case studies), employee training and development (lectures for new agents of insurance companies or seminars for service and marketing personnel of automobile agencies), teacher training (experts located hundreds of miles apart analyzing a teacher's performance), or training a group to learn sign language through lecture and demonstrations (Bunyan et al., 1978). Television has also been used extensively in adult basic education. "Operation Alphabet," "Your Future is Now," and the Kentucky Educational Television high school equivalency (GED) series are examples of those efforts.

More recently, the PLUS (Project Literacy U.S.) effort to raise citizen awareness of adult illiteracy and its effects on society is an example of a much wider effort to educate adults through television. Wiesner (1987) indicates that television's effect upon undereducated adults, however, depends upon the quality of the support systems available at the local level, including classes, tutors, and public awareness and support.

Television has also been the basis for the advance of *distance education* in recent years. Credit and noncredit courses and programs are offered by several universities and businesses on a wide variety of topics. Public television has not only survived but maintains a prominent place among the commercial networks even though donations and contributions provide most of its support. Lectures, panel discussions, interviews, dialogues, and demonstrations are featured for viewers. Telecourses have been attempted by a number of broadcast stations in order to literally take the campus to the student; one successful example is the British Open University. The development of a consortium of organizations has helped provide opportunities for adults to obtain a bachelor's degree. Some of these consortia often contain institutions from more than one country (Heinich et al., 1982).

A number of presentation strategies are suitable for instructional applications through television. These include interviews, voice-over narrative, panels, lectures, and demonstrations (Gayeski, 1983). Most require little in terms of design, scripting, and production, but they must be planned carefully and produced with occasional change and variety in format to prevent boredom.

Although television has served adult education extensively, Wiesner (1987) sees an even greater future for it. As consumer level grows and costs are reduced, larger audiences will begin to participate, particularly in underdeveloped countries that have not had the resources to utilize this medium extensively for educational purposes. "In the coming decades, television will continue to play an important part in extending education beyond the classroom. Therefore, educators will have to confront the issue of cost-effectiveness and struggle to balance media production values with academic requirements for accuracy, relevance, and currency" (Wiesner, 1987, p. 17).

Computer Technologies

Computers have become an integral part of almost everyone's life. Whether by the microcomputer in the home or office, an electronic bulletin board, or a large data base with the family's financial and medical records, our very existence is often influenced by computers in many ways. Education is no exception. College, schools, businesses, public and private agencies, the military, and religious organizations are utilizing them in many teaching modes.

Although computers are more suitable for an interactive learning format with adults, there are some strategies that work well where the adult is primarily in a receiving or passive mode. Even here, some variety or somewhat frequent breaks in the instruction must be programmed into the process.

Drill and Practice. In this form of instruction, the computer provides for reinforcement of certain knowledge and skills. Adult basic education students find these kinds of exercises most useful in learning mathematics, but even more important are the vocabulary building exercises or foreign language classes taken by speakers of any language. Several levels of difficulty may be developed within the same drill-and-practice program, which can include both positive and negative feedback (Heinich et al., 1982).

Tutorial Instruction. In this instructional mode, the computer emulates a human tutor or teacher. In general, a program presents concepts, principles, practices, and related information about the knowledge to be learned. Then questions or problems are given to the learner, and an appropriate response is requested. When an incorrect response is given, the computer may move to remedial information or recycle to the previous instruction. Teaching technical information or skills to new employees or a refresher course to employed technicians or engineers are frequent uses for this instructional mode (Heinich et al., 1982).

More discussion about the use of computers is found with other teaching strategies. However, as we have noted, computers can be utilized effectively to enhance learning even when the student assumes a primarily passive mode in learning.

CHAPTER FOUR

Using Action Strategies

"Boy, these seats are hard," thought Joe as he wiggled back and forth in his chair. The teacher was throwing out ideas that were interesting, but it was getting harder and harder to concentrate on what he was saying. What was that old saying Joe had heard someplace before—something like "The mind can absorb only as much as the seat can endure"? He sure was reaching that point now! Well, what other choice did he have? He really needed to learn how solar energy systems work, and this course came at the right time. But Mike Simpson was putting a system in his new house; maybe he could offer to help Mike and learn in the process. The teacher had mentioned a couple of good books that had just come out and that were available at a local book store. Maybe if he read the books he would have enough ideas to be of use to Mike. Then he could learn the how-to-do-it by helping him. Yeah, that sounded like a good idea—do some reading and practice on Mike's house. That would be better than just sitting here and certainly better than practicing on his own house. Let's give it a try!

Joe's dilemma is fairly common in adult-learning situations. Most adults are not well-trained students. They are not used to sitting quietly and listening passively to ideas presented by another. Quite the opposite. They are accustomed to doing something themselves about their problems and their needs. They are used to being active. So, it should be no surprise to us that when it comes to learning tasks, the average adult behaves in much the same way as when he faces any other task. The adult looks around for something that might work and tries it. The criteria for method or resource selection are more likely to involve the amount of time, effort, and money demanded by the resource than any close analysis of the efficacy of the learning methodology. Trial and error, asking a friend or neighbor, and checking a how-to-do-it manual are still the most popular ways for adults to attempt to learn something. These may not be the most efficient means of learning but they are approaches the individual can use and still remain active and in control of the situation. This has led adult educators to advocate action strategies for the teaching of adults.

Overview of Action Strategies

Action strategies are teaching activities in which the learners are physically as well as intellectually active during the learning process. Examples of such strategies include the following: in-basket activities, case studies, simulations, role playing, skits, self-tests, field trips, and direct experiences such as microteaching. Because the amount of learner participation is so great, the amount of control or responsibility for the learning also tends to move from the teacher to the participant.

Action strategies have long been recognized for their effectiveness with adult learners. After reviewing hundreds of reports on the effectiveness of instructional strategies, McKeachie (1974) concluded that although most traditional principles of learning are not valid in all cases, some "do stand up fairly well in this more complex domain. For example: (a) active participation is better than passive learning if active learning means something more than writing out an answer one already knows" (p. 187). Knowles (1970) simply states: "Given a choice between two techniques, choose the one involving the students in the most active participation" (p. 294).

Adult Learners and Action Strategies

The great advantage of participative strategies is that they seem natural to adult learners. As adults we like being in charge of things. We might not always like the responsibility, but we like even less being manipulated into doing things that seem silly or meaningless to us. This suggests that our first standard regarding the use of action strategies might well be: *Such approaches must seem natural and meaningful to the adult learner.* The apparent appropriateness of any instructional activity will, of course, depend largely on the learners' attitudes. However, their attitudes are usually less important than their success in meeting objectives. Thus the appropriateness of the activity to the participants' learning objectives is the best guarantee that the activity will be perceived as relevant.

Most adults will readily agree that they prefer to be active rather than passive in a learning situation. This greater enjoyment of more active approaches is obviously an advantage to their use. However, many of our fellow adults have been conditioned to believe that learning should be hard work, not fun. Until they realize that learning can be both hard work and enjoyable, caution might be needed in the use of active learning strategies. In any case, a second warning

worth suggesting is: *Avoid active strategies that might appear childish or irrelevant to the adult participants.*

Obviously one of the reasons we frequently avoid a formal learning situation in favor of a self-directed but less productive learning approach is that we don't want to commit the time necessary to meet the requirements of the structured learning activity. Time is a very precious commodity to most adults. They will often sacrifice quality of effect for a saving of time. Because active learning strategies frequently demand more time than passive approaches do, another standard for practice might be: *Make sure the time needed to conduct action-type strategies is available and its use agreeable to adult participants.* Individuals with a pressing need for detailed information are likely to respond more positively to a situation in which that information is delivered in a concise, orderly manner. To press them into an active search for answers that are readily available elsewhere can be a waste of their time and energy.

Learning Styles and Action Strategies

Although it seems that most adults do prefer to be active in their learning endeavors, we cannot be certain that *preferred* learning style is equivalent to *most efficient* learning style. However, it does seem logical that adult learners who are more active and who have more control over their learning activities will, for the most part, choose learning approaches that are more conducive to their own style of learning.

One cognitive factor that relates to this issue is learning mode. Some of us learn better through an auditory mode while others need to see something to remember or understand. For others, learning efforts are fruitless until they do something with the lesson. For learners who are kinesthetically inclined—who need physical movement as part of their learning activities—action strategies offer a more effective approach. Perhaps, including this additional sensory modality—movement or kinesthesis—in the action strategies makes them better learning approaches for the majority of adult learners. After all, it has long been an accepted instructional principle that the more senses are involved in the learning activity, the more likely students are to learn and remember.

Teachers and Action Strategies

The degree of control that a teacher feels must be maintained over a learning activity could easily influence that person's preference for or rejection of action strategies. Control can be maintained in such approaches, but the manner in which the leader does this will differ from situations in which participants are more passive. In action approaches, control comes through careful preplanning of activities and through attention to such elements as timing, selection of materials, and interpersonal relations. The teacher accustomed to maintaining control by dominating the situation may have trouble using such tactics in action situations.

Action strategies also call for different skills from the teacher. Structured and well-organized presentation strategies must give way to patience and question-posing skills. Ability to analyze processes affecting the learning situation becomes vital as the emphasis switches from content to process. Group-facilitating skills, for example, are more frequently called upon in action strategies than in other activities. So are timing skills, for such activities are often much more effective if a question is posed, information injected, or efforts redirected at the right moment.

The time and effort needed to search out resources and carefully plan each part of the learning activity make special demands of the teacher. Case studies, role plays, and field trips do not just happen. Not every administrator is able to offer teachers the material or financial resources necessary to put such activities together. Even when they can, appropriate activities may need to be redesigned or newly created to fit the expressed needs of a particular group. The teacher's role becomes that of learning-activity designer and planner and learning facilitator instead of leader or presenter.

Teacher-centered approaches tend to give way to learner-centered approaches in action strategies. Emphasis is on what the participants are doing, not on what the teacher is doing. The teacher has to be willing to move with the action and to change plans when unanticipated events occur. Such reaction may be as much a part of a person's educational philosophy as practice because it takes a certain faith in people to risk such change and experimentation. But a teacher who demonstrates such confidence in learners and lets them know they are in charge of their learning has a chance to have a lasting effect on their development. In learner-centered approaches, the leader and the participants are sharers in both the successes and failures. The excuse "I did my job; they just weren't ready to learn!" will not work.

Learning Objectives and Action Strategies

The presentation of information is not a suitable objective for most action strategies. On the other hand, when the purpose of the learning activity relates to the use or evaluation of such knowledge, action strategies become very effective approaches. While ability to apply or analyze cognitive information might be gained through insightful discussion with others, these are certainly appropriate objectives for involving action methodologies. Some form of practice or doing is frequently necessary before we can transfer such cognitive skills to general use. This becomes even more necessary if the content we are learning is to be synthesized with other information or if we are to pass judgment on its worth. Thus we can see that although action strategies may not be appropriate for the sharing of content at the knowledge or understanding levels, they are effective at higher cognitive levels.

Such approaches are also effective in teaching psychomotor skills. One criticism of traditional approaches to education has been that most teaching stops short of helping learners make the newly taught skill or behavior their own. Options may be presented well, reasons for choosing a certain approach stated clearly, and decisions for action posed convincingly; but if the new behavior never becomes internalized—that is, never practiced to the point of being as easy as the old way of acting—it will be forgotten or abandoned in actual practice. Action learning experiences provide not only an opportunity for practice but an opportunity for *safe* practice. This element of safety is important when mistakes in practice could involve serious injury or great financial waste, such as in driving skills or health care. However, from the psychological point of view, it is always important for learners to feel free to try out new behavior before making it part of their repertoire.

Examining the relationships among people or other variables, assessing the impact of various elements contributing to a certain outcome, or clarifying the processes involved in a complex situation are the special strengths of action approaches to learning. As such, they can be particularly useful in laying the groundwork for the development of attitudes or value sets. This is vital to reaching objectives in the affective domain. However, when such goals as the development of interpersonal skills or appreciation for superior products are being pursued, such insight alone is not always sufficient. The encouragement of meaningful others and the dedication of one's own efforts to the accomplishment of a worthy goal supply psychological elements that are as essential as cognitive elements when pursuing goals in the affective domain. Action strategies such as gaming or role playing, which involve the learner in a struggle to resolve an issue and, at the same time, to clarify processes involved in the interaction, provide techniques for accomplishing both of these essential elements and thus are excellent ways of reaching affective goals.

How to Use Action Strategies Effectively

Time is usually listed as the number one payment demanded of those who would use action strategies to accomplish learning goals. Usually, it takes longer to prepare such learning activities and longer to conduct them. Preparation frequently calls for the collection and setting up of equipment and resource materials as well as careful planning of the activity. The location or creation of a suitable strategy is but the first step. To be effective, care must also be given to personal and interpersonal relations among the learners, to alternative strategies for the times when action may not go as planned, and to the timing of the various steps involved in the methodology. Such time is not always available. If that is the case, it may be better to choose another strategy but to resolve that the next time this lesson is to be taught, the resources, strategies, and time will have been found to prepare an action approach.

In certain instances action strategies can actually save time. Many gaming situations are designed, for example, to condense the action within a time frame that makes it feasible to deal with processes that in reality are spread over days or months. Simulated models can lead a learner through activities in a fraction of the time it would take for direct experience. Case studies can present in a few minutes the essential elements of a situation that took years to develop.

Another major condition affecting the use of such strategies is the financial and material resources available to the facilitator. This is indeed a concern but today need not be overwhelming. Many collections of useful action strategies are available through such sources as University Associates of Palo Alto, California, or other publishing houses. Besides, the argument can always be offered to concerned administrators that such simulated experiences are actually much cheaper than individualized, on-the-job experience would be.

The rules and regulations of institutions and agencies at times conflict with good educational practice. Questions of insurance and responsibility, of public image and precedence, or of reaction of other staff members can be raised when different teaching strategies are used. Perhaps even more discouraging, though, is the complete disregard of many institutions for teaching methodology. No incentives are offered for attempts to improve instruction. In either case, the determination of the instructional leader to do a professional job may be the sole determinant of whether such rules or attitudes change, or remain to discourage good practice.

Educators considering methods that call for learners' active participation must certainly keep in mind the attitudes and expectations of the participants. Many adults have a definite idea of what school should be, based on experiences of childhood. Until they can be reeducated to understand that not every-

thing that has been done in school is productive of new learning, novel approaches to instruction may turn them off rather than on to learning. At the same time it is important to give adults credit for being reasonable and insightful creatures. Explaining the rationale for using different strategies or helping a group evaluate the effectiveness of their learning experiences can encourage adult participants to appreciate strategies that may not be what they are used to but that do seem natural to them. The rule remains: Use approaches that seem reasonable and that do not leave the learners with a feeling of discomfort.

The learners' physical status may affect the feeling of comfort in the learning situation. Adults who come to a learning activity after working all day may appreciate interludes, when they can be quiet, relaxed recipients, instead of constantly active. Individuals with physical impediments may be leery of situations where movement or vision problems can occur. Parents or others on call may be reluctant to participate in a field trip or similar activity if that means they will be out of reach of a phone for a considerable time. Again, adult learners will adjust to many of these situations if the learning strategy is obviously effective, but such training in the art of learning how to learn is something the teacher must offer them. While some teachers struggle with the advisability of scheduling a field trip, their students are wondering why they should sit in a classroom and discuss a situation when they could go a few blocks down the street and actually observe it!

In-Basket Exercise

The in-basket exercise derives its name from the manager's in-basket or mailbox. It is a simulation strategy in which items that might appear in a manager's box are presented to participants, who must then make a decision on the proper strategy for responding to each item. Usually participants work alone for a set period of time before moving into a discussion phase in which rationale for and outcome of the various reactions to the problems posed by the in-basket items are examined.

Strengths and Limitations. Such activities are particularly suited for management training and can be designed to apply to specific problem areas. The dynamics of the activity usually uncover a variety of factors impinging on the situation. Consequently in-basket exercises offer some of the following advantages:

1. They involve the participant in situations similar to those faced on the job and evoke personal decisions and analyses of the causes and effects of these decisions from each learner.

2. They are rather easy to construct and involve the use of few resources beyond the paper upon which they are printed.

3. Each exercise can be designed to deal with problems specific to the organization or the position for which the individual is being trained.

4. Learners are offered the opportunity to experiment with new behavioral patterns in a relatively safe environment.

5. Exercises can be easily adapted to fit time constraints and most other situational variables.

6. No special skills beyond those of any good teacher are demanded of the instructor.

7. Such activities call for the exercise of higher order cognitive skills.

8. In-basket exercises are involving and interesting to most participants.

The use of in-basket activities is not suited to all types of training situations. People who are not accustomed to dealing with print correspondence would have difficulty relating to this activity. Other limitations include:

1. The reaction of a learner to a situation in a classroom might be radically different under the pressures of the actual work environment.

2. At times, participants react to problems they see in the described situation rather than to the problem the instructor attempted to pose. The limited time devoted to orienting participants to the simulated situation often leaves them with varying perceptions of the environment.

3. The development of new insights and skills is dependent upon the quality of the discussion that follows the exercise. Strong proponents of a less insightful approach could influence less experienced participants.

4. Complete analysis of the situations posed by the in-basket exercise can often be very time-consuming.

Designing In-Basket Exercises. Is an in-basket the appropriate strategy? In-basket exercises are not just an enjoyable way of learning but also fun to create. They allow instructional leaders to pose relevant questions in creative ways and challenge them to approach learning objectives in a holistic manner. Thus, it is vital that the designers ask themselves two questions before they begin work on a new in-basket exercise. What is the specific purpose of this learning activity? The educational objectives must be carefully thought out and must guide the design throughout. The second question is why is the in-basket exercise the chosen strategy for accomplishing these objectives? If other methods will meet the objectives more fully, forget about designing an in-basket exercise.

In practice, an in-basket exercise is an ideal way of getting a group to examine a previously ignored aspect of a problem. For example, one group examining the management of continuing education functions expressed little awareness of the impact of value sets on the educational environment. A specially designed in-basket dealing with familiar problems, each of which was affected by value conflicts among those involved, became an ideal occasion for diagnosing and discussing the impact of attitudes and values on the continuing education process.

An important element in the learning process is providing alternative strategies for the resolution of a problem. This aspect of learning is frequently ignored, especially among experienced adults. It is so much easier to grab at past solutions—especially if they were successful—than to examine all the potential options. Such practice can easily interfere with learning, for the same old tired solution seldom leads to improvement in practice. Thus, when learners evaluate the new behavior, they see no improvement, abandon the practice and return to their original behavior in that situation. When a number of options are explored, learners may still choose the old solution, but when that approach proves unsatisfactory, they have a number of other ideas from which to select. This is one of the advantages of using a strategy like the in-basket. Participants see that a number of different ways of resolving a dilemma are possible and that their favorite techniques may not seem so great to others.

Another advantage is the holistic approach encouraged in the analysis of problem situations. One group we worked with insisted on redesigning the staffing patterns within the proposed organization before working on any of the problems posed in the exercise. Indeed, staffing patterns had contributed to the difficulty of decision making in most of the instances posed, although that was not the area we had posed for analysis. Because the reality of human interaction is complex, teaching strategies that encourage holistic approaches can be appropriate.

In-basket activities can be especially significant when all participants are members of the same organization and can apply the insights gained to their common situation. This encourages immediate and mutual application of new behaviors that have been tried and evaluated in the safe educational environment. However, in-basket exercises can also have distinct advantages when the participants represent different situational and experiential backgrounds. Varied insights can contribute significantly to the creative resolution of difficulties.

In like manner, such activities can be used either to develop a general impression of or to examine in detail some process within the overall situation. Discussing the implications of a certain action on various parts of the organization promotes awareness of the total situation. However, the exercises may be restricted to a detailed examination of a specific process within the general structure.

What Issues Will the In-Basket Examine?
Once the objectives have been set and the in-basket exercise selected as the appropriate strategy, the educator must decide what issues to examine. Much of this, of course, will be influenced by the clientele, the insights and priorities of the instructional leader, and the situation. But one of the first decisions to be made is whether to use issues that have broad application to the total system or that concentrate on issues relevant to some component of the general system. The effect of general policy, of public relations, of communication patterns, of supervisory tactics, of human relations, or of

organizational staffing patterns are examples of general issues that can suitably be used in an in-basket. The patterns, procedures, or problems of a unit within the system are examples of issues that could be used when the decision has been made to concentrate on a certain component of the system.

What Situations Can Be Used? Either the actual work situation of the trainee or a completely contrived one can be used as long as the situation closely simulates reality. The learning objectives will determine the feasibility of the site selected. Perhaps more important is the level of the position assigned and the characteristics of other staff members with whom the learner will have to interact. Variety should be built into the situation, and stereotypic models that are likely to encourage stereotypic solutions avoided. Slip a character or two into the staff to add a little spice to the situation! But have the learner operate at an appropriate level to satisfy the training objectives.

One component that must be built into the situation is a rationale for completing the exercise in a specified time. Such time pressure forces participants to make decisions and specify courses of action. It is also convenient to have individuals within groups arrive at the discussion stage at the same time. The restricted time frame also prevents the learner from avoiding responsibility for action by resorting to delaying tactics or by using resource people to make the decisions. This time pressure can be established by scheduling a trip out of town, a meeting important enough to outlaw disturbance, or an already overloaded itinerary. Time pressures can be increased during the process of the exercise by having unexpected problems arise, unannounced visits occur, or unavoidable telephone calls interrupt—as they so often do in our everyday lives.

What Materials Should Be Used? The actual working materials of the in-basket exercise can be any of those typically found on a desk: memos, letters, contracts, telephone messages, personal notes, minutes of meetings, forms needing signatures, or newspaper clippings. Variety can be added with tape recorders that are activated at certain times to simulate telephone calls, announcements, or news broadcasts. What these materials must do is present with sufficient clarity and urgency a situation that demands some reaction. The problems or situations must reflect training session objectives but should include enough variety to challenge even the most experienced participant. Setups can add to the action by presenting an apparently simple problem that will be complicated by some item following later in the exercise. Such situations can also be useful in teaching the value of prioritizing work or being flexible. The teacher should build into these items the communication breakdowns and policy inconsistencies so typical of most organizations. Contradictory messages from different levels of the structure or different individuals on the staff can also be used.

Since the purpose of in-basket exercises is to examine the implications of decisions and action strategies, such exercises must be designed and conducted so that they press participants to specify in detail their reaction to the situations. Because we are not accustomed to describing proposed action in writing, participants tend to be vague. "Talk to the secretary about this" may be a typical response but does not indicate what direction or strategy will be followed in such a conversation and thus is not an adequate response. Some developers of in-baskets deal with this tendency to avoid full descriptions of action by including specific questions as an addendum to a piece of material in the basket. Others urge participants several times during the course of the exercise to be specific and detailed.

Leading an In-Basket Exercise. The typical skills demanded of a facilitator are those needed to lead any exercise of this kind. Because many adults have never experienced this type of training, care should be taken to explain the goals, procedures, and terminology used in the exercise. Clarifying the setting in which learners are to operate and guaranteeing that their answers or attempts at resolving issues will not be used against them is even more vital. Selling them on the value of such an exercise in contrast to more traditional approaches to learning may be necessary for some groups of adults. It is always important that adults see the meaningfulness of an activity.

Once participants have completed their individual reactions to an item in the exercise, the size of the group will affect the further processing of the material. The leader could review the exercise with each on a one-to-one basis. Because of the value of using the insight and experience of the other adults in the group, it is usually better to proceed through open discussion among all members. If the group is large, divide it into groups of five or six persons. If care is taken to ensure diversity in such grouping, this size will enable all participants to share their proposed action and yet provide the group with a variety of input. Such small groups are also more likely to reach consensus on a preferred course of action, if that is a desired outcome of the exercise. The leader can always lead a summary discussion on the more interesting points or implications noted by the various groups if reporting by each group is undesirable. Frequently, participants expect and want the leader to go through the exercise and indicate a preferred action in each

situation. This can be another way of summarizing the exercise.

Evaluation of in-basket activities may be especially important if the exercise is newly created or if participants are not accustomed to this kind of activity. Ideally, the facilitator will devise some means of judging whether competencies of participants have increased or if practices on the job have improved. Such feedback is the ultimate assessment of training activities. However, in this situation, evaluation of the materials and self-evaluation by the learners may be particularly important. Two things that the leader can listen for that will provide excellent feedback on the value of the materials are:

1. Did the participants have any difficulty with the reality of the situation or the materials?

2. Did the materials stimulate consideration of all the issues the designer wished to have considered?

Participants can evaluate their own learning through such questions as these: Have you decided to do anything differently in the future? What is the most important thing you learned from this exercise? Can you understand better now why some people act the way they do?

Adapting the In-Basket. Because of the highly involving and participative nature of in-basket exercises, most adult learners find them interesting and productive. Some will desire greater structure or more detailed analysis of the issues. Facilitators can adapt to these situations by providing more detailed analysis through a formal wrap-up of the exercise after the participants' discussion. They can also recommend additional reading or study for those desiring additional analysis or research on the topic.

The leader who wants to be in strict control of the progression of the learning activity might have problems with this type of exercise. In-basket exercises are designed for the learner to make individual decisions and to test these decisions against those proposed by other members of the group. The teacher's role is not that of presenter but of facilitator: preparing the material, orienting the group to the exercise, promoting discussion, and evaluating or summarizing. However, adjustments can be made to increase the leader's control over the exercise should teacher or learner characteristics call for a more teacher-controlled approach.

Concepts, principles, or strategies that affect good management of the situation can be presented or reviewed by the teacher before or during the in-basket activity. Although such teaching would ordinarily be done before engaging in an in-basket, it could be made part of the orientation process or briefly reviewed before group discussions begin. This approach might relieve the concern of the leader who fears that participants will rely solely on past experience and ignore recently taught rules or principles in their decision making or discussion.

A variety of footnotes, asides, or addenda might be appended to materials as a means of focusing the learners' attention on specific aspects of the activity, especially when working with a relatively naive or inexperienced group. Such reminders might also be inserted into the discussion process by general announcements or asides to specific groups or individuals.

The major adjustment to content requirements is usually in material design or adaption. Most in-baskets, for example, can readily be customized to reflect the "back-home" situation of the participants, but it could take more effort to revise an exercise so that it meets the specific level of objectives desired in a certain situation. For example,

an otherwise appropriate exercise that deals only with the application level could be revised to promote synthesis or evaluation goals. This might necessitate the addition of materials that would broaden the concern of participants to similar but different situations or to long-range effects of their selected strategies. Perhaps this could be dealt with by appropriate announcements or insightful questions during the process of the in-basket activities.

Time is a factor that frequently concerns the director of an in-basket activity. The time needed can be reduced somewhat by having the participants do their individual analyses of the materials in a truly individualized and self-paced manner—perhaps as a homework or premeeting assignment. If this is not desirable, a break can be scheduled immediately after the individual analysis section so that those finishing can move into the break period rather than wait for others to complete that section of the activity. Input of the leader might be integrated into the discussion process of individual groups rather than added at the end of the activity. Summaries can be prepared in written form and distributed to members at some time after the activity. However, in-basket activities do take a considerable amount of time and frequently call for some flexibility in how such time is allocated.

The attitude of the group may also call for adjustments to the exercise, since inexperienced groups may need more orientation from the teacher. Groups in which participants are not acquainted with one another or in which they come from widely varying backgrounds need time to get to know one another. This is one reason why many facilitators are reluctant to use action strategies with newly formed groups and prefer to wait until some rapport has developed between instructor and participants and among group members. Adjustments may also be necessary for groups in which members are well acquainted to prevent hidden agendas, such as on-the-job competition, from interfering with the in-basket process.

The learners' physical state might also influence the manner in which an in-basket exercise is conducted. This is an excellent way to liven up a group that has grown lethargic from being passive participants during the presentation of factual material or to prevent the after-lunch doldrums from setting in. But there are also times when groups are too tired to engage in such involving activities.

Example of an In-Basket Exercise. The materials shown in Figures 4.1–4.4 (see pp. 90–91) were designed to demonstrate to a group of trainers in the real estate industry the value and use of in-basket activities. Since time was severely limited, the number of pieces of material used in the activity was also limited. This limit was also used to stimulate participants to add materials specific to the needs of their own situations, training objectives, and trainees.

Since the author was not experienced in the intricacies of the realty business, the goal of analyzing interpersonal relations among office staff was selected. This was an area of concern to the trainers and one that was judged as fitting to this type of exercise. Completed materials were also field-tested on real estate agents to assure the appearance of reality.

A Realtor's In-Basket

Instructions: This learning activity allows you to practice some of your problem-solving skills in the relative safety of a training situation. It is called an *in-basket exercise* because each sheet of paper represents an item of correspondence that might be waiting for you on your desk. Participants should write out their solutions to the problem presented by each item in the in-basket. Normally, we do not interact with employers, associates, and others solely through written communication, but for the purpose of this exercise, please write out your action as clearly as possible. You will have approximately fifteen minutes to determine and describe your action. Each person will work this problem independently.

The Situation: Assume that you are *Chris Bright,* a realtor associate in the firm of Moore Realty. This is your first job in realty and you want to do a good job. You have been on the job for six weeks and really enjoy the work. You have even managed to sell a few homes—with no serious problems. You grew up on a ranch and feel you know something about rural property, but you've heard there is money to be made in commercial sales. How do you get into that? Maybe you could take a course somewhere. *Edward Moore* is the owner of the business. He seems nice and has been patient in explaining things when you ask. He is so busy though that you hate to bother him. But you are really glad to know that *Phil Moore* is not his brother—only a cousin. That guy is really a crooked politician, but his opponent is one you admire for having the interest of the whole community at heart. You have gotten along well with the four older associates in office with you, especially *John Reardon.* He is one super salesman! He has taught you a lot in the past six weeks and inspired you with all the extra time he devotes to his family and to the community. *Sandra Smythe* is just the opposite. Oh, she's a good salesperson too, but she is also a volatile, high-pressure type that everyone in the office treats with kid gloves. She and John outsell all the rest by far. The one person in the office you are not sure about is *Dwight Wellington.* He was just hired two weeks ago but seems to have been involved in a number of things in his young life. He is a lot like Sandra; the two talk and laugh

MOORE REALTY
1200 South Main
Hart, Texas

MEMORANDUM

Tuesday

TO: Chris Bright

FROM: Edward Moore

Attached is a description of a piece of property that
we have been asked to list for sale by a Mrs. Elsie
Strack of Winona, Minnesota. I believe her husband
inherited it through his side of the family, but now
that he has died, she wants to get rid of it. I know
you are not really familiar with apartment sales, but
we need to get someone besides Jack into the area. As
they say, "There is no better time than today."

Let me know what you need, but try to get this on the
market as soon as possible. I can meet with you for a
few minutes before 9:00 a.m. on Wednesday, but after
that I'll be out for the rest of the week.

EM:jy

Figure 4.1
In-basket exercise item #1

HAPPINESS IS
BEING BUSY AS A BEAVER

Chris —

Your client, W. B. Adams,
came in early this morning.
I think I am selling him
or that Stevenson prop-
erty we've been trying
to get rid of for so long.
I'm showing it to him
first. Just relax and
put your feet up on
your desk. I'll be back
by noon and we can talk
about working as a
team!

Dwight

Figure 4.2
In-basket exercise item #2

WHILE YOU WERE OUT

TO _Chris Bright_

DATE _Wed._   TIME _8:25 AM_

NAME _Mrs. VanNorman_

OF _1101 Viewcrest_

PHONE _555-1278_

TELEPHONED	☒	PLEASE CALL	
CALLED TO SEE YOU		WILL CALL AGAIN	
WANTS TO SEE YOU		RETURNED YOUR CALL	

MESSAGE:

"Please use more caution in showing her home. (She kept talking about it being in a family neighborhood and the difficulty of a young divorcee fitting in. Maybe you should call her back.) _Judy_

Figure 4.4
In-basket exercise item #4

MOORE REALTY
1200 South Main
Hart, Texas

Dear Friends and Associates,

As all of you great people here at Moore Realty know, Phil Moore is running for the City Council. In my opinion, this is an EXCELLENT OPPORTUNITY to get someone on the council that understands what we do and appreciates how important Realtors are for the development of the city. Our profession needs PHIL.

I am personally organizing the Realtors of our community to support Phil and can see no better way of starting than by assuring everyone that the MOORE AGENCY is 1,000% behind Phil. Make your checks out to "Moore for City Council" and do it today. (If you are short of cash, I'll personally lend you the money till payday!)

NO NICKELS, please! We want to make our support impressive. Make Phil feel he needs us as much as we need him!!!

Figure 4.3
In-basket exercise item #3

91

together a lot. *Judy Young,* who runs the clerical staff, has been a great support. She slips little words of wisdom in constantly without being intrusive. It is 8:45 Wednesday morning and you just got in to the office. Car trouble! But it's okay and your first appointment is not until 9:00 A.M. You have been working with Bill Adams for a couple of weeks now and have not been able to satisfy him. But you made a few phone calls last night and put together a package that you know will sell him. It will have to be represented carefully—he is easy to put off—but just wait till he comes in at nine! This is going to be the deal that impresses everyone at the office. But you better get through your in-basket; you have only fifteen minutes to do so.

Simulation Games

Although there is general agreement that simulation involves a useful or workable model of some aspect of reality, there is great diversity in the manner in which educators label, classify, and discuss the use of such models. This lack of agreement is compounded when words such as gaming, structured experience, experimentation, and modeling are added to the discussion. Guetzkow, Schultz and Sullivan (1972) surveyed people in various fields using simulation techniques and suggested: "Most simulation studies can be described as *the use of a process to model a process*" (p. 4). In his analysis of the use of simulation, Cunningham (1984) argued that simulation can be used for at least four distinct purposes: experimental, evaluative, predictive, or educative. Such an analysis, based on the purpose of the simulation, allows us to differentiate experimental models developed to test hypotheses and mathematical modeling used for predictive purposes from simulation games and structured experiences designed to provoke the in-

teraction and thought conducive to specific learning goals. In addition, incident simulations and in-basket activities can be classified separately for they tend to use an evaluative approach.

The following discussion will center on simulation games and structured experiences designed to reach specific learning goals. While role playing does use simulated life situations for educational purposes, it will be dealt with separately because of its distinctive characteristics.

There are two basic assumptions behind the use of simulations for educational purposes. The first contends that there is no structure of reality or human process that cannot be represented by some workable model. *Workable* in this context means a model that represents reality sufficiently well that those experiencing the model will gain insight into the reality. And this precisely is the second assumption; namely, that the experiencing of modeled reality—together with the guided reflection and interaction established by the learning facilitator—does promote learning.

Strengths and Limitations. Respected authorities in adult education are frequently quoted by advocates of simulation approaches to learning. Bergevin (1967) insisted that certain essential human behaviors could be learned only by experiencing them. Kidd (1973) not only labeled as myth the notion that learning was basically the storage of information but also called for the involvement of the learner in the learning process. Lewin (1951) demonstrated the frequent need for the "unfreezing" of an adult's previous insight or behavior as part of the learning process and acknowledged the value of experience in this process. In general, adult education has been labeled as a field interested primarily in the *process* of learning; consequently, a teaching strategy defined as "a process to model a process" would be of natural interest to many in the field. Some specific strengths of simulation approaches to adult learning are:

1. Simulation games and structured experiences generally arouse the interests of the adult participants and enhance their involvement in the learning activity.

2. There are few learning strategies expressly designed to examine process; yet, many of the issues that form the content of adult learning endeavors are complex matters involving the understanding of processes or relationships. Kidd (1973), for example, pointed to training in leadership and human relationship skills, training in sensitivity to people and situations, and training in problem solving as areas in which simulation is particularly effective.

3. Because learning, for an adult, involves change, and change is usually risky, simulated situations that provide a safe environment in which to test newly formed insights or conclusions or to practice unfamiliar behavior are very valuable.

4. Simulations allow the presentation of complex models or situations. This enables the learning director to deal with the total model or with specific segments of it. It allows for the introduction of chance or for attempts at replication.

5. The opportunity to integrate both new factual knowledge and that gained through prior experience with the practice of newly formed skills can make simulations a powerful approach to learning.

6. The openness and flexibility of simula-

tion approaches enable participants to use the learning strategies and styles they prefer. Reading, listening, discussing, and moving about as well as global or analytical approaches can be tried.

With all the apparent advantages of simulation, one might well ask why such approaches are not used more frequently by adult educators. One apparent reason is cost; yet, there may be a less obvious but more pervasive reason. In the eyes of many, activities such as gaming, structured experiences, and simulations are just not standard educational practices; consequently, their use is to be questioned. Definitely, some adult participants feel this way for they have been put off by poorly designed or inappropriately used simulation techniques. But in the main, it appears to be educators themselves who show distrust of simulation techniques as appropriate educational tools. It is easy to find articles in educational journals questioning the value of simulation because no one has proved these approaches to be superior promoters of learning. Such mistrust is likely to remain with us for some time due to the complex nature of evaluating the effectiveness of simulation games (Bredemeier & Greenblat, 1981; Reiser & Gerlach, 1977). Specific limitations of simulation approaches include:

1. To the degree that the simulation is unable to represent the real situation, it could instill inaccurate information or inappropriate skills. This can be a confounding problem, since the more completely the simulation duplicates a real situation, the less generalizable are the skills developed. On the other hand, the simplifying of the model in order to concentrate learners' attention on specific tasks can result in

solutions that work well in the simulated activity but that are much too simple for the complex world of reality.

2. Large amounts of time, money, and other resources are frequently involved in the use of simulation. This applies both to the designing, purchasing, or adapting of the simulated activity and to its use.

3. The learners' awareness that the situation is not real can engender a "play" mentality regarding the learning activity. The enjoyable nature of the activity may stop participants from taking seriously the lessons of the simulation or from moving beyond the limits of the experience.

4. It is difficult to talk about *the* learning that occurs in *the* participant as the result of a simulated activity because so many variables are involved. Ability, experience, and learning style of the participant (as well as the leader) influence learning outcomes but so do the activity variables such as the role assigned or the participants with whom one interacts.

Selecting, Adapting, or Designing Simulations. Many simulation and gaming activities have been learned in informal ways. A meaningful learning experience in a continuing education situation may be remembered, duplicated or adapted, and used back home in one's own training efforts. Today there are groups such as University Associates and publications such as the journal *Simulation and Games* that have collected and described hundreds of structured activities. Nevertheless, each user must review and probably make some adaptations to each simulated activity used. Some suggestions for selection and adaptation follow:

Will the Exercise Help You Reach Your Objectives? It is especially important for the educator of adults to clarify learning objectives when considering the use of simulations. Attempts to model a process can become complex. The educator who selects a simulation while remaining unclear about learning objectives is likely to use some criteria such as "It will provide a change of pace" or "We really enjoyed that activity last spring." This approach, at best, will accomplish a change of pace or an enjoyable interlude, but it can hardly be described as the modeling of a process. Moreover, the probable result will be confusion on the part of the learners at being put through an exercise that has no relation to the learning task. "Nice—but a waste of time!"

The objectives best served by simulation approaches are usually at the higher cognitive levels or more complex stages of the affective domain. Simulations can also be used in the development of psychomotor skills, but even here they reach their full potential when allowing for the interaction of several variables on the practice of the skill. Analysis of what one wants to accomplish is most productive when it goes beyond specific skills to the identification of relationships, variables, and processes affecting the situation being modeled. This demands insight into the reality of what is being taught, for it is only when we know the important aspects of the system being modeled that we can decide what skills, what information, and what strategies are essential to those who must perform within that system.

How Real Should the Model Be? Models can duplicate an actual situation and as such provide a very realistic setting in which to practice certain skills. At the other extreme, a model can simulate a process essential to effective practice in certain situations and yet have little other resemblance to those situations. Both approaches can produce effective learning experiences. However, the exact duplication of a real or imagined situation places limitations on the transfer or generalizability of the learning. In fact, such an approach can teach strategies that are ineffective as soon as the situation changes, even to a small degree. Thus, game designers who use an actual situation as the basis for their simulation generally try to open some aspects of it to more general application. This can be done by leaving anonymous or obviously fictionalizing some aspects of the model. Caution must be exercised during the use of such a simulation to make sure that the players do not find a solution that allows them to proceed through the simulation with ease but that would not work in the real situation.

The use of a structured activity, game, or simulation that has no obvious identity with the actual environment in which the learners must operate can also have its drawbacks. It is difficult for learners to make the connection between the learning activity and back-on-the-job practice. This can readily cause both motivation and transfer problems. However, it is often the only approach that allows sufficient isolation and manipulation of a vital process to be an effective teaching/learning strategy. The caution here is that the game designer or selector be familiar enough with the situation being modeled to understand the essential elements (people, organization, goals, resources, constraints, values, processes) affecting actual practice. Such insight into the system permits the selection of effective simulation devices that bear little apparent resemblance to the actual situation.

How Should the Simulation Be Structured? Simulation design calls for both technical and creative ability and usually requires considerable field testing and rede-

sign. Rather than suggest a step-by-step process for such design, we offer some basic questions to keep in mind:

1. What level of expertise or skill development can be anticipated in those who will lead or participate in the simulation?

2. Are the assumptions or theoretical bases upon which the model is built readily evident to the participants or must they be clarified before the learning process can proceed?

3. Are the interactions or interrelations of important components of the model obvious or must they be made more evident?

4. What would make a logical starting position from which to begin the simulation?

5. How much time should be dedicated to this activity?

6. How can chance, excitement, and insight be built into the activity?

Such concerns for simulation or game design should be balanced with principles of adult curriculum design. Can the activity have obvious external applicability to real-life tasks so as to appeal to the average adult's desire for learning activities that have meaningful application? Can they be made intriguing enough to guarantee motivation? How can the differing background experiences and levels of previous learning of any group of participants be accounted for and perhaps used in the modeling process? In addition, two very special concerns of adults must be recognized in the design process. According to the common perception of many adults, games and structured activities can easily appear to be activities more suited to children and play than to adults and learning. Effective simulations will be designed so as to have obvious usefulness. In addition, the general tendency of simulated approaches to contain elements of competition and to call for risk-taking action can put a great deal of pressure on adult participants who usually do not appreciate such threats. Ways of avoiding such pressure need to be built into the experience.

Leading a Simulation. Many of the cautions raised about the difficulties and dangers of leading simulation activities have grown out of an inaccurate assessment of how adults learn or a weak model of what a good teacher is. Nevertheless, there are special skills that an effective facilitator should employ. First among these are an interest in and an ability to attend to process. As noted several times above, the distinctive quality of simulation approaches is the modeling of process. Teachers so absorbed in communicating content that they seldom attend to process will be poor leaders of simulations or other process-oriented strategies. This is also true of those who prefer to know ahead of time exactly what will happen during each minute of class. Flexibility and willingness to let adult participants have some control over the direction in which an activity will go are essential characteristics of the leader of simulations. Because simulation approaches involve interactions among individuals, another important facilitator skill is that of interpersonal relations. In conjunction with this is a sense of timing, that is, when to intervene in the interaction among individuals or in the simulated process itself. Listed next are several steps in the process of leading simulation exercises that call for special leadership skill.

Be Clear About the Objective(s). If the major purpose of the simulation or game is to model a process, the good facilitator needs a thorough understanding of that process. It certainly helps if the leader also knows the content or setting involved, but it is the understanding of the process that is essential. Since simulated approaches are often used to provide practice of a process, the leader should be aware of why a simulated approach was chosen for such practice and of what secondary outcomes might be expected. Occasionally, simulations are selected to set the tone for a further learning activity. This can be a very effective use of simulation, but the leader must be conscious of the process being highlighted and its relation to later activities in the learning experience. The same is true of the use of a game or structured activity to provide a common experience for a group of learners. The interactions that occur during a simulated or structured experience can be essential to group learning, but they can also lead to feelings, concerns, or hidden agendas among participants that can interfere with further learning activities. This concern about understanding learning objectives and simulation outcomes has led some to suggest that a leader should experience a simulated activity before attempting to lead it. When it is not possible to really do so, a fantasy exploration of the activities and relations of people in the various roles and activities of the game may be useful.

Understand the Procedures. It is very frustrating to adult learners to wait for the teacher who has to interrupt the learning process in order to figure out what comes next or to locate some piece of equipment that has been forgotten. Because simulations model a process or some aspect of it, it is essential that the materials supporting the simulation be realistic. Some groups have justified spending millions of dollars for simulated training devices. In most situations such a financial investment is not possible, but this does not excuse the leader from gathering or constructing adequate and realistic support material.

Concerns about adequate support materials can also be applied to the need to be conscious of timing constraints, roles to be played, and procedural steps of the activity. It is helpful to think through the activity and estimate how long each segment of the simulation will take. Such estimates may be inaccurate, but they do provide a tentative time schedule for the process of the activity and thus some guidance for the facilitator. Although such activities can have an impact on a group over an extended period, such as a semester-long class, it is seldom a good idea to interrupt a simulation in process with the intention of "picking up where we left off next time we meet." Processes and relationships broken off in such a manner are difficult to reestablish. In thinking through the roles individuals will adopt and the procedural steps of the learning activity, try to anticipate the questions that group participants may have. While preparation will seldom predict every question or potential glitch in process, it does tend to prevent many potential interruptions of the simulation.

Prepare Participants for the Activity. The orientation of adults to the simulated activity is vital to their effective learning. It includes establishing the purpose of the game or simulation, assigning and clarifying roles to be played, and setting the scene for the activity.

Frequently, simulated activities will have surprise endings or hidden confrontations built into them. This has led some facilitators to the practice of "just springing the activity on the group" without any preparation. This is seldom a good idea. While it is not necessary to give away the secrets of the game or activity and often is not even useful to reveal the expected learning outcome, adult participants have a right and a need to be reassured

that the activity does have a useful purpose and that some simulated confrontation may occur. Adult learners can rightfully grow resentful if it appears that they are being treated like children, having their time wasted, or being tricked into taking positions that make them look foolish. Yet most adults are willing to risk new behavior and enter into a gaming situation once they are reassured that the experience has a purpose and that their experimental behavior will not be held against them.

The leader should not take lightly the task of assigning roles to be played. Many simulations have broken down, or at best limped along, because participants found it impossible to carry out the roles assigned them. A good practice here is to assign people to roles that you believe they can fill and then check with them to see if they feel they can carry out that role. The important thing is not how well they can act but how comfortable they feel in carrying out their assignments. A leader who knows the needs of the individual learners may also assign roles according to each person's need to experience certain relationships. The leader who does not know the individuals well enough to assign them roles may not be ready to lead that group in a simulation.

Many simulated activities call for grouping participants. Practice has shown that it is usually better to group participants heterogeneously so that the varied backgrounds of the adult participants can be used to advantage. Balancing the teams according to apparent ability in the area under consideration is also important. Including two or three less experienced or more hesitant individuals on a team with other experienced, expressive members can provide the interaction and reassurance most needed by such learners—provided other members of the group do not become so competitive that they threaten the less competent. Group size can also affect the value of the experience to participants. Ideal size must be judged by the purpose of the activity and the task assigned to the individual groups. For example, groups that must reach consensus and act on an issue should be smaller than groups that benefit most from shared experience or opinion.

In setting the scene for the start of the simulation, leaders should reflect on the fact that this may be a new and unusual experience for the adult learner. Reassurance that this is a worthwhile and safe activity and clarification of the general procedure of simulation are important to such adults. All have the right to know the timing aspects expected. But perhaps the most essential task in getting the simulation started is adequately preparing the participants for the roles they are to play. Although many activities deliberately leave some relationships unexplained, the participants need to know enough so that they enter the experience without extreme hesitancy. When a group plunges into a learning activity with expectancy of learning something and anticipation of enjoyment, the leader has accomplished the greatest part of the instructional task.

Monitor the Simulation. The task of monitoring the simulation is often the easiest part of the leader's duties. One should, of course, be aware of any participant who is confused, hesitant, or disturbed by the actions of another participant, but this should be done during any learning activity. During a simulation the primary duty of the facilitator is to keep the activity running smoothly. This may mean supplying or replacing materials used in the simulation, clarifying rules of the game, or encouraging individuals to become more involved in the activity. Many leaders find it helpful to note meaningful incidents as they occur. Such comments can be useful in raising questions or pointing out examples during the postgame discussion. Well-

designed simulations often flow so smoothly that the leader is tempted to take part in the experience. Is this a good idea? Chartier (1981) cautions: "If this is done, however, this person has relinquished the role of facilitator and has turned the control of game flow and the postgame discussion over to the group. There is nothing wrong with this, but one must be clear about what has been done and act accordingly" (p. 252).

Discuss the Simulation. The postactivity discussion may be the most productive part of the simulation. Because simulated activities frequently involve the total person, participants often like to talk about what happened to them or how they felt at a certain point in the activity. It is important that the facilitator not only allow but encourage such talking out of feelings. Failure to do so can leave feelings of inadequacy, resentment, or even animosity toward the facilitator or other participants, whereas talking out and understanding why certain things happened during the activity often dispel such unhealthy interpersonal feelings. But even more important are the positive benefits that can result from analyzing emotional involvement in a simulated activity. For example, a realization of the emotional involvement that participants experienced in a simulated activity might be a startling revelation of the degree to which many people are caught up in the reality being modeled. It can help one understand the opinions and attachments of others or the forces applied by various social environments. But it can be most revealing in helping one understand one's own emotional involvement in certain activities.

Apart from dealing with the emotional and interpersonal aspects of the activity, the discussion should also reinforce the process being modeled. Because better understanding of the process is precisely the purpose of the simulation, the leader should know beforehand what aspects of the process need to be discussed. In some cases this discussion might center on the purposes or causes of the process, while at other times the procedures or variations encountered in the activity might be more germane. Many times, the facilitator will be more interested in transfer of the insights gained and will want to talk of potential applications or back-home situations. Because this time of reflection upon a shared, often intriguing experience has such high potential for learning, careful thought should be given to ways of making it productive.

Adapting Simulations. Simulation activities usually involve adult learners extensively and use such a variety of ways to present the major objectives of the lesson that they need little adjustment to meet the individual learning differences of participants. However, they often do need to be adapted to reflect more naturally the actual environments of the learners. A little creativity in materials used, physical arrangements, or procedures established can sharpen the perceptions of participants regarding potential applications.

Similarly, the number of participants or the fact that some have had much more experience with the process being modeled can be turned from a potential problem to a distinct advantage. Participants can be separated into smaller groups for the experience and brought back together to share their different experiences with the same process. Members with sufficient experience can be used as process observers rather than regular participants and thus add a different viewpoint to the discussion.

Group leaders who want their members to experience a simulation or game but who feel incompetent or unwilling to lead the exercise may do well to invite an outsider to lead. This would have the advantage of making the simulation a separate activity in the learning sequence. Such different activities can often be examined more objectively by those involved. Certainly this would be preferred to a perfunctory conducting of the activity by a reluctant leader.

Simulations, by definition, deal with processes. Thus, they are best employed to accomplish higher-order cognitive or affective objectives, although some also teach psychomotor skills. If the simulation models the process well, application of the learning experience to a specific situation or objective can usually be accomplished through the postactivity discussion. However, subsequent objectives may call for adding other techniques to the simulation. For example, the simulation may have led the participants to an appreciation of a new procedure that an agency wishes to adopt. Now a brainstorming session is needed to uncover as many potential applications as possible. Similarly, objectives dealing with change, practice, application, or evaluation that support the lesson of the simulation could readily be linked to that activity through some additional technique such as small-group discussion, field trips, or even new simulation or practice sessions.

Time and physical arrangements are the two major situational factors that frequently call for adjustment in the use of simulated activities. Often there is little that can be done to shorten the time frame needed for the activity. If the time required is not available, the simulation should not be attempted. Remember, the time required includes the postactivity discussion. However, one must also realize that there will often be considerable variance in the length of time it takes different individuals or groups to go through a simulated activity. The game that took two hours last week may hold the attention of this week's group for less than an hour. Thus, the use of simulation demands flexibility from the leader in adjusting to time requirements.

On the other hand, physical arrangements and supportive materials can be adapted in countless ways. Always be careful not to change the elements essential to the modeling of the process; this presupposes an understanding of the process and the manner in which it is being modeled. Apart from that, accommodations to the local situation or creative additions by the facilitator usually make the lesson more enjoyable or more easily applied.

Example of a Simulated Activity. An interesting example of an educational game that has been used in many different situations is known variously as Prisoner's Dilemma, Chicken, Tit for Tat, or the Cooperation Game. Luce and Raiffa (1957) attribute the game to A. W. Tucker and discuss applications of the simulation to social science, economics, and psychology. Hyman (1978) dedicated a complete book to analyzing and describing uses of Prisoner's Dilemma, which he said he had been "using for years with my university students, with youngsters, and with teachers in in-service workshops" (p. v). He sees its application to be to "value decisions on such matters as air pollution, Middle East foreign policy, equal rights for women, drug abuse, civil rights for all races and religions, conservation of water and oil resources, and economic prosperity" (p. vi). University Associates described it in their *Handbook of Structured Experiences for Human Relations Training,* volume III.

In its basic form, the game poses the dilemma of two persons who have been arrested, charged with a crime, and imprisoned separately. The officer in charge tells them they have two choices: to confess to the crime the police are sure they committed or not to confess. If they both confess, they will be prosecuted, but the police will recommend a lesser sentence. If one confesses and the other does not, the police will work out a plea bargain and minimal sentence for the con-

fessor but will throw the book at the non-confessor. The prisoners are not sure how much evidence the police have but feel confident that, if neither confesses, they will probably be charged with some lesser offense and receive a small sentence. However, as long as they cannot communicate, neither is sure what the other will do.

In terms of time spent in prison, the prisoners' dilemma can be envisioned in the following way:

		Prisoner A	
		Not Confess	Confess
Prisoner B	Not Confess	A = 1 yr. B = 1 yr.	A = 6 mos. B = 6 yrs.
	Confess	A = 6 yrs. B = 6 mos.	A = 3 yrs. B = 3 yrs.

Other versions of the game follow similar formats. For example, the issue of absentee tenement owners and the repair of their neighboring buildings might be posed as follows. If both improve their tenements, both can charge higher rents and make better profits. However, if one repairs and the other does not, the one repairing suffers because of increased investment with little potential for increased income. The nonrepairer experiences increased income with no increased investment. The dilemma of the tenement owners and the percent of return on their investment can be graphed as follows:

		Owner A	
		Not Repair	Repair
Owner B	Not Repair	A = .06 B = .06	A = .03 B = .12
	Repair	A = .12 B = .03	A = .09 B = .09

The simulation can be couched in terms of any similar dilemma. Most frequently, however, discussion of the theory behind the game is delayed until participants have actually experienced the dilemma of choosing between cooperation or competition.

One effective way of playing the game is to divide the participants into pairs or small groups. All players are told that the object of the game is to score as many points as possible. Points are scored based on the combined decisions made within each of the pairs. Some point-scoring categories, similar to the following, are established.

		A	
		No	Yes
B	No	A scores −3 B scores −3	A scores −6 B scores +6
	Yes	A scores +6 B scores −6	A scores +3 B scores +3

Role Playing

Role playing as an educational strategy is particularly effective in helping participants understand the motivation behind their own behavior and that of others plus the emotions that can be aroused by such behavior. It has the added advantage of allowing practice in dealing with difficult or troublesome situations. J. L. Moreno is generally credited with introducing the practice of role playing to modern educators through his advocacy of the technique for counseling. It has been used widely, especially for training in the military and in industry (Shaw, Corsini, Blake, & Mouton, 1980).

"Never call it role playing" is the advice of Zoll (1969) as he begins his description of the potential uses of role playing in the training of managers. He expresses a concern common to many adult educators who em-

ploy the technique; that is, adults intent upon learning can react negatively to the idea of "playing." Reality practice, role experimentation, and action learning are descriptive titles that may be more acceptable to some adult learners. Whatever words are used, it is important to maintain the attitude both among facilitators and learners that role playing is a very effective and legitimate educational tool.

The unique feature of role playing lies in its ability to reflect the thinking-doing-feeling nature of the adult learner. In the normal course of living, we do not separate these functions. In role playing we have one of the few educational strategies that integrates thinking with doing and feeling. The potential impact of such a strategy can be appreciated when one considers that in the normal course of living we avoid many potential learning experiences because of the difficulties or dangers involved. They are just too risky to our physical beings, to our bank accounts, or to our psychological health. But through the simulated experience of a role play, we may actually be able to enjoy this experience in the supportive, enriched atmosphere of an educational environment.

Strengths and Limitations. Major characteristics of role playing include the following: (a) integration of thinking, doing, and feeling into the same educational activity; (b) opportunity to experience and experiment with various roles that might be too threatening to initiate in reality; and (c) encouragement to evaluate alternative approaches to action rather than presentation of solutions to be learned.

These characteristics make role playing especially appropriate for the accomplishment of the following objectives:

1. Role playing encourages the learner's active participation and focuses attention on specific, concrete applications

of the concepts or skills under consideration. It is so flexible that it can be redirected even during the actual conducting of the role play.

2. Conceptualization of appropriate behavior is integrated with practice of that behavior, supplying reinforcement for both the principles of action and the skills vital to carrying out the newly developed insights.

3. The focus of the individual's attention can readily be directed to personal concerns. This allows the adult learner to concentrate on felt needs in addition to being directed to the concerns of the instructional leader.

4. Role playing is conducive to demonstrating principles that may be abstract or upon which a group has difficulty concentrating. Thus it can provide the common experience important to collaborative efforts to analyze a situation.

5. Behavioral and attitudinal change is more likely to occur because appropriate or inappropriate behavior can be experienced and alternative skills practiced.

6. A greater appreciation and understanding of the role of feelings in interpersonal relations is likely. This applies not only to the understanding of how others might feel or react in a certain situation but also to a deeper understanding of how feelings influence one's own behavior.

7. Role playing is effective in the practice of interpersonal skills for it promotes reflection on the impact of the skill together with practice in its use.

8. Role playing is usually fun. Most adults soon learn to enjoy the opportunity to experiment with new behavior, especially in a situation in which it is possible to try out new roles without embarrassing or endangering oneself.

In terms of limitations, not all content and certainly not all levels of cognitive objectives are suited to role playing. The transfer of information, especially at the knowledge and comprehension levels, can usually be done more effectively through other techniques. Even when the objectives of the activity call for application, synthesis, or evaluation, care must be taken that the solutions derived through the role play are not overly simplistic or overly personalized. In fact, one of the main challenges to facilitators of role-playing activities is to guard against stereotypic playing of roles and consequent generation of stereotypic answers to problems. Other limitations include:

1. It is a difficult strategy to use effectively before an atmosphere of trust has been established between facilitator and participants and among the members of the group. The total involvement of the learner in a role can lead to inadvertent self-disclosure and expression of feelings both during the enactment of a role play and in the personalizing of feedback during a postactivity debriefing.

2. Concerns about adverse emotional impact upon participants have led to many published warnings about the potential hazards of role playing with adults and have resulted in a reluctance on the part of some teachers to use the strategy.

3. Situations in which time is limited can make the effective use of role playing difficult.

4. When objectives call for active participation from everyone but the

number of participants is large, role-playing strategies need adaption.

Designing Role-Playing Activities. There are two basic types of role play: (a) the structured role play and (b) the spontaneous role play. In a structured role play, the objectives are set, the situation defined, the characters described, and the instructions given for conducting the activity. Some activities are even scripted; that is, a complete script is provided for the role play. The participants simply read through the script, perhaps adding a few ad libs here and there. A spontaneous role play provides little of the above. The characters or the situation may be well defined, but the participants are free to take the enactment where they will.

In role playing, the idea of structure can include many things. Generally, it refers to all those ingredients determined before the activity begins. As such, it includes the problem setting, the announced purpose or objectives of the activity, all role descriptions, the format used to introduce key issues, and any physical equipment or materials used to support the activity. However, the structure of a role play can also be restricted to the essential relationships that exist among the key elements or personnel involved in the simulated situation. Those relationships give the distinctive nature to role-playing activities.

Structured Role Plays. These activities possess distinct elements that lead to success as learning activities. When preparing original role plays or selecting prepared activities, consider the following essential ingredients:

1. The purpose or objectives of the activity must be clear. If the situation accurately reflects reality, several goals can be pursued through the same activity. This can be either good or bad depending upon the degree to which participants are likely to give adequate attention to each desired objective and to their ability to avoid oversimplification of reality. The study of simulated situations has the advantage over the study of actual reality in that issues are simplified and thus are more readily examined and analyzed. Generalizations of learned strategies to overcome similar problems are also more likely when problems studied are not complicated by all kinds of nonessential issues. However, over-simplified problems increase the potential for treating the problem as play.

2. Important relationships among key people and issues in the problem situation should be identified clearly. A major strength of role playing is its ability to clarify relationships and to help individuals recognize and deal with them. Thus, some conflict, or at least variety, is desired among the various roles. Such potential conflict need not be identified beforehand. The broad range of human interrelations is often best elucidated by a surprise emergence of hidden conflict or confrontation. In the design or selection of role-playing activities, these relationships should be given greatest attention.

3. The setting for the role play usually includes orientation to the problems and purposes of the activity, descriptions of the character or role, and explanation of the situation that is to be played out. Additional guidelines are often provided for participants who are to play an observer role. It is usually better to use a simulated situation that provides potential for broad applica-

tion of issues that arise rather than one closely resembling the real-world environment of the participants. Similarities to the real situation may distract from the learning of principles by prompting members to defensive behavior or to the seeking of immediate solutions.

4. Because the postactivity discussion or debriefing of participants is a vital part of role playing, good examples usually provide a format, some suggestions, or at least a number of references that will be useful for such a discussion. This supplemental material can encourage the facilitator to think through the issues that are likely to be raised, their implications for the individuals involved, and the methods that can be suggested for the continuing development of the participants.

Unstructured Role Plays. These usually develop much more spontaneously. A problem emerges, conflict between two or more individuals appears inevitable, several learners assume appropriate roles, and the interaction begins. The objective is to clarify the problem and let the structure emerge developmentally. Thus, the participants' background and experience become the sources from which problems emerge, roles are clarified, and conflicts among individuals or between individuals and the organization arise.

Teachers can preplan spontaneous role plays. In preparing a learning activity, they should foresee situations that will be conducive to interaction. Thus, a leader can think through the roles or situations that would benefit from enactment and perhaps even select group members for the various roles. However, experienced teachers know that in such situations it is best to have several op-

tions available. In adult-learning situations, the expected is far from inevitable.

Prepared role-playing activities are available from many sources. Specialists in various disciplines have gathered examples useful to teachers in their fields. Some well-established sources for use with adults are Maier, Solem, and Maier's (1975) *The Role Playing Technique: A Handbook for Management and Leadership Practice;* Shaw et al.'s (1980) *Role Playing: A Practical Manual for Group Facilitators;* and the University Associates' series of handbooks for group facilitators.

Suggestions for Using Role Plays. Before proceeding through the process of a role play and offering suggestions regarding each segment, it is important to note that participants can be organized in at least two ways for the role-playing strategy. Multiple-role-playing approaches divide the total group into several small ones so that each person is engaged in the role-playing activity. The single-group role play has only one role play going on at any time. Those not actively engaged in the various roles act as observers.

Multiple role play has some distinct advantages when used with adults. Participants who are less inclined to engage in acting out roles before a group often feel less embarrassed when going through those same roles with two or three other people who are similarly engaged in a role. The pressure of analyzing one's reaction to another's words or acts, and perhaps sounding critical of that person, is also lessened when the comments are directed toward a character played by many people rather than toward a role modeled by one individual. Such shared analysis is often improved because it is based on the reactions of the several individuals who experience that role rather than on that of a single person. This multiple-role-play approach also has the obvious advantage of engaging all participants in active participation in the learning activity.

Maier et al. (1975) insist that the single-group role play also has some distinct advantages. It provides a single shared experience that all members of the group can reflect and comment upon. It provides each role player with more solid feedback in that a number of people observe the behavior and comment on it from their various perspectives. The single-group approach also allows for a number of variations, such as team approaches to a role. For example, pauses can be called in the action to enable players to consult with their team on the type of behavior to experiment with when the action resumes.

Setting the Climate. There are three orientation processes important to the role-playing strategy. The first is setting a learning climate for a role-playing strategy. The second is establishing a climate of trust among group members. Finally, there is the orientation to the specific role play being used. All three orientations are important, especially for adult learners.

The notion that role playing is more playing than learning has ruined many attempts to use this strategy in an adult education setting. Most adults have never experienced such approaches to learning and do not recognize their value. Therefore it is vital that the teacher orient participants not only to meaningful objectives of the learning session but also to the meaningfulness of the technique being used. Most adults can appreciate the unique strength of role playing when they realize that it reflects well the thinking-feeling-doing of real life. They also understand the need to pose a problem so that all can analyze and discuss the same issue. A short reflection on such points and the clear linkage of the role-playing strategy to the objectives of a particular learning session can

provide the necessary positive orientation to the use of role play.

Establishing trust among the group members and between them and the group leader is also essential. Because this usually takes a period of interaction, many experienced facilitators hesitate to use role playing in the early stages of group formation. Before trying out new ideas or suggesting unusual solutions to problems, they prefer waiting until the group has accepted that the group facilitators will not embarrass or belittle the participants. Establishing trust between a group leader and group members encourages trust among members. Make explicit the need for concern for other members of the learning group before beginning a learning activity based on role playing. Remind the participants that learning involves change and that change is not always easy for adults. Some impediments to change or defensive behaviors resorted to by those facing change can be discussed. But regardless of the orientation given to role playing, the facilitator must be concerned that trust and understanding be maintained throughout all role-playing situations. The emphasis should always be on trying out new behaviors and evaluating their usefulness rather than on evaluating how well a person handled a problem or a role.

Introducing the role play usually includes (a) clarifying the learning objectives, (b) defining the characters involved, and (c) setting the scene in which the action is to take place. In some situations, it is best to spell out the objectives as clearly as possible. At other times, it may be sufficient to assure the group that there is a valuable purpose to the activity and use the unexpected revelation of the purpose during the course of the activity as a means of added impact. In either case, the leader should evaluate the background experience and the present state of knowledge of group members to determine whether additional preparation is necessary. Sometimes lectures, films, or other techniques for delivering information may be used to prepare learners so they may benefit more fully from the role-playing activity.

In describing the roles, a facilitator should remember that role playing differs from acting. An actor tries to present someone else on stage. A role player experiments with his or her own behavior in a simulated situation. For this reason role descriptions should be open in that the learner need not be as concerned with filling in all the details of the role as with dealing with the issues being raised. Roles must be specified to the degree necessary for the desired interactions to occur, but if the players need to keep referring to their role descriptions during the course of the enactment, the characterizations are too complicated. Just as in reality, not everyone is aware of all the pressures or needs motivating an individual, so in role playing not all vital information on every character need be revealed to all participants.

Setting the scene is usually best done in general terms rather than in an attempt to reflect a specific situation. Participants who believe that they recognize some real-life situation can easily become defensive or bring all kinds of hidden agendas to the enactment. Generalization of the insights gained during the activity is more probable if the experience can be applied to several situations.

Conducting the Role Play. The first step in acting out the role play is matching participants with roles in which they will be comfortable. It is important that group members be able to see themselves in the roles they are to play, not that they be able to put on a good show as certain characters. One method of doing this is to ask participants to volunteer for roles they would like to try. Another approach is to assign roles based on your insight of group members and offer basic advice on acting out the role—

somewhat in the manner suggested by Maier et al. (1975):

1. Accept the role and be yourself.
2. Make up your own lines.
3. Don't act as you think someone else might act.
4. Feel free to make up facts, if necessary, but don't change the role or situation by doing so.
5. Don't reread your role description once the action has begun.
6. Trust your own feelings and experience and try out new behavior.

Once the action has begun, it is better for the facilitator to keep a low profile unless some kind of intervention is needed. Interrupt the activity if some member finds it difficult to carry out a role or if the interaction wanders away from the direction needed to accomplish the activity's purpose. If the action does reach an impasse, the leader has several options: (a) roles might be switched or new players introduced into the roles, (b) a total group or several small group discussions of the impasse could be initiated, or (c) several methods of breaking the impasse might be outlined and the action allowed to resume. Stop the action soon after the objectives of the session have been achieved. Sometimes this can be accelerated by announcing a time limit shortly before ending the role play.

Feedback and Analysis. Two things must be accomplished during the postsession analysis. All participants must be encouraged to talk through feelings that might have been aroused during the role play. In addition, the events of the session must be reflected upon and related to the learning objectives.

One way of initiating discussion is to invite those playing the central roles to reveal how they felt about the activity. If the facilitator noted meaningful events during the role play, participants can more easily discuss what thoughts, feelings, or frustrations were motivating them at those moments. The purpose of talking through the emotional aspects of the interaction goes far beyond the discharge of any resentment or emotional hang-ups among participants, as important as this might be. Role playing has the potential of helping adult learners appreciate and understand the influence of their emotions upon their behavior and the vital role feelings play in interpersonal relations. This opportunity for learning should never be neglected. Sometimes the observers may have been in a better position to notice emotional interaction than the actual participants. Be certain to invite their input.

Relating role-play experiences to the objectives of the learning activity is also essential. Group leaders sometimes forget that an experience, in itself, is not a learning activity. It is an opportunity for learning. For experiential approaches to learning to be most productive, group discussion and analysis are important. The rich and varied backgrounds of most adults make it easy to generalize and apply the lessons of the activity. This can be stimulated by posting objectives, by handing out printed questions, or by switching to some other effective strategy such as small-group discussion. As in so many other learning situations, it is good for the leader to conclude the role-play analysis by summarizing and referring once more to the general lessons learned.

Useful Techniques. There are a number of techniques that leaders can use to increase the effectiveness of role playing. One effective approach, especially when the action is slow or the role is difficult, is role rotation. This can be done in a variety of ways. For example, in a confrontation situation that does not seem to be moving toward resolution, the main players can be asked to reverse roles and to continue the action as the new characters. Another version of role rotation is serial role playing. Several participants can discuss the character before the action begins and take turns in the character role as seems appropriate. A simplified version of this can be used when a participant gets stuck or over-involved in a role. The facilitator asks one of the observers to substitute in that role. Multiple role playing is also useful, especially to help participants appreciate the interaction going on among various characters. In multiple role playing, participants experiment with several different roles in a problem situation.

Various other techniques are described by Shaw et al. (1980) in their book on role playing. Doubling is an approach in which a third participant is asked to act as the inner voice of one of the role players. The empty chair technique uses a prop to represent a person who is important to the situation but whose actual presence might block the carrying out of the role play. The mirror technique is used to reflect another participant's understanding of a solution or option suggested by one of the role players. Renner (1983) speaks of physical movement, such as changing chairs, as a way to break the action or to help individuals step out of roles. He also suggests that participants might find it easier to go the wrong way before trying more effective solutions.

Adapting Role Playing. Adults unaccustomed to or uncertain about the value of role playing may find it easier to experiment with simultaneous approaches to role playing. They can do so without the pressure of others observing their behavior and yet benefit from the comments of fellow participants who attempted similar enactments. If a single role play is being used, they might prefer not to be participants or to be involved gradually through some technique such as serial role playing. While such techniques may help, the most important thing that can be done for all adults entering a learning activity in which a role-playing strategy is being used is to remind them of what to expect. Role playing is an opportunity to experiment with new behavior, to express feelings, to examine the consequences of new thoughts, and therefore, a time to reserve judgment and be accepting of one another.

Because many role-play situations call for examining interactions among a few individuals, the question of how to involve the other group members is frequently raised. There are several ways of involving everyone either as a participant or as an observer. For example, a number of minor roles can be created which will allow more people to feel part of the action and yet not interfere with the major intended interaction among the central figures. If the group is large, variations of simultaneous role playing can be used. Each subgroup could be composed not only of players but also of observers. Another approach is to assign several participants to each role. The groups assigned a specific role can be given time to discuss strategies for carrying out the role and to select one of their members to lead the actual enactment. One or more group members can support the role player by sitting behind the person and offering suggestions during the action.

However, the most common method of involving everyone is through assigning less involved tasks such as observing. This can also be done in a variety of ways. The leader can prepare checklists calling for close attention to important interactions or certain details about the objectives of the learning activity. Or the observers themselves can discuss the strategies that might be involved in resolving the problem and prepare their own checklists of things to observe. Such efforts to involve everyone usually lead to enthusiastic discussions after the actual role play has concluded.

The facilitator needs to be open, flexible, friendly, and able to "see the trees *and* the forest" (Shaw et al., p. 4). The use of role playing strategies demands a willingness to relinquish absolute control and allow the participants to experiment with new behavior. This calls for a process-oriented or student-centered teacher, but the value of content expertise should not be ignored. Such activities often uncover root issues or raise questions not commonly discussed. Participants have a right to expect insightful guidance from the moderator. One possible solution for the teacher who feels uncomfortable either as the content expert or the process facilitator is to invite a consultant and have one individual guide the role-play enactment and the other lead the postactivity discussion.

Role playing is not an effective strategy for communicating information. It is more useful for demonstrating abstract ideas or for practicing interpersonal skills. These skills can vary from simple practices such as welcoming people to an office to complex interactions such as settling grievances. This strategy can also be used with objectives calling for change or new behavior by making it an evaluation device to study the consequences of such change. Playing out the consequences of the change can give practice to those who will have new responsibilities, or it might provide additional insight that calls for voiding the proposed change. Role playing can be a strategy for reaching objectives at the higher cognitive levels and for affective and psychomotor objectives.

Three situational factors could interfere with the use of role playing as an effective strategy: time, physical facilities, and a supervisor who does not appreciate such learning activities. Few adjustments can be made regarding time. If there is not enough time—and some flexible use of it—to carry out the role play and the postactivity discussion in one setting, it may be better to select another teaching strategy. The opposite is true of physical facilities and other support materials. While it is nice to have abundant room and customized materials, the emphasis in most role plays is on abstract interactions, not on props. This is no reason to neglect them when they are available, but usually adjustments can be made. The unappreciative supervisor is a different matter. Perhaps the best strategy is the one suggested earlier for all role playing: Do not use until a trusting atmosphere has been established.

Example of a Role Play. Problems associated with interpersonal communication are the content of many structured and non-structured role plays. One of the most famous and frequently used role plays was created by Norman Maier and published in several of his works (e.g., Maier, N. R. F., & Verser, G. C., 1982, pp. 579–581). It is known as "The Appraisal Interview" or "The Evaluation Interview" and is presented here because it is an excellent example of the type of role-play activities available in the literature. We have adapted this version to apply to an educational rather than a business setting. This is a simple thing to do with many good role plays: They have universal application and can readily be made situation specific. Readers seeking further discussion of role playing in general or this role play in particular are advised to consult the writings of Maier. He offers suggestions on facilitation of the role play as well as lessons that might be drawn from it.

The Evaluation Interview—Role Playing*

Chris Smart, one of five department heads in your program, is about to enter the office of Sandy Dean, the program leader. These are the only two participants in this role play. The roles that they are to assume

*Adapted by permission from Norman R. F. Maier and Gertrude C. Verser, *Psychology in Industrial Organizations,* Fifth Edition (Boston: Houghton Mifflin, 1982), pp. 579–81.

are described below. Please read only the role description for the person you are to play. Then participate in this evaluation interview.

Role for Chris Smart, Department Head

One assistant director, six professional staff, and two clerks report to you. You feel that you get along fine with your group. You have always been pretty much of an idea person and apparently have the knack of passing on your enthusiasm to others in your group. There is a lot of "we" feeling in your unit because it is obvious that your group is the most productive.

You believe in developing your staff and always give them strong recommendations. You feel you have gained the reputation of developing your employees because they frequently go out and get much better jobs. Since promotion is necessarily slow in a school such as yours, you feel that the best way to stimulate morale is to develop new people and demonstrate that a good person can get somewhere. The two clerks in your unit are bright and efficient, and there is a lot of good-natured kidding. Recently one of them turned down an outside offer that paid forty-five dollars a month more, for she preferred to stay in your group. You are going to get her a raise the first chance you have.

The other department heads in the unit do not have your enthusiasm. Some of them are dull and unimaginative. During your first year as department head you used to help them a lot, but you soon found that they leaned on you and before long you were doing their work. There is a lot of pressure to produce. You got your promotion through your efficiency, and you don't intend to let other department heads interfere. Since you no longer help the others, your efficiency has gone up. But some of them seem a bit sore at you. Tom, your assistant, is a better leader than most of them, and you'd like to see him made a department head. Since the school has some dead wood in it, Sandy Dean ought to recognize the fact and assign to such units the more routine jobs. Then they wouldn't need your help and you could concentrate your efforts on jobs that suit your unit. At present, Dean passes out work pretty much as it comes up. Because you are efficient you get more than your share of these jobs, and you see no reason why the extra work shouldn't be in the form of a "plus." This would motivate units to turn out work. When you have suggested to Dean that some of the more routine jobs be turned over to other departments, it has been—reluctantly.

You did one thing recently that has bothered you. There was a development and change in plans and you should have told Phil Downs (a fellow department head) about it, but it slipped your mind. Downs was out when you had it on your mind and then you got involved in a hot idea that Tom, your assistant, had and forgot all about the matter with Downs. As a result, he had to make a lot of unnecessary changes, and he was quite sore about it. You told him you were sorry and offered to make the changes, but he turned down the offer.

Today you have an interview with Sandy Dean. It's about this personnel development plan in the school. It shouldn't take very long, but it's nice to have the boss tell you about the good job you are doing. Maybe there is a raise in it; maybe Sandy will tell you something about what to expect in the future.

Role for Sandy Dean, Principal (Dean)

You have evaluated all of the department heads who report to you and during the next two weeks you will interview each of them. According to school policy, you are to evaluate each department head's performance annually giving recognition for jobs well done and correcting weaknesses. Today you have arranged to interview Chris Smart, one of the

department heads. Below is the information and evaluation as contained in your files.

☐ Chris Smart: ten years with the school, two years as department head, married with two children.

☐ Evaluation: Highly creative and original, and exceptionally competent. Department is very productive and during the past two years, the group has shown steady improvement.

During the past six months you have given Chris extra work, and it has been done on schedule. As far as excellence and dependability are concerned, Chris is your top manager. However, Chris' cooperation with other department heads leaves much to be desired. Before you made him head of a department, his skill and knowledge were available to everyone. Gradually he has withdrawn and now acts more as a lone wolf. You have asked other supervisors to talk over certain problems with Chris, but they say they get no suggestions. Smart tells them there are things to do, listens disinterestedly, kids them or responds sarcastically. On one occasion he allowed Phil Downs, another department head, to make a mistake that he could have prevented if Chris had only told him about some changes that had been made. Department heads are expected to cooperate on such changes.

Furthermore, during the past two weeks Chris has been unwilling to accept two assignments—said they were too routine, that their department preferred more challenging assignments, and advised you to turn the routine work over to other department heads. To prevent trouble, you followed his suggestions. However, you feel that you can't give his department all of the interesting work and that if Chris persists in this attitude there will be trouble. You can't play favorites and keep up the morale of the total group.

Smart's failure to cooperate has you worried for another reason. Although that group is highly productive, there is more turnover among the staff than in other groups. So far you have heard no complaints, but you suspect Chris may be treating people in an arbitrary manner. If Smart talks to you and other department heads as reported, it's likely this "boss" is even more off-handed with subordinates. Apparently the high productivity of this group is not due to high morale, but to Smart's ability to use people to do the things for which they are best suited. This won't work for long. You hope to discuss these matters with Smart in such a way as to recognize good points yet correct weaknesses.

Case Studies

In their 1953 work on teaching human relations through cases, Cabot and Kahl suggested that, while the physical sciences can be studied and taught through the scientific method and generalizations derived from it, the analysis of human interaction is much too complex and variable to rely on standards generated through an objective approach. They argued that the study of a number of cases demonstrating varied examples of personal interaction in similar situations produced a better understanding of human behavior. The success since then of the Harvard Business School, with its renowned reliance on the case method, certainly lends credence to their argument.

The distinction must be made here between the occasional use of case studies in an approach using various teaching strategies and the exclusive use of case studies in what is sometimes called the case method approach. In the integrated approach, case studies often serve as a change of pace with the major learning objective being the synthesis of insights gained through various teaching techniques and the testing out of these insights in a practical setting. The case method approach, with its reliance on cases as the major vehicle for learning, concentrates on developing analytical skills and presumes that the learner's involvement with some case studies will promote an understanding of the problem-solving process. Certainly both approaches have merit, but the following treatment of the case study will concentrate on its occasional use with adult groups.

What is a case study? Generally this term refers to a description of a real and relevant situation that is complex enough to warrant analysis. The realness of the situation does not mean that the case must be an exact rendition of some physical reality, although some insist this should be so. A case must be real in the sense that the actual situation portrayed—or the various real or imagined elements combined into a single study—reflects the reality of human interaction. It can present an overview, such as the general operations of a continuing education office, or can concentrate on a specific area, such as programming or marketing. But the case must contain sufficient detail for the learners to benefit from an analysis and discussion of it. This of course depends on the objectives of the learning activity and on the case writer's ability to reflect the complexity of human interaction in the specifics selected for description.

Strengths and Limitations. Case study approaches are process-centered rather than content-centered. As such, they are seldom useful strategies for conveying factual information but are more suited to higher cognitive objectives such as analysis and synthesis of ideas. Because they are process-centered, they tend to involve learners in the learning process. This results in some of the following advantages:

1. Case studies tend to develop or sharpen problem-solving skills. This depends on the quality of the cases selected, of course, but in general the reflection on and discussion of complex reality with a group of peers and an informed facilitator results in various interpretations and suggestions for resolution. The realization that in most human problem situations there is no one best answer promotes decision-making processes that search out and evaluate various options for resolving the problem.

2. Independent study is promoted. In the case study process an individual is encouraged to make a decision and defend it. To do so, it is usually necessary to search out additional resources.

3. Case studies provide ways to gain insight into one's own way of viewing reality and making decisions. In working through cases, one tends to rely heavily on one's own prior learning and experience, a procedure typical of the common behavior of adults. Having one's experience and decisions challenged—in a supportive learning environment—can help refine thinking processes.

4. Interaction among participants can promote the development of communication skills. Some facilitators insist on formal written and oral presentations of each participant's analysis of the case as a means of sharpening communication skills.

5. Case studies can be valuable in evaluating what has been learned by a group of participants. The analysis performed by each individual should reflect how well previously taught concepts have been integrated into that person's behavior.

Case studies can consume a great deal of time. This is one reason many facilitators hesitate to use them. Yet the infrequency of their use in itself can be a problem, because the ability to learn from case studies is a process that is perfected through practice. Adults not familiar with this approach may feel uneasy in that they, rather than the teacher, have become the analyzer of the situation. Other limitations of this approach are:

1. Feedback on decisions made in a case study can be limited. Suggested behaviors that were not adopted in the real situation can be analyzed and evaluated by the participants, but full feedback on actual results of their use is not available within the case study framework.

2. Some adults feel that case studies are more slow-paced than other action-type strategies. Good cases are complex and call for constant analysis and reanalysis. As noted above, full benefit of the case study approach comes only with repeated use of the process.

3. The learner is frequently frustrated by limited understanding of the situation. Details that appeared important to the case writer were included in the case description, but these may not be the details that appear important to the learner. The complexity of the problem posed may add to this frustration.

4. Adults may be turned off by the fact that they do not see the case as their problem. If it does not appear meaningful, participants may be tempted to put little effort into their analysis of the case.

Designing Case Studies. Cabot and Kahl's (1953) description of a good case study is still worth noting.

A case must be *real* in the sense that the reported interactions between the people in it have actually occurred. The description of it should be brief but detailed, presenting verbatim conversations and sufficient background material to establish the social context within which the interactions took place. Names and places should be disguised to prevent embarrassment to original participants, but always in a way that does not modify substantially the original situation. Value judgments—whether any particular social situation is good or bad—should be scrupulously kept at a minimum. No analysis should be included to indicate why things happened as they did, unless such an analysis is made by some character in the case whose relation to the social situation is evident. Nor should a case be written to illustrate any particular theory, but, by presenting the complexity of the original situation, exemplify, like life itself, many theories. (pp. xxii–xxiii)

Zoll (1969) adds three practical considerations: (a) the case must fit the objectives of the learning encounter both with regard to the objectives of the teacher and the background and needs of the participants; (b) the setting and language of the case must be such that the learners can relate to the situation; and (c) the case must fit the time available (p. 11).

Sources of Case Studies. There are many sources for prepared and tested case studies dealing with managerial training. The Harvard Business School is well known for its collection and dissemination of case studies. The *Harvard Business School Case Bibliography* gives short descriptions of many cases useful with administrators. Textbooks of cases dealing with settings as varied as human relations or marketing and arbitrations are available in many libraries. Some professional journals, such as the *Harvard Business Review,* occasionally publish case studies. But finding case studies in fields other than those related to managerial training can be difficult. Occasionally, stories in

newspapers or news magazines can be used as they appear or with some modification. However, the difficulty of finding appropriate case studies suited to their needs has moved many teachers to develop their own case descriptions.

Writing Case Studies. Developing a case for a specific audience with a specific goal in mind is the ideal situation—provided one has had some experience in writing and using case studies. Even the less experienced facilitator may enjoy success by writing a personally experienced event and testing it for clarity and completeness. This may call for a significant amount of time and effort by the facilitator, but it is also likely to produce a significant learning activity. It produces a case not only closely related to learner needs and experience but also one that the teacher can amplify and respond to more readily.

In his book, *Dynamic Management Education,* Zoll (1969) offers ten suggestions for writing case studies. In general, he suggests that, in gathering material for the case, one must support the information garnered from interviews with as much written material as possible. Concentrate on presenting the facts in a situation and distinguish them from assumptions of involved persons. If facts conflict with theories or interpretations, this may be simply a reflection of what often happens in reality. Base the length and complexity of the case on the objectives for the learning situation and on situational factors such as time and the experiential background of participants. Collect all the material available for your case, but as you write, select what is most appropriate for the intended audience. Try to create a picture of a real situation but disguise or change details that could embarrass or distract people involved. Test the case on appropriate individuals to ensure clarity and completeness and to guarantee that those who supplied the information approve of the final format.

The experienced adult educator will want to review potentially usable cases for elements likely to encourage adult learning. For example, is the case presented in a manner that will be interesting and meaningful to the adult participants? Interest can be stimulated by including actual or simulated dialogue between persons involved and appropriate letters, memos, or news articles. For the case to be meaningful, issues meaningful to the participants must be highlighted. This implies that the writer should go beyond interesting dialogue to supply essential detail regarding administrative structure and interpersonal relations. Another point to be considered is the degree of uncertainty participants might feel in making decisions or suggestions regarding the case. Adults are reluctant to speak out on an issue only to find they have missed the point because an essential bit of information was kept from them. However, this does not imply that everything must be supplied through the written case itself. Supplemental lectures or suggested readings are often used to provide theories or principles useful in analyzing the case.

Teaching notes are a useful addition to a case study, especially if several people are involved in its facilitation or if continued use and evaluation of the case are projected. Cameron (1982) suggests that such teaching notes include statements of the intended uses of the case and the learning outcomes anticipated of the students. Estimates of the difficulty level of the case and the analytical and technical skills needed to deal with it should be supplied. The author's analysis of the case together with suggested questions for the students are most helpful, as is a teacher's guide to be used during the class or in suggesting outside resources.

A final point is that the cases we have found most useful do not contain heroes and villains. No character does everything right; none is always wrong. This extends beyond

individuals to value systems or theories proposed. There is no obviously good way of dealing with most situations every time they occur. There is no one theory that solves every problem. This is the way human interaction usually occurs. This is the way cases best reflect reality. Moreover, adults soon realize that if certain individuals are always right or wrong or if certain strategies are always successful, there is little value in discussing these actions.

Suggestions for Using Case Studies. The orientation of adult learners and facilitators to the case study approach is important. This is essentially true of all action strategies but differs in the use of cases for they do not immediately involve the learner in action as do simulation and role play. Case studies call for considerable preparation before interaction occurs. Learners must be carefully briefed both on the rationale for using a case study to accomplish this learning objective and on the learning outcomes they can expect from the activity. Cases can be frustrating. They contain somebody else's problems, and they present situations that cannot be rearranged. The student cannot say, "I never would have organized my staff that way!" or "We would never have gotten involved in that issue." Nor can learners interact with described characters by asking for more information or reasons for behavior. Teachers must help learners through this initial frustration or they will lose interest in the case.

The orientation of the group facilitator is also important. Teachers not accustomed to the use of cases are often directive in their use. They may spend a lot of time introducing a case, indicating potential problems, and listing questions to be answered. They may even dominate the group's discussion of the case. Proper orientation to the use of cases promotes an awareness that the case study approach is basically a learner-centered approach. It is best suited to objectives like the development of analysis skills or problem-solving abilities. Teachers who want to use cases to point out factual data or to teach "correct" solutions may use cases as examples, but they are not using the case study as a teaching strategy.

Preparing Learners. Adult students not accustomed to learning through case studies will benefit from the following advice from Zoll (1969), who points out "six habits of fuzzy thinking" that can interfere with the analysis of a situation:

1. Inexperienced participants want to fix the problem or do something about it rather than analyze the situation.
2. Broad generalities are offered instead of identification of specific problems.
3. Criticisms or value judgments supersede analysis.
4. Total blame is placed on certain individuals or policies.
5. Excuses are offered based on past events or decisions.
6. Similar situations experienced are discussed in place of analysis of this case. (pp. 32–33)

Learners can be encouraged to examine each case carefully by reflecting on the *process* of analysis. This begins by examining one's own statements and by listening to what others are trying to say. It includes withholding judgment until all the facts are in, questioning rather than making pronouncements, and reflecting on the *whys* as well as the *whats.* Also important are listening skills: probing to understand rather than criticizing, appreciating different points of view, and supporting creative approaches.

The following suggestions for teaching students the process of analysis have been offered by Cameron (1982):

1. Try to take an insider's perspective and develop an overview of the situation and the people involved.
2. List basic problems facing various participants and distinguish between symptoms and real issues.
3. Organize and critique the information available.
4. Develop both options and criteria for evaluating such options.
5. Make sure that recommended actions are feasible and capable of solving the problems identified.
6. Always act from the viewpoint of a participant in the situation. (p. 8)

The Teacher's Role. The manner in which the facilitator structures the case review and moderates discussion of it will have a great influence on the adult participants' learning of the process of analysis. Dooley and Skinner (1977) have developed a matrix to help the instructor examine the components of the case study process. In their eight-step process, the teacher is the major actor in the first three steps by presenting background knowledge and stimulating interest in an area, by pointing out interrelationships and priorities to consider in various situations, and by explaining problem-solving techniques and their application. Next, the leader shares with the participants in examining the application of these principles in a specific case. In the final four steps, the leader's role is vital but the percentage of time the leader talks is less than 10 percent. While the learners analyze and determine cause and effect relations, the leader probes and clarifies. While learners set priorities and plans of action, the leader challenges. When learners debate outcomes, the leader raises the issue of personal attitudes. Finally, the leader waits and gives only appropriate feedback while the learners debate alternatives and implications.

Adapting the Case Study. Case studies achieve their greatest potential when learners begin to examine prior beliefs and attitudes. The student who is looking for answers or confirmation of preestablished behavioral patterns will benefit little from the case study process. However, such reevaluation of one's ideas can be anxiety producing. Time and care for the establishment of a safe learning environment may be necessary before such adults can benefit from the challenge and counterchallenge of case study procedures.

Adults often rely on past experience and tend to be analogous rather than analytical in their approach to problems. If a solution worked in this case, why not use it in a similar situation? Such participants need to be led through a process of learning how to analyze situations and solve problems. Helping them understand that problem-solving skills are more useful than having answers to the problems will be a valuable prerequisite to learning through the case study approach.

Traditionally, case studies and their support material have been presented through print media. This may cause some difficulty for adults who do not learn well through reading. Supplementing cases with diagrams, models, or preanalysis discussions of people or situations may be useful for them. Facilitators should also be aware that movies, plays, and recordings can be used effectively for case studies.

The analysis process is the most important aspect of case studies. Useful outcomes or solutions tend to be diverse. Thus, the teacher must convey the attitude that it is appropriate to question, to challenge, and to offer divergent suggestions. This differs from the traditional teacher-centered educational setting, in which the student is rewarded for coming up with answers prized by the teacher. Teachers who insist on taking an authoritative stance and who want to be reinforced by the admiration of the students will

have little success with the case study strategy. Perhaps such teachers might best reserve the use of case studies to occasions when they are absent from the classroom.

On the other hand, a facilitator who believes the case study approach may be a valuable strategy but who has had little or no experience with its use may do best by trying short cases or critical incidents (described elsewhere in this book) with an adult group. Such a teacher may feel more comfortable supplying learners with outlines for the analysis and discussion of the case. Such aids are fine; just don't try to analyze the case for the learners! If the teacher has concerns about the value students are deriving from case studies, it can be helpful to share them with the adult group. This can facilitate the group's appreciation for the value of examining their own concerns rather than insisting on their correctness. Adults are more likely to learn from teachers who are also learning than from those concerned about their image.

It is important to have the teacher's goals and the goals of the participants clearly in mind when using the case study strategy. Objectives are essential to selecting or developing a case and to orienting the participants. Although case studies are well suited to objectives directed toward the development of analysis and problem-solving skills, they have limited use in the teaching of some skills essential to problem solving. Factual information, concept development, and theory awareness relevant to a problem are often necessary to the treatment of that problem. However, methods other than the case study approach are better at conveying such information.

Case studies used as examples of application have limited didactic uses. For example, they can be used to point out principles applied in action or examples of conflicts in human interaction. They might also begin a discussion of some theory exemplified in the case. In certain situations, case studies could be directed primarily to the improvement of participants' communication skills. However, all such objectives violate the major value of case studies, that is, improvement of analytical skills.

Content dealing with business topics or management skills is much more likely to have a good selection of cases available. The only way to use case studies in many other content areas is by finding appropriate descriptions in reports or news sources or by writing your own cases.

Time is a major consideration when selecting case study approaches. Participants must have the time to read through, analyze, and select ways of resolving issues raised in the case. It is difficult to rush this process or the equally valuable interaction and discussion time, although in some situations, cases may be distributed ahead of time for individual analysis and discussed when participants have gathered together. Time is also necessary for selecting or developing appropriate cases. Previous experience with the use of case studies and a broad collection of cases at hand can help reduce time needed.

Example of a Case Study. Following is a brief example of a case study. It is based on an evaluation study we conducted. Other documents, such as the project's final report, are used in conjunction with the case study. Because of space limitations such support material is not included here; the final report is available through the Educational Resource Information Center (ERIC) (#CE 042 047).

Case Study: Planning an Evaluation

The state agency for Adult Basic Education (ABE) has asked your department to conduct a statewide evaluation of the Adult Basic Education program in the state. The agency's major goal is to find out how comprehensive the program is: Is there a program available in all parts of the state to serve the needs of area adults from the lowest literacy levels through a high school diploma? The final evaluation report will be distributed to all ABE programs throughout the state to inform them of the current status of the program and will be sent to the federal government to satisfy its requirement that the ABE program be evaluated every three years.

Your department is the adult education department at a major state university. Here faculty members have a flexible time schedule, and travel is not a problem. Two department members are willing to spend a major portion of time on the evaluation, and the department head is willing to help out some. All three have many contacts with ABE personnel throughout the state.

In your state, adult basic education is a large operation. Each year the state agency gets approximately five million dollars from the federal government and about seven million from the state to run the program. These funds are distributed to approximately fifty regional administrative units for directly establishing and conducting classes in adult basic education (low-level reading and math), English as a second language (includes those who are illiterate in both their native language and English and those who just need to learn English), GED (high school equivalency training for passing a standardized test), and several locally adaptable programs through which adults can earn a high school diploma. Regional units vary greatly in size. Some are rural and cover vast geographical areas while others are urban. Many have a high number of minority students. Some rely heavily on learning centers for program delivery while others conduct classes in a variety of locations. Most programs are attempting to develop linkages with numerous community agencies that also try to provide services to disadvantaged students. Altogether, these units employ about two thousand full- and part-time teachers, counselors, and administrators and serve about 125 thousand adults per year. Over the years the state agency has collected much statistical data on the number of students attending each program and on local program budgets. Agency personnel are willing to provide you this information. Everyone knows there is diversity in programming throughout the state, but no one is sure what type of services are best serving the needs of adults.

Your immediate task is to develop a rough outline for the state office personnel to show them how you plan to do this evalua-tion. A planning meeting has just been called. At this meeting there will be at least one of each of the following: (a) the faculty member who will be in charge of conducting the evaluation; (b) the head of the department; (c) a graduate student who hopes to be employed by the project; and (d) another faculty member. At the end of this meeting your group must have a plan that states the type of evaluation you are going to conduct, the way you are going to collect and analyze information, a projected timeline for the evaluation, and an outline of how you are going to spend the sixty thousand dollars that the state will give you to conduct the evaluation.

Using Interaction Strategies

Jim has agreed to teach one evening session of a course being held at the local community college. All class members are local farmers who are attending to learn how to improve the quality of water and wildlife in the ponds on their land. Jim directs the local office of a state agency funded to provide services to farmers. By teaching the class, Jim hopes to make the farmers aware of these services. How does he organize the class to do this? Jim realizes that just telling the farmers about the office and giving them some information on water and wildlife will probably not result in future use of his services. Thinking it over, he realizes that he must get participants to relate their problems to the knowledge base and services available through his office. Having made that decision, Jim has many interaction strategies in mind for organizing this class.

Overview of Interaction Strategies

Interaction strategies are teaching techniques that rely heavily on discussion and sharing among participants. Students are active during the learning process in clarifying their own thinking and sharing their ideas with one another. Examples include discussions and participation training, buzz groups, audience reaction and listening teams, brainstorming, colloquies, forums, critical incidents, problem-solving groups, committees and committee hearings, and learning teams. Because of increased learner participation, the amount of teacher control is less in situations using discussion strategies than in those using presentation-type strategies.

Adult Learners and Interaction Strategies

Education is a transactional encounter in which both the teacher and learner bring a set of values to the learning situation (Brookfield, 1986, p. 20). Discussion strategies provide techniques for the learner to react to the ideas, experience, insights, and knowledge of the teacher or of peer learners and to generate alternative ways of thinking and feeling. They provide the mechanism for learners to reflect upon their experiences and to use adult education to determine what is significant and meaningful about these experiences. Such a method is both democratic (Bergevin, 1967) and fundamental to adult education (Knowles, 1970). Students have an opportunity to organize their thoughts, develop rational arguments, and defend their academic and emotional stances on issues related to the learning activity.

Interaction strategies also promote depth in the learners' mental processing. The challenge of applying new knowledge to problems raised by peers or of interpreting it in terms of one's own experiences promotes deep processing of information, which in turn leads to improved retention and recall of information. After reviewing several research studies, McKeachie (1974) concluded: "Thus, interaction between students and peers and between students and faculty produces favorable educational outcomes at several levels" (p. 177).

Learning Styles and Interaction Strategies

Adults differ widely in their learning styles. Interactive strategies can capitalize on the strengths of many learning styles and preferences that may not have been used in traditional, formal schooling. Discussion strategies are compatible with learning traits such as field-dependency. Field-dependent learners are global thinkers who usually prefer learning in social situations. Strategies that promote interaction allow students to synthesize pieces of information from the learning activity into a meaningful whole. The less structured, free-flowing discussion allows field-dependent learners to examine areas of interest and to test others' perceptions of the applicability of their ideas.

Much traditional schooling involved only print and aural modes of learning. All learning was expected to take place through reading, writing, and listening. Unfortunately, many adults learn best by verbalizing. The adult's vast reservoir of experiences encourages and supports verbalization among adults as a means of acquiring or clarifying new information. The physical action involved also seems to help adults who learn best kinesthetically.

Discussion strategies complement preferences for learning with others and for having a degree of control over the learning situation. Interaction and sharing among participants are stimulated by discussion strategies that allow students to work in groups and to interact not only with the material but also with their peers. Because the teacher does not control discussions, students are able to manage their own learning and direct it to their needs and interests.

Teachers and Interaction Strategies

Interaction strategies require that the teacher transfer some control of the learning situation to the students. As a facilitator, the teacher relinquishes direct control over the learning activity. Instead of being linear, learning branches. Both linear and branching activities start from the same source. However, while the linear follows only the path dictated by the teacher, branching may divert in many directions. It may end at the same place as the linear approach, or it may result in an entirely different conclusion. Because branching is rooted in students' experiences, it has great potential learning value.

Although some control is given up with the discussion strategy, the teacher does not abdicate responsibility for the learning activity or influence over its direction. Teacher control is maintained through various devices. In planning the activity, the teacher determines the discussion strategy that will be used and the exact topic for the discussion. Once in the classroom, the teacher can control the amount of time for discussion and the size, composition, and reporting technique of the groups. Each of these factors influences the structure of the activity.

Teachers need specific skills in order to successfully use discussion strategies. In the planning stage, they must be able to conceptualize the topic for the learning activity. Several years ago, Bruner (1963) emphasized that ideas can be learned at many different levels. Because of this "spiral curriculum," teachers must master their content above the knowledge level. They must understand it at the conceptual level. To encourage students to interact intellectually with the content, the teacher must first conceptualize it thoroughly and then design activities that will enable the students to analyze the concept and apply and evaluate it.

In conceptualizing the topic, the teacher

must anticipate possible directions that student discussions might take. This is a prerequisite to planning discussion activities. Once that has been done, activities can be structured to arouse awareness of paths that students might be unlikely to generate because of their lack of knowledge or experience in the area. Direction can be given that clearly focuses the group. Decisions can be made about the best size for the group and the most appropriate interactive strategy to accomplish the learning goal.

In the classroom, the teacher must be a good listener and observer. While the students are interacting, the teacher must either function as a discussion leader or circulate throughout the class to "overhear" the students' arguments. Although several discussions may be going on simultaneously, the teacher is responsible for gathering enough samples of the content of each group's discussion to understand the logic of how each group's conclusions were derived.

However the teacher must also attend to the process going on within the group discussions. Is something interfering with the learning process? Is some area of information or some principle of practice lacking that inhibits resolution of a question or problem being discussed? Or, is some hidden agenda or conflict among participants distracting members from the learning objectives? Is more time needed for the group to make significant progress? Such questions must be resolved if discussion or interaction strategies are to be fully effective.

The teacher's listening skills are tested further during group debriefings. It is a common practice with discussion strategies to have the groups share the results of their discussion. In this process, the teacher must be able to coordinate the contents emanating from each group and to link these insights to the teacher's goals for the course and the existing knowledge base for the field. Both

functions require thorough preparation and acute attention to the learners during the discussion process and reporting.

Learning Objectives and Interaction Strategies

In situations where group interaction is used, the purpose of the learning activity is to stimulate thought at the highest cognitive levels by filtering new knowledge and concepts through prior experiences. New knowledge may be introduced, but interaction strategies serve primarily as a means of processing information that is presented through some other source such as a reading, lecture, film, panel, case study, or role play. However, because of the vital influence of prior experiences on adult thinking and learning, discussion groups as a learning activity are a distinct tradition in adult education.

Gagne (1965, p. 291) observes, "the discussion class is *not* primarily concerned with learning at all, but with the transfer (generalizing) of what has already been learned." He acknowledges that discussion should naturally be enjoyable to learners since generalizing is "intellectual fun" (p. 290). However, experience has indicated that adults do enjoy discussions especially when they result in applying, analyzing, or evaluating new information.

Learning objectives in the affective domain are also more likely to be obtained through interactive strategies than through presentation techniques. Knowles (1970, p. 294), for example, suggests that experience sharing or group-centered discussion is appropriate for teaching attitudes or values. Many reasons can be given for why this is so. A supportive situation is especially important for attitudinal change or learning. The more cohesive the interacting group, the more support the learner is likely to feel. In addition, loyalty to group members has been reported as not only encouraging change but also promoting adherence to the change.

How to Use Interaction Strategies Effectively

Space and time constraints, the stage of development at which the group is operating, and various organizational factors must be considered when planning interactive strategies. Generally it takes more time to work through material when using interactive techniques than when using presentation approaches. It is also harder to predict time frames for such exercises, because the composition of the group and members' experience and interest in the topic can significantly affect progress. The physical environment may be easier to envision, but preplanning is still important. This is especially true when the activity calls for the interaction of several groups. Is there room to separate the groups physically so all will be able to interact without disturbing others? Break-out rooms and round tables may be important. Situations where groups are to report to one another call for special planning, for such occasions can readily become boring.

Effective learning in group situations demands skills that must be learned and practiced. Most groups have some members who are adept at such skills and others who are not. Time spent planning the most effective mix of participants can be very beneficial. The instructional leader must also make judgments about the attitude of the group toward use of interaction strategies, the ability of group members to interact constructively, and the stage of group cohesiveness. Such factors determine the amount of structure that must be given to exercises and the type of orientation to the learning activity that is most profitable.

Organizational factors affecting the successful use of interaction strategies include the attitude of supervisors toward such activities and the long-range goals as well as the immediate objectives of the sponsoring organization. Many believe that education is primarily the presentation of new ideas, while others feel that a teaching/learning transaction is incomplete until participants have adopted the new practice on the job. The networking that frequently grows out of interactive strategies will be appreciated by the latter group but not by the first. Similarly, situations in which a mastery approach to learning is preferred to a competency-based approach may be much more conducive to interactive strategies.

Discussions

Many different definitions have been offered for small-group discussion as a learning tool but most involve three basic elements: (a) a group of people, (b) brought together for face-to-face oral communication, (c) for the purpose of sharing knowledge or making a decision (Bormann, 1975; Brilhart, 1982; Gulley, 1968; Kahler et al., 1985). Much argumentation and research has been conducted regarding the ideal size of a discussion group. The consensus is that the group should be "small," but the definition of small has varied from four or five to twelve or fifteen. In reality, the ideal size depends on the purpose of the discussion. Some groups are formed mainly to discuss various aspects of an issue or to exchange information. In such cases it is important that the membership be large enough and diverse enough to represent various points of view. However, when the major purpose is to reach a decision or plan an action, diversity and numbers can be an impediment to action.

Modern technology has moved us past the need to bring discussion participants together for face-to-face interaction. In many effective discussions, participants are brought together via telephone or television hookups. Physical presence may not be necessary, yet the rapport essential to open and honest communication—figuratively to look someone in the eye and say what you mean—remains a vital aspect of effective discussion sessions.

While it is true that groups joining together for discussion frequently do so for the purpose of exchanging ideas or reaching a decision, this process is frequently used to build group cohesiveness or to sharpen members' skills in dealing with group processes. Grouping students to study group process rather than to concentrate together on some topic or outside goal will be examined later under "Participation Training". However, the idea of defined purpose does distinguish educational discussions from social converse or "gab" sessions—including those that occur in the classrooms of unprepared teachers!

Discussion strategies have been very popular in adult learning. Discussion and interaction are natural ways of learning, especially when those involved have had experience with the content under consideration. In fact, most adults experience some learning nearly every day through informal discussions. The approach is also natural in that it allows the adult to be active in the learning situation and to exert some control over its direction.

Groups can be organized to accomplish three distinct purposes. Some discussions are designed expressly for the learning of content. Such groups are usually characterized by a strong leader, who is charged with the introduction of new knowledge or the structuring of strategies for such input. Discussions within formal classrooms are often of this type. Material is presented through lecture, film, case study, or some other means, and discussion is used for deeper processing of the content. Other groups are structured to allow participants to share insights or experiences. Exchange of information is encouraged, and the teacher is careful not to dominate the interaction. The third type of discussion is oriented to task rather than subject matter. The group is organized to solve a problem or arrange for a task to be accomplished. Learning is involved, but the task rather than individual needs gives direction to the discussion.

Strengths and Limitations. Flowery language is often used to extoll the virtues of group discussions: "Small groups are the very warp and woof of daily living" (Brilhart, 1982, p. 5), "characteristic of democracy" (Gulley, 1968, p. 4), "the heart of any sound program of communication" (Bormann, 1975, p. 1), and "force an individual to do straight thinking and come to a definite decision" (Kahler et al., 1985, p. 88). Because they are so much a part of human life, they are an easy and comfortable way of introducing adults into formal learning situations. Specific strengths include:

1. Active participation in the discussion process tends to keep the learner physically and mentally active and thus inclined to process information more deeply.

2. Discussions promote the development of listening and speaking skills.

3. Interaction with other adults often leads learners to awareness of differing views of a situation and more tolerance for other stances.

4. Participants have some control over the content and direction of the discussion thus making it more likely that their needs and interests will be considered.

5. Group cohesiveness developed during discussions may continue to be expressed in other collaborative work or learning efforts.

Limitations are present even in this highly regarded approach to learning. While conversation and interchange of ideas are natural, the fact that there are more than two individuals in a discussion group and that the interaction has a specific purpose calls for some control and skill from participants. Few adults have studied the discussion process or have been trained to be practiced participants or leaders. Other limitations:

1. Generally it takes more time to develop a plan of action or consider a content area as a group than as an individual.

2. A few members can dominate the group, directing the discussion to their own interests and ignoring the wishes of others.

3. Group pressures can lead to concern for efficiency rather than satisfaction, authoritarian approaches rather than collaboration, or consensus rather than divergent thinking.

4. Time and space constraints can interfere with the effectiveness of small-group discussions.

Suggestions for Discussion Groups. Discussions can be such powerful strategies for accomplishing a variety of objectives that it is important for the instructional leader to clarify the learning goals and structure the discussion to meet those goals. For example, discussions designed to evoke a sharing of ideas on a subject require a certain type of preparation for the participants. Reading selected materials, reviewing a list of questions, or sharing some appropriate experience could prevent a discussion from becoming what some critics have described as a sharing of mutual ignorance. A problem-solving group, on the other hand, needs to understand the situation and define the problem before entering into a discussion of alternative solutions or a planning of action.

Similarly, purpose can give direction to the selection of participants. Situations requiring different views of the subject call for a larger, more varied group of participants. However, when the objective is to reach a decision or to plan an activity, smaller groups or groups formed of participants with previous experience in working together may be indicated. When working with several groups simultaneously, the instructor must decide whether participants will be allowed to form their own groups or whether membership in groups will be assigned. Occasionally, it may be important to structure—unobtrusively— some groups while allowing others to form naturally. Similar considerations may influence the decision whether to appoint leaders and recorders for groups or to allow such leadership to emerge.

Promoting Communication. A variety of books and articles have been written regarding communication within small groups. Some detail formal rules of order. Others analyze interpersonal relations. Such treatments go far beyond the scope of this writing and are recommended to readers who need deeper analyses of communication in small groups. The following section will simply offer some basic suggestions for improving interaction in adult discussion groups.

Conversation often results from a need to say something rather than from a need to communicate. Thus, adults will speak out in small groups because of a desire for recognition, a feeling of obligation to the group, or a simple preference to hear themselves speak rather than to listen to others. Group leaders need to recognize this and train participants to be aware of the differences between conversation and profitable discussion. This can be done in the orientation to the discussion session or program. The importance of listening rather than lecturing to one another, of informing rather than arguing, of supporting rather than attacking in the overall learning process can be introduced then but will have to be reinforced whenever interaction strategies are used.

The communication or interaction rate of a group is readily influenced by the interpersonal relations of participants. Such relationships are impossible to ignore and are difficult even for individuals experienced in group learning to deal with until some rapport is developed. This provides a rationale for keeping the same participants in groups at least for the first few meetings and for holding initial discussions on topics that tend to be exploratory or at least nonthreatening.

Another recommendation: Check frequently to make sure everyone is discussing the same topic. Discussions that are disappointing to participants and that seem to go nowhere are often symptomatic of a lack of agreement or understanding of what the true topic of the discussion is. It is surprising how easily this can occur with adult groups. Meaningful topics often carry with them emotional overtones that can be stimulated once the dialogue begins. These, combined with differing experiential backgrounds and varied life tasks, push the adult participants to different interpretations even of the *topic* under consideration. It often takes a careful observer to note that, although the same words are being used, different topics are being discussed.

Leadership in Discussions. The larger the number of participants or the more complex the issue being discussed, the more important it is for the group to have an experienced leader. Such leadership in discussion groups has two dimensions, one relating to content and the other to process. The leader's essential abilities and insights vary according to these dimensions and according to the major purpose of the group. Problem-solving groups demand different leadership than groups discussing content. All of these types of group leadership have received much attention in the literature. Gulley (1968), for example, dedicates three chapters of his book to leadership in discussion groups. Bormann (1975) begins his discussion of the leader's role by saying: "The most influential role [of the leader] has been the subject of much fiction, drama, poetry, and conjecture; and, lately, it has been the concern of many systematic empirical investigations" (p. 242). Brilhart (1982, p. 217) even provides a self-test so readers can determine what type of leader they tend to be. Such literature is recommended to the reader for in-depth information on the role of the group leader.

One important observation: Adult discussion groups tend to move through stages rather quickly. The group that needs strong control and tight structure in the early stages of development is likely to soon move beyond that to a greater sense of security and self-direction. Often three or four meetings are sufficient for the development of cohesiveness and directedness. The leader who cannot change leadership style as the group matures will experience great difficulty.

Adapting Discussions. While auditory and kinesthetically inclined learners may relate well to the interaction of discussion strategies, adults with other learning styles or preferences may not. Instruction leaders could use print materials as advanced organizers or distribute summaries of discussions for such learners. The structure-oriented learner might relate well to a prepared outline of potential directions for the discussion. (See Gulley, 1968, pp. 216–231.) The timid participant, the poor listener, and the adult prone to argue rather than discuss need help from the process-oriented discussion leader.

A good discussion leader shares control over the learning activity with participants. A teacher not prepared to do this might put effort into training one or more of the participants to be a group leader and then personally withdraw from the discussion process. Similarly, instructional leaders with little feeling for group dynamics or insight into learning processes might turn responsibility for the guidance of the discussion over to others. The teacher anxious for structure might experiment with assignments preparing learners for discussions or giving specific guidance to participants regarding directions the discussion is to take.

While the discussion process can be used to share information, it is better suited for addressing higher cognitive levels. Adults sharing ideas on the application, analysis, or evaluation of material make a more effective use of this interactive process. Discussion groups in which group cohesiveness and openness develop can also be effective situations for affective change. Much of the literature on change recognizes the small group and the support provided an individual through the group as important ingredients for change.

Because interpersonal communication is essential to discussion sessions, every effort should be made to enable participants to talk and listen to one another with ease. Crowded conditions make this difficult, but adjustments such as the following can help. Keep groups small and use round tables when possible. Separate groups physically, even moving some to other rooms when feasible. Control the general noise in the room; as noise from machines, traffic, or other people increases, the volume within each group also rises, eventually creating an intolerable situation.

Time is another situational factor that can interfere with the discussion process. Adults must be given adequate time to examine a topic and learn from each other. Moreover, discussions are difficult to time because some groups exhaust a subject or reach a

plan of action much more quickly than others. Rather than plan a specific amount of time for a discussion, a leader may be more effective by observing the progress of the discussion and making a judgment as to when to terminate it.

Participation Training

The purpose of participation training is to teach students how to learn more effectively from the discussion process. This is done by involving participants in a learning discussion and then having them reflect upon the *process* they experienced. A moderator familiar with group process guides the analysis.

Groups can be formed as cohesive units for one of two purposes: the group can be a means to an end or the experience of group cohesiveness itself can be the primary end. In the discussion process, the group becomes a means or a setting in which the learning of some meaningful content can occur. The greater the cohesiveness of the group, the more likely members are to share personal ideas, insights, beliefs, and feelings. In participation training and other procedures designed to examine the interactive process, group cohesiveness promotes greater revelation or sharing of factors affecting the learning process of group members. The content being discussed takes on a secondary importance to learning about how one learns through the discussion process. A third class of groups could be added here—the task-oriented group. However, those groups are dedicated primarily to the accomplishment of some task, as in the case of steering committees or problem-solving groups. Because learning and group process both become secondary to accomplishing the task, task-oriented groups will not be considered in this section.

The literature on adult education is replete with examples of groups formed for the purpose of learning how to learn. The authoritative book on participation training is Bergevin and McKinley's (1965) *Participation Training for Adult Education*. In addition, Bradford, Gibb, and Benne (1964, p. 215) list understanding the group process and the learning process as two major purposes of T-group experience. Sensitivity groups vary in their specific purposes but most promote a greater awareness of communication, interaction, and learning processes as means to those ends (Egan, 1970). Similarly, fishbowl or group-within-a-group techniques examine communication and social interaction among group members and have been used to promote more effective learning within groups. We have also used an expanding group strategy (see description later in this section) to encourage participants to examine group process issues.

Strengths and Limitations. A simplistic way of defending the value of participation training is to say that the better one understands a process the more likely one is to perform that process well. Participation training's major purpose is a better understanding of how individuals learn through the discussion process; other strategies attempt to teach such learning skills only indirectly. Other strengths:

1. It provides a realistic setting in which adult learning is likely to occur and in which the learning process can be analyzed.

2. It promotes the development of basic tools essential to learning in groups such as listening, observing, communicating, and reasoning.

3. It enables participants to examine and appreciate the effect of climate and emotions on the learning process.

4. Individuals who have experienced such training are usually adept at analyzing and adapting to various group-learning strategies.

5. While analyzing the learning process, participants also have an opportunity to explore meaningful topics of common concern.

6. This strategy can challenge individuals to examine basic presumptions and to think through positions on important issues.

Participation training has certain limitations that are more likely to emerge when the strategy is imposed on an unenthusiastic group or introduced by an inexperienced moderator. As in any situation in which human emotions are aroused, training sessions can stir strong negative reactions as well as positive ones. Some group members may refuse to examine their learning processes or to share with others their thoughts on topics. Other limitations:

1. The procedure demands a willing group of participants and an insightful leader for full effectiveness.

2. It often takes several sessions before participants begin to appreciate the benefits that can be derived from participation training and as many as thirty hours of training for full comprehension of the process.

3. There is a tendency for participants to be distracted from examining learning processes during their discussion of interesting content.

Suggestions for Participation Training. A simplified outline of a participation training program would include the following: (a) orientation to participation training, (b) examination of elements essential to learning through discussion, (c) selection of a topic for discussion, (d) practice of discussion, (e) evaluation of the discussion, and (f) repetition of this process until the group has come to a thorough understanding of how they learn through the discussion process. Each step will be examined briefly in this section. For fuller explanations of the procedure, consult Bergevin and McKinley (1965) or other resources on participation training.

The orientation to participation training should make clear to all that its purpose is to help them understand and appreciate the processes involved in group learning. Group members must value such understanding of learning processes, or they may be frustrated by the time spent on process rather than content. Participants should also become acquainted and comfortable with each other because the effectiveness of the training sessions is dependent upon their willingness to be honest with themselves and others. As in most adult groups, tension will be lessened by explaining the procedures to be followed and by answering any questions participants might have.

During training sessions presentations on the theory and principles of group learning can be very productive. For example, the nature of learning or of human development might be discussed or principles of communication or group interaction examined. Calling attention to the effect of threat on human learning can also be useful. However, the spirit of such didactic interludes should be more one of sharing insight or asking questions than an authoritarian insistence on absolutes. The dominant approach to learning in participation training should always remain experiential—discussing, reviewing process, and sharing insight.

Selecting meaningful discussion topics can be difficult for newly formed groups. Until participants are willing to trust one another to the point of discussing ideas that differ from their own and until they are willing to investigate topics that might call for a change in their current way of thinking, they are likely to suggest topics that are safe, that is, topics that may lead to a sharing of information but that will not push other members to change their thinking or behavior. As members become more confident with one another and more concerned about using the practice discussions to examine meaningful topics, they begin talking about subjects of genuine interest. They are also concerned that all members of the group are interested and willing to discuss that topic.

Discussions among members of newly formed groups may last only a few minutes. Later the same group may dedicate an hour or more to the investigation of a topic. This willingness to give time to a topic is usually a sign that participants feel they are learning something from the discussion. Theoretically, this indicates that group members are fulfilling their individual responsibilities. They are sharing their insights and beliefs; they are sharing in the decision-making process of the discussion; they are concerned about impediments to one another's learning; and they are informing the group when the discussion moves to an area that lacks personal meaning. When this happens, the group becomes a unit that accommodates itself to the essential needs of the total group yet supports and encourages the learning efforts of the individual.

One obvious but often overlooked essential of good discussions is that everyone discuss the same topic. It is not at all unusual for small groups to talk about two, three, or even four different topics at the same time without members being aware of it. Some may be using the same words but be talking about different ideas. Others may be discussing the same topic but different aspects of it. The result is a general dissatisfaction with the discussion by all—except those who were more interested in hearing themselves talk than in learning from one another! Checking to be sure everyone is discussing the same topic is essential for those using participation training.

A good observer will note things happening during the discussion process that encourage or hinder learning. Occasionally, the observer should interrupt the discussion to point out something that is blocking progress so that it can be eliminated and the discussion can continue. More often such items are part of the observer's objective critique during the evaluation of the discussion. The observer's role is to lead the evaluation, but all group members should share their insights and feelings. The observer should also restrict observations to the *process* of the discussion, not the content. The temptation to share opinions and insights on the topic is great, but such diversions tend to distract from the essential message of participation training. Unless group-learning processes are attended to, the learning of content is seldom effective.

Adapting Participation Training. People who are attuned to the value of attending to process components in the learning experience are much more likely to appreciate participation training. The same is true of people who are sensitive to the internal dynamics of groups. Those who learn best through auditory modes and those who prefer interactive approaches would also appreciate such training. Other adult learners need to be oriented to its value, especially in group-learning situations, before entering fully into the process of participation training.

Not all instructors of adults are prepared to lead participation-training sessions. Because participants learn mainly through an experiential, interactive process, the instructional leader must promote a climate that is learner-centered and that encourages in-

dividual responsibility. It is very difficult for a teacher who prefers to dominate a learning group or who needs to follow a precise schedule to be an effective trainer. Such educators might consider inviting a guest instructor to provide participation training for their students.

Many educators believe they have a responsibility to promote learning-how-to-learn skills in all teaching situations. Yet they are held captive to the expressed objectives, most often content specific, of the program in which they are teaching. There obviously is no room in their course for a formal program in participation training. However, in most learning situations there are many informal opportunities to reflect on the fact that how we learn information does affect how it is remembered. Also, occasions of difficulty in mastering content can be used to analyze learning processes. Moreover, teachers of small groups have many opportunities to turn attention to the potential of group interaction and learning and to give guidance in promoting this potential.

Promoting learning skills within groups calls for situations where group members can develop cohesiveness and rapport with one another. Factors such as group size or time limitations, which prohibit interpersonal interaction and group formation, are not good occasions for examining group-learning processes. Perhaps a teacher's efforts are more effective in helping students understand their own learning process in such situations.

Examples of Participation Training

The first two strategies described here, the fishbowl and expanding groups, are most useful in studying group process. Although they may help adults gain insight into content areas or psychomotor skills, their power lies in teaching interaction skills. In this they can be considered versions of participation training.

Fishbowl

The fishbowl strategy involves group members in observations of one another. It derives its name from the analogy of people observing the activities of fish within the controlled environment of an aquarium or bowl. While some group members discuss a topic or perform a behavior related to the assigned task, other members observe them. The observers may be assigned to watch for a certain type of behavior, to listen for a specific type of content, or to observe certain group members. Since they have a passive role, observers will often physically withdraw from the group. After the active group members have completed their activity, the observers will provide feedback to the group. Often the activity is repeated with the active participants and the observers switching roles.

The major purpose of the fishbowl strategy is to provide immediate feedback to members concerning the processes that go on within a learning activity. This feedback can relate to anything happening in the group and can range from physical behavior to communication patterns to the quality of ideas expressed. Because group members are required to observe other group members, evaluation is a natural result of this approach. The value of this strategy is directly related to its nonthreatening nature. When observation is by peers and in a small group, pressures are minimized. Because participants have an opportunity to discuss the feedback immediately in an informal setting with their peers, defensive responses are not stimulated, and criticism can be viewed constructively.

Because of these strengths, the fishbowl strategy is especially useful when used with training activities and role playing. In training activities, the observers may be watching just one person, as in a simulated situation, or may be observing several, as in interview training. Regardless of the number of active participants, this strategy fosters group discussion and interaction in the evaluation of the activity. Likewise, role-playing situations that may be threatening because they involve self-concept and attitudes can be structured to be supportive through small groups and the fishbowl strategy. Such a combination allows more class members to practice the role play, reduces the pressure on the role players of having a large audience, and casts those not doing the role play as active listeners and evaluators.

Suggestions for Using Fishbowls. Fishbowl approaches depend on two factors for their success: good activities that engage the group being observed in meaningful and natural activity and specific assignments for observers that lead to meaningful feedback to other group members. The facilitator must be clear about the purpose of the fishbowl. For example, if communication patterns of individuals are to be observed, the active group must be put through an exercise that encourages a variety of communication exchanges by each member. The observers must be given specific individuals or patterns to observe and be told what to look for. Opportunity for feedback between individuals and among all members of the group is to be provided.

Expanding Groups

While most discussion groups remain constant in size, the expanding group strategy allows the size of the group to change during an activity. Groups start with a small number and are increased in size with each round of the activity. For example, groups may initially have only two or three members. After the first round of discussions, the groups can be expanded to four or six members by combining two groups. In the next round, they may again be doubled. This expansion continues until there is only one group containing all class members.

The expanding group strategy capitalizes on the strengths of various group sizes and allows for a change in the internal dynamics of a group. The intimacy of very small groups at the beginning of the activity fosters the initial input of ideas. As groups expand, their ideas can be subjected to further analysis and development. However, since ideas carried forward assume a group identity, the tendency for a person to become defensive of an idea is lessened. As the group expands, isolated ideas can be categorized and organized into broader concepts. This can lead to the broader development of relevant ideas and the rejection of irrelevant ideas.

Expansion also allows for a change in the dynamics of a group. Members supporting a minority idea within a small group may find allies for it in the expanded group. Ideas rejected in one small group may be resurrected and further developed in a larger group. Group members who were reticent to reject a colleague's ideas in a small group because of their being identified with their originator may be more critical of ongoing ideas in a larger group. Thus, the expansion process not only allows ideas to seek the highest possible level of development and support but also allows members to vary their participation level in accordance with the group size they find most comfortable.

Final rounds of the expansion process may suffer from repetition and unmanageable group size. If groups start with two or three members and are doubled, by the third round they contain eight to twelve members and are at the maximum for effective group interaction. Because ideas have been close-

ly scrutinized and many alliances formed by the third round, subsequent rounds with larger groups frequently become a reporting episode with further actions decided by structured voting procedures rather than by in-depth discussion.

Suggestions for Using Expanding Groups. The expanding group strategy is especially effective with discussion involving controversial issues. For example, group members may be given a list of approximately ten statements about issues of concern to the group. These should be written in such a way that a few words will elicit divergent opinions on the concept in the statement. Group members should be given a few minutes to decide whether they agree or disagree with the statement. They must take a position on each statement and record it on their sheet. Once individual decisions are made, groups of three can be formed. The task for each triad is to reach consensus on each statement. Is it best to agree or to disagree with each of the statements as written? The facilitator can expect lively discussions at each round as the groups are expanded. By the end of the third round, most groups will have reworded many of the objectionable statements. If the statements are well written, the final rounds may degenerate into straight votes because of the passion invested in each decision during the previous rounds. Regardless of the final actions, the overall goal of lively discussion and critical analysis will be accomplished through the various rounds as the group expands.

Buzz Groups

Buzz groups are small clusters of learners who are temporarily grouped together for a short period to address a topic presented by a facilitator. Adults usually engage in educational activities voluntarily, so they are unlikely to resist participatory learning techniques. Most agree "the importance of ensuring that new knowledge, concepts, skills, or frameworks of interpretation are presented to adult learners in a manner which is comprehensible in terms of their own experiences is a major reason for using participatory learning methods" (Brookfield, 1986, pp. 11–12). Thus, wide use is made of participatory discussion strategies of which perhaps the most flexible and widely used is the buzz group.

Buzz groups simultaneously allow several students to actively explore ideas with other learners and to relate new ideas from the teacher and fellow students to prior experiences. To effectively use this strategy, the teacher must do several things. In the planning stage, the teacher must decide how the buzz groups will be organized and the exact wording of the task that will be presented to the group. Here, care must be used to assure that the higher-level processes of application, analysis, synthesis, or evaluation are elicited. Prior to the buzz session, some presentation of the topic to which the session will be related must be made. During the actual buzz session, the teacher circulates and carefully listens to each group. The teacher is responsible for taking brief samples from each group and constructing from them a general picture of the nature of that group's discussion. After the buzz session, the teacher coordinates a follow-up activity. This may involve such things as debriefing by a spokesperson for each group, a summary by the teacher, or a plan of action for implementing ideas generated by the group. Throughout the process, the teacher should observe as many learners as possible in order to gather valuable behavioral information for evaluating the learner's progress.

Strengths and Limitations. Buzz groups have several advantages that have made their use popular in adult education. Foremost is

that they allow many learners to get involved at the same time. Instead of a limited dialogue between the presenter and a few students as exists in a typical question-and-answer session, students in every group are simultaneously interacting. Other advantages are:

1. Each student has more time to express and explore ideas and to get reactions from others.

2. Adult learners can relate their experiences to the ideas defined or principles enunciated by the presenter and share in the insights of other group members.

3. The buzz group provides an opportunity to get feedback on the interpretation of the material presented.

4. Satisfaction of group members is usually greater when they are allowed to express their opinions and ask questions regarding material presented.

Buzz groups also have some disadvantages. A major one stems from their popularity. They are used so much that some students may find them tedious. Other limitations include:

1. Although buzz groups are efficient in the total amount of critical thinking and activity that they stimulate, they are time-consuming. Usually ten or fifteen minutes are required in order for the groups to organize, clarify the task, and engage in critical discussion. Additional time may be required for debriefing.

2. The quality of the group's discussion is closely related to the appropriateness of the topic or task defined by the teacher. If it is not

clear, time is wasted and students become frustrated.

3. Within the small group, participants do not have the teacher's reactions to their ideas or to those of the group.

4. Some adults may be threatened by the implied expectation for them to participate in a discussion with people they do not know well.

Suggestions for Organizing Buzz Groups. Because the purpose of buzz groups is to allow learners to discuss an issue and to raise critical questions, the two key ingredients in organizing them are size and time. Buzz groups are small. They can range from three to twelve members. The group must be small enough to allow all members to contribute fully to the discussion, but it must also be large enough to remove any feelings of forced participation or to prevent dominance by anyone. A group of three permits maximum participation by each member. However, a group this small may be threatening to some members. Such anxiety may either cause total withdrawal from the activity or foster latent hostility by a learner. A grouping of three also suffers from potentially limited input. While it is easy for everyone to participate, divergent viewpoints or experiences may not exist with such a small group. On the other hand, when groups become as large as eight, it is more difficult for everyone to participate. Courteous members may not get a chance to participate at the appropriate time, and the focus of the group may wander as various members try to inject their ideas. As a result of the limitations at each extreme of the range, buzz groups of five or six individuals are a common practice in adult education.

The second critical factor in organizing buzz groups is time. The buzz session must be long enough to allow for adequate discus-sion of the topic but not so long that the groups digress to unrelated topics. Two techniques can control the time factor. One allows for a maximum of teacher control. The teacher merely states the amount of time budgeted for the buzz session. This decision is based on the teacher's judgment and experience. The teacher acts as the timekeeper and usually gives a warning shortly before the limit expires.

The other approach is more flexible. At the beginning, the teacher announces the approximate amount of time allocated for the session. As the discussion proceeds, the teacher circulates among the groups and listens. As the groups reach closure, the teacher makes a quick decision and announces the amount of time remaining. While this method allows for situational flexibility, it may be more confusing for the learners and may hinder their task orientation in the group. Typically, ten to fifteen minutes are allowed for a buzz session.

The teacher also exerts control over the buzz session by the method of group formation and by the topic. In forming the groups, the teacher can either assign learners to a specific group or allow self-selection. There are advantages to each approach. Teacher assignment facilitates the rapid formation of groups. Sometimes the purpose for using a buzz session mandates certain combinations of learners. At other times, the freedom of the learner to select a group may be as important as the actual discussion. Occasionally, a teacher may need only assign specific functions such as a group leader or recorder. The combination of the discussion topic, immediate situation, and teacher preference for control should collectively decide this organizational factor.

Adapting Buzz Groups. Most adults adapt easily to buzz groups. This strategy enables group members to express their ideas and share their perceptions within the limits of the topic being discussed. Buzz groups enable all members to hear different points of view and weigh the merits of others' discussions about their ideas. This is particularly important when all or most of the members do not know the others in the group. Using buzz groups with varied memberships enhances the opportunity for everyone to become better acquainted with and appreciative of other participants in the learning activity. This, in turn, improves the opportunity for learning as ideas and knowledge are exchanged among a greater number in the various small groups.

Although students have a great deal of freedom for exploring ideas, teachers have much control over buzz groups. They can structure the topic for the buzz group and determine the way it is introduced. They can modify the group by size, time, and assigned roles to elicit discussions in the directions they desire. Various groups can be assigned different topics to cover a wide range of subjects in a short time period. Therefore, buzz groups are a very flexible means for allowing the instructor to quickly organize the learners and to get them interacting with others at a high cognitive level on topics related to the class.

A major advantage of buzz groups is that they can be combined with other techniques. Buzz groups are often used to process information presented through another technique. For example, they could be used to synthesize and evaluate knowledge presented in a lecture, film, or slide-tape show. They could also be used as the working unit for those involved in a case study. Besides eliciting reactions to other content material, buzz groups can be used to generate information. Such groups could identify individual, group, or community needs for a needs assessment. They could also be used prior to a large-group presentation or discussion to identify potential items for the session. Whenever the

teacher has a need for involving the learners in a short, intense discussion related to classroom topics, buzz groups are an option with possible benefits.

Example of a Buzz Group. Phillips 66: One popular version of the buzz group is known as the Phillips 66 technique. It was developed by J. Donald Phillips (Kahler et al., 1985, p. 116) and is especially applicable to large-group sessions held in auditoriums. In this approach groups are formed by asking people in every other row to turn around and talk to people in the row behind. Groups of six are formed quickly in this manner and are given six minutes to discuss the topic assigned by the facilitator. The approach has the advantage of splitting up cliques and associates sitting together and bringing diversity into the buzz groups. It can have the disadvantage of limiting the depth of the discussions either because of the time factor or because individuals are reluctant to speak out without knowing others in their group.

Brainstorming

While buzz groups are used primarily as a follow-up activity to deal with a prescribed content, brainstorming is an interaction strategy used to generate ideas or to help determine the exact nature of content to be discussed. This approach encourages group members to think creatively and to expand upon ideas of fellow group members. The primary purpose of brainstorming is to create a pool of ideas on a topic. These ideas can then be processed in several ways.

Because the purpose of brainstorming is to encourage a group of people to think creatively about a topic, innovative, unique, or untried ideas as well as practical, obvious, or tested approaches are equally accepted. Ideas may be linked together, modified slightly, or piggybacked onto someone else's ideas. Ownership of the ideas is not important. The ultimate goal is for the group to interact in order to produce the largest possible pool of ideas related to the topic.

Brainstorming requires a facilitator, who initiates the activity by posing a problem or topic area and by asking for ideas from the participants. The facilitator is then responsible for recording on a device such as a chalkboard or flip chart a few key words that capture the essence of each expressed idea. During this process, the facilitator tries to maintain a constant flow of ideas from the participants and to prevent the group from diverting their creative energy to criticism or discussion of the proposed ideas. Nothing that inhibits creativity is to be tolerated.

Strengths and Limitations. Brainstorming is useful for encouraging divergent thinking by a group and for stimulating group members to expand creatively upon the ideas of others. This interaction elicits new ideas. Other strengths include:

1. Brainstorming is a strategy for getting many ideas out before a group.

2. It can encourage participants to think beyond their traditional approaches to solving problems and their day-to-day procedures for dealing with issues.

3. Well-run brainstorming sessions draw out ideas too divergent to be suggested through other techniques.

4. Brainstorming encourages the involvement of all participants yet relies on ideas suggested by individuals to stimulate thinking by other group members.

One of the major limitations of brainstorming is that the immediate discussion of interesting and potentially fruitful ideas is not possible because such discussion would thwart the generation process. Other limitations include:

1. Brainstorming has no quality control. It is undirected. The experiences and motivation of the individual group members and the maturity of the group will affect the number and type of ideas generated.

2. Because the emphasis is on creative exploration, many of the ideas may not be useful; only later discussion and analysis can determine their feasibility.

3. Members of the group can dominate the process by their suggestions, or the first few ideas generated can set a direction for thinking.

4. There is no guarantee that all relevant areas will be mentioned or that creative ideas will be suggested.

Suggestions for Brainstorming Sessions. The facilitator's role is to set a climate that will encourage the generation and expression of ideas. This may be difficult in newly formed groups or in situations where participants feel threatened by other members of the group. One technique for overcoming hesitancy to speak out is to hold a light-hearted warm-up session before serious brainstorming begins. One approach we use is to challenge the group to come up with twenty uses of a brick within a two-minute time frame. Usually some humorous or impractical suggestions are offered, and the idea of brainstorming is clarified for participants.

Basically, there are three rules to brainstorming: (a) all ideas suggested are accepted and recorded in public view, (b) no criticism of any suggestion is allowed, and (c) everyone must share any idea that seems even remotely appropriate. The facilitator who can get a group to accept these rules is well on the way to a successful brainstorming session.

One difficulty in leading brainstorming sessions is capturing and publicly recording all the suggestions made by group members. The assistance of two or three recorders to note ideas on a chalkboard or flip chart can help. Ideas can be synopsized, but care must be taken to retain the original intent. Occasionally, the generation of an idea may be so important that a tape recording of the session is appropriate.

Brainstorming is usually followed by an interactive strategy for further resolution of the ideas suggested. Small-group discussion of various kinds can be used, but some clarification of suggested ideas is usually appropriate before the brainstorming group is disbanded. This is the time for evaluating and clarifying ideas.

The purpose of the brainstorming session often dictates the follow-up strategy. If some consolidation and ranking of suggestions is desired, a modified delphi technique could be used: Each participant indicates the ideas that person considers most important. Feedback of the total group opinion is provided and some discussion allowed. Further rounds of ranking and discussion may be appropriate. At other times, the purpose of the brainstorming may be served more appropriately by preserving individual opinions. Some version of a Q-sort or priority ranking could be used. In still other situations, small groups may be assigned one or more of the suggested ideas for analysis. The purpose might be to develop plans for the implementation of those suggestions.

Adapting Brainstorming. One very popular adaptation of the brainstorming strategy is known as the nominal group technique. The approach was developed in the 1960s at the University of Wisconsin by Delbecq, Van de Ven, and Gustafson (1975). The title comes from its use of participants as individuals—only nominally (in name only) as a group—for the initial stage of idea generation. This approach calls first for the silent generation and priority ranking of ideas by each group member. This is followed by a public listing of ideas usually by asking for each person's top-ranked idea and then moving on to second- and third-ranked ideas until everyone's list is exhausted. As in brainstorming, the purpose of the listing stage is to record as many ideas as possible. Once this is completed, group members are allowed to discuss the ideas. Participants may ask questions of other group members to clarify an idea, and they may use this period to argue either for or against any of the listed ideas. After the discussion, a vote is taken in which group members are asked to rank the ideas that have been generated. Ideas receiving the highest number of votes are retained. The exact number retained may vary with the purpose and content of the nominal group activity.

The strength of the nominal group approach is that it prevents individuals or early suggested ideas from dominating the number or direction of ideas generated. Its weakness is that it lessens the stimulation of other group members' ideas.

Brainstorming and the nominal group technique can be used whenever group input is desired for generating ideas related to a topic. They could be used for any stage of the curriculum-planning process. Ideas may be related to potential student needs to be addressed, specific content to be explored, potential avenues for investigating the topic, and possible ways of evaluating the learning. Besides initiating ideas, the nominal group technique provides a structure for reaching rapid group closure on the topic.

Other approaches can regulate the structure for idea-generating activities. For example, group size can affect these strategies. Larger groups potentially offer a greater number of resources for more ideas. However, with a large group it is more difficult for each member to participate, and spontaneity may be restricted. In determining the exact group size, planners should consider any information about the participants' preference for group size, type of content, and available facilities.

Example of Brainstorming. Brainstorming and the additional features of the nominal group technique were recently used in one state to generate the content for a conference. In response to a state agency's request to produce a list of state goals for adult basic education, a group of approximately twenty experienced practitioners convened. The two-day conference started with a brainstorming session. Participants were divided into three groups: teachers, administrators, and state agency personnel. Following a fifteen-minute period of silent individual listing of ideas, each group generated a list of possible goals for adult basic education in the state. Using the discussion and ranking period of the nominal group technique, ideas were explored and group consensus reached. Each group produced within a few hours a list of ten possible goals for the state's ABE program.

Since the content of each list was influenced by the homogeneous composition of each group and because the total number of goals from the three lists was too large, a modified nominal group technique was used with the entire group. Instead of generating new ideas, the participants discussed and ranked the thirty ideas from the three previous lists. Through debate and consolidation of ideas, the group of twenty reached consensus on eight goals for the state's ABE program. A similar process was used to deter-

mine strategies for accomplishing those goals.

Listening Teams

Interaction strategies can also be used to focus listening. Listening teams are small groups of learners who are assigned to listen for specific information during a presentation. The assignment of topics prior to the presentation provides the listener a structure for organizing the information presented. The division of labor among several individuals or groups allows the listeners to specialize in one aspect of the presentation with the assurance that others are critically analyzing other aspects of the presentation. Through discussions after, all points of the presentation are shared.

Teams usually range in size from four to seven members. Although each member listens and takes notes individually, the group convenes after the presentation to process the information together. Because group members have been organized to listen, the ensuing discussion starts easily and is quite focused.

Strengths and Limitations. Listening teams are a powerful strategy for helping learners preview a presentation and for assuring that they analyze the major elements of it. Other advantages include:

1. A facilitator can assign listening topics that alert learners to the major elements of the presentation and that stimulate questioning.

2. This strategy provides a way of summarizing and synthesizing a presentation as well as integrating the participants' experience into the discussion.

3. Listening teams inject a degree of audience participation into a formal presentation.

4. Presenters are more likely to consider the interests and concerns of their audience when they know that the participants are going to respond to what was presented.

5. Responsibility for assigned listening tasks can promote the development of listening skills among adult learners.

Limitations of listening teams generally result from the way they are structured. Team members may not be competent to analyze the topic assigned or may be distracted in their listening by the structure imposed upon them. Other disadvantages include:

1. Those listening carefully for material related to their topic may overlook other ideas.

2. The organization imposed by the facilitator may hinder the learners in organizing the information in a manner more natural to them and more likely to be retained.

3. Listeners may be assigned a topic of little interest to them, or their interpretation of the presentation may be of little interest to others.

Suggestions for Listening Teams. Kahler et al. (1985, p. 128) advise us that, "Listening team members must be carefully selected. It is important that they be persons who are well informed concerning the subject under consideration, yet persons who have no biases or axes to grind." This is especially true when the team is to react publicly to the presentation. If the teams are to meet separately and discuss what they heard among themselves, careful selection remains important since competence in various aspects of the question must be represented in each group.

Adapting Listening Teams. When using the listening team with groups experienced in interaction, the facilitator may not want to assign specific listening tasks to individuals beforehand. Participants can be allowed to impose their own structure on the presentation, and differences in learning style and past experience can be counted on to direct varied input into the discussion.

In large gatherings or situations where it would be difficult to organize group discussions, one listening team can be used to respond to the presentation. Members of the team are carefully selected to represent expertise in the various areas that will be covered in the presentation. Their task is to make the presenter's comments more applicable to the local situation or to raise questions ignored in the original presentation.

Audience Reaction Team

This strategy is similar to the listening team approach. However, members of an audience reaction team need not restrict their remarks to the end of a presentation. They may interrupt the presenter at any point to seek clarification or to direct the trend of the presentation to the needs or interests of the audience. This technique is especially useful when the subject matter is complicated or difficult for the audience to follow or when the presenter(s) would benefit from audience input during the presentation.

Because adult learners may be unfamiliar with this technique, the chairperson or moderator should explain the process clearly. Members of the audience reaction team are usually given a prominent place to one side of the stage or near the spot where presentations will be made. They are introduced, and their qualifications are announced to the audience. Often a rationale is given for the use of the audience reaction team. It is also helpful if a presenter invites some response from the team early in the presentation so that the audience becomes accustomed to interruptions from the team. Upon completion of the presentation, each team member is allowed to give a short reaction to the content.

Because the audience reaction team is similar to the listening team, the reader is referred to that section of this chapter for an analysis of strengths and limitations, suggestions for practice, and ways of adapting the strategy.

Colloquy

A simple definition of the word *colloquy* is "to talk with." As a structure for a learning situation it retains this basic notion of talking together but establishes a format that makes such conversing feasible among members of a large audience. This is done by combining some of the features of the panel and the forum.

A panel of three or four experts presents information, insights, or opinions to an audience. The audience is represented by its own panel of three or four members who interact with the panel of experts. Usually this small group representing the general audience is selected beforehand from the total group and is given a prominent place on a stage with the panel of experts. The group can question the experts, challenge their opinions, or offer ideas representing the views of the larger audience. Occasionally, colloquies will be structured so that any member of the audience can interrupt the presenters to ask for more information or to express an opinion. However, as can easily be imagined, such lack of structure can readily lead to a complete breakdown of interaction. Only in situations where the larger group is very experienced with interaction and where the chairperson is extremely skilled can such an open-ended structure be expected to work.

Strengths and Limitations. The major advantage of the colloquy is that it involves the audience in the learning interaction. That it does so in a limited manner does not negate the fact that the questions and concerns of the audience are likely to be brought into the conversation and addressed specifically. Other strengths:

1. Presenters are pressured to attend to audience needs and to be precise about the information and opinions they express.

2. The format encourages the exploration of various sides or aspects of an issue.

3. The colloquy provides formative feedback to all involved so that direction or emphasis in the discussion can change to meet interests, needs, or levels of competence.

4. The format stimulates thought, because participants are involved in taking sides or identifying with positions expressed.

5. It can interject audience participation into a discussion at timely and relevant occasions rather than restrict such participation to postpresentation situations.

Any attempt to accomplish so much—the presentation of material by several individuals and the questioning and commenting by the larger audience—is bound to have problems. Some limitations are:

1. There is seldom enough time for presenters to express all their ideas and at the same time allow for all the comments and questions of the audience representatives.

2. Because of time and participation constraints, opinions are difficult to change.

3. Extreme positions may be taken by an expert or an audience representative and block the general resolution of an issue.

4. The colloquy is difficult to control and demands a skilled chairperson and cooperative panelists.

Suggestions for Conducting Colloquies. In colloquies, it is especially important that those in leadership positions be skilled both in content and procedure. Presenters must realize that they cannot limit their remarks to carefully worded statements prepared beforehand. They must respond to the expressed needs of the audience even if it means dealing with unforeseen aspects of an issue. Those representing the audience also need to be flexible; they cannot simply represent themselves but must know the needs and interests of all participants. The moderator or chairperson needs to exercise very delicate control by moving the group through a careful consideration of the content while allowing each participant the necessary freedom to delve into specifics important to that person.

Several things can be done to prepare a group for a colloquy. The audience can be given some general information about the content so that all participants are close to the same level of readiness. If those who are to represent the audience are involved in this preparation, questions and comments of group members can be noted at this time. Both groups of panel members can be instructed on the importance of such things as encouraging questions and comments, controlling extraneous remarks, and occasionally synthesizing or summarizing to give direction to the discussion. Some indication of the type of control that the leader will exercise could also be advantageous. All must recognize that the chairperson is in control, yet the chair must reassure participants that they will not be cut short and will be allowed to express opinions—even if controversial.

Kahler et al. (1985) offer summary advice on the use of the colloquy worth quoting here. "Program planners who wish to vary their program procedure should consider the colloquy as a technique with many advantages. It should not be used too often" (p. 84).

Adapting the Colloquy. More audience participation could be promoted by allowing individuals from the audience to replace panel representatives at various times during the colloquy. This might stimulate small groups within the audience to caucus and send a representative to the front. Other strategies could also be integrated into the colloquy format. For example, buzz groups might be used to stimulate small-group formation and expression of concerns.

Forum

The forum is an educational strategy that gives each participant a chance to express his or her views. It has been defined as a "form of public discussion in which a group seeks to explore a problem by means of questions, answers, and brief statements under the guidance of a skilled chairman" (Wagner & Arnold, 1965, p. 182). Occasionally the forum is used with some other technique such as a lecture or film, but it can stand alone as in a town meeting or political caucus. Similarly, the name *forum* has also been applied to a series of public meetings in which the audience is invited to express opinions either in reaction to a presentation or in open discussion.

Forums usually begin with orientation both to topic and procedure. Because the objective is to encourage participants to express their viewpoints, content orientation is restricted to an overview of issues. The procedural orientation is often more detailed as a means of imposing order on the interaction. Methods for recognizing speakers, procedures for the use of microphones, limitations on comments, and general directions for the discussion are explained at this time. The chairperson then guides the interaction according to the preestablished rules.

Strengths and Limitations. The forum is often held up as the theoretically ideal strategy for group learning, for it involves everyone in active participation. It attempts to carry all the positive aspects of the small-group discussion over to large-group interactions. Thus, specific strengths of the effective forum include:

1. The forum allows all group members to be actively involved in the learning situation.

2. The format provides formative feedback allowing all participants to recognize how they are communicating to others and what concerns are affecting the interaction.

3. A group can reach consensus or at least a common awareness about an issue affecting all members.

4. A forum allows participants to apply information to their own situations and to let others know their opinions on common concerns.

The limitations of the forum relate to the difficulty of accomplishing meaningful discussion while involving a large number of participants. Other limitations include:

1. Some comments that are relevant to individuals will be irrelevant or of little interest to the majority.

2. Because of time and interaction limitations, the forum can fail to move through disagreement or misunderstanding to consensus.

3. In spite of stated procedures intended to encourage participation by all, a few can dominate a forum.

Suggestions for Organizing Forums. All participants are entitled to know what a forum is, when it will begin, and what the rules for discussion are. If the forum is to be used with a presentation, that should be announced at the start. Immediately before beginning the forum, the rules of the discourse should be announced or distributed. These should include the goals and objectives of the forum; any limitations on content area, questions, or comments; methods by which individual speakers will be recognized; time limits, including any on the length or number of comments from an individual; and guidance on the use of a public-address system, if one is used. The chair should also take advantage of this opportunity to teach participants to be better discussants. For example, the value of preparing brief, clear comments rather than rambling diatribes and of listening to others' comments could be pointed out. Impressing on participants that the purpose of a forum is to reach a group goal rather than satisfy individual needs can be very helpful.

In preparing for a forum, the leader should also think through methods for promoting the essential processes of such a discussion. The group must be stimulated to think deeply about the problems to be discussed. Are a formal presentation, handouts, or directive comments from the chair necessary for this? Pausing to summarize discussion, to formulate meaningful questions, or to clarify unclear comments or questions needs to be done regularly. It is also useful to have a system prepared for referring difficult questions or problems to an appropriate resource person. Finally, the discussion must be brought to a satisfactory conclusion. This is more likely to happen if alternative closures have been thought through than if left to chance.

Adapting the Forum. Very large numbers of participants can be accommodated if forum procedures are adjusted so that the first stage of discussion takes place in small groups. At an appropriate time, the small groups are joined together and further discussion occurs among representatives of each group. Other members listen to representatives share ideas discussed in the small groups. More than one round of small-group discussion can be used.

Controversial topics are bound to stimulate emotional behavior in some participants. If this is objectionable, some kind of filtering system can be set up. For example, throughout the audience several "reporters" might be stationed whose task is to listen to participants and to announce the comments of groups and individuals. These reporters would be the only ones allowed to speak to the whole group. Another filter used frequently is restricting questions or comments to written form, again to be read by an appointed representative. A simple but crude form of control is the installation on all microphones of switches that can be operated only from the stage. However, participation should be encouraged, not stifled.

Committee

The committee is a "small group of people given an assigned task or responsibility by a larger group (parent organization) or person with authority" (Brilhart, 1982, p. 3). Although committees are generally thought of as task forces, they can be an effective teaching strategy if the task assigned is one that calls for committee members to acquire knowledge. This aspect of an assigned task is also the element that distinguishes the committee from a problem-solving or action/ discussion group. Once the task is given, the

committee is usually free to plan its own process for accomplishing it—often under the direction of one member appointed leader either by the parent organization or the committee members.

The task given the committee has a major impact on the type and amount of learning that occurs. Tasks can vary greatly according to the needs of the parent group. Some committees are formed to obtain information or plan action; others are organized to formulate policy or set goals; still others are charged with carrying out some action or organizing a program. Most learning that occurs relates to what is necessary to accomplish the assigned task. However, the interaction of committee members usually results in serendipitous benefits. Frequently, major learning outcomes of the committee approach fall in the affective domain. Group members form networks that carry over to other activities, and loyalty to the parent organization is strengthened considerably.

Strengths and Limitations. As representatives of a larger organization, committee members often have access to resources that they would not ordinarily be able to tap. And, because the working/learning group is small, it can frequently be more productive than the larger group it represents. Other strengths include:

1. As a small group of people who meet together regularly, committees can develop into very efficient groups.
2. Because committees tend to have specific tasks to accomplish and are often required to report back to the larger organization, committees are likely to move consistently toward closure of the learning or work task.
3. Committee members learn through action, thus getting both practice in the

learning task and feedback on the effectiveness of their learning.

4. Committee members develop a stronger allegiance to the parent organization and create networks among other members of the larger group.

5. Committees are in a very favorable position to educate other members of the parent organization.

The committee approach to instruction has definite limitations. Individuals within the group may resent the assignment given or disagree with its importance. Committees tend to be structured, so some adult learners may fail to accept responsibility for the learning or work tasks and give only limited effort to their accomplishment. Other limitations include:

1. The assignment given the committee may be unimportant, unclear, or posed in such a manner as to limit the learning involved.

2. Committee members may have hidden agendas that interfere with the learning tasks.

3. Because the task is assigned and not necessarily their own, participants may give only perfunctory service to the work or learning tasks.

4. The task to be done for the represented group may overshadow any obvious need for learning and consequently absorb all of the committee's energy.

Suggestions for Using Committees. The assignment given to the committee and the people appointed to the group need to be given serious thought. In phrasing the task, an instructional leader should be specific. Committee members should perceive the

assignment as a real problem or a meaningful task. It also needs to be within the experience of the group and accomplishable in the time frame available. Learning elements involved in doing the task should be specified to the degree possible. Thought should be given to the mixture of people best suited not only to the completion of the task but also to the enhancement of the learning. Because the committee chairperson often has a dominant role in the committee's work, this person needs to have some competency in directing learning efforts or should be given the help to do so.

Some organizations prepare guidesheets to outline policies and procedures for committees. These can be very helpful especially for inexperienced adults or those working together for the first time. Usually a simple problem-solving process is suggested, the first step being to identify and clarify the problem. This vital element is often overlooked by groups that want to rush into offering suggestions for solving a problem before they know what it really is. Besides, this identification process can be ideal for learning—not only for learning content but also for developing skills in processes such as identification and evaluation of resources, assessment of needs, and setting of objectives. Once the issue has been clarified, alternative methods for its resolution can be discussed. This is an occasion for practicing discussion and decision-making skills. The third major step calls for planning procedures for carrying out the solution or set of actions selected by the group, again an excellent occasion for teaching both content and process skills.

Adapting Committees. Various types of committees can be used to accomplish learning tasks. Standing committees have an element of permanence, and their members tend to form long-lasting relationships. A different kind of learning task can be accomplished through such interaction than can be accomplished through an ad hoc committee that is assigned a specific task and that may meet only a few times, then disband.

Parent organizations as well as individual leaders often have a hard time giving an assignment to a committee and then releasing it to work on the task. The leader's urge to maintain control can limit the effective use of the committee strategy. Teachers with these tendencies might do better sticking to task-oriented committees. Leaders with less need to maintain control can make good use of advisory groups such as quality circles.

Committee Hearing

The televised coverage given to congressional committee hearings has made this a well-known strategy for eliciting information. By definition, the committee hearing is the questioning of a person or several persons by a group. It is basically an interview to which the dynamics of group interaction have been added. It can be structured to deal with several individuals by questioning more than one at the same time or by interviewing them in sequence.

The major uses of the committee hearing are to solicit the information or opinions of knowledgeable people, to stimulate interest in an area, to orient a group to a problem, or to get a speaker or consultant to be specific in addressing the needs and interests of a group. It is especially useful for probing deeply into an issue or for directing the comments of a hostile consultant or of one unfamiliar with the group's needs or interests. It can be a time-saver when it keeps the consultant from wandering to details of no interest to the group. However, it can be time-consuming when each committee member pursues his or her own interests or views.

Strengths and Limitations. The interaction of group questioning adds a dynamic that can spark the interest of a larger group observing the committee hearing. However, the greater intrinsic value of the hearing lies in its problem-solving power. It is an excellent way for a committee to become informed on an issue. Other strengths include:

1. There is flexible control over the investigation of the issue, and that control lies in the hands of the committee, thus enabling the members to direct the flow of information.

2. It allows for cooperative thinking and questioning in which members can concentrate on certain aspects of a problem or take time to think while others lead the discussion.

3. The verbal interplay among participants can create high interest among observers.

4. The committee hearing can provide good training for group members in information-gathering and problem-solving procedures.

The limitations of the committee hearing result from difficulties usually found in a group performing a task that an individual could accomplish. Disorganization, repetition, and pursuit of goals that interest only a few are possible. Other limitations include:

1. Committees can be disorganized and members can interfere with each other's learning.

2. A hearing can be hard on the person being interviewed; the questioning can jump from issue to issue or the probing can become intense.

3. Committee hearings can be very time-consuming.

4. The public image of a committee hearing may be one of discord, hostility, and self-seeking, an image that could detract from its use as a learning strategy.

Suggestions for Committee Hearings. Hearings need not be restricted to the questioning of hostile witnesses on issues of public concern. Many formal classroom situations could benefit from a committee-hearing approach, for it could motivate a small group of students to dig deeply into an issue while preventing a guest lecturer from wandering to inappropriate topics. Many experts would appreciate such a strategy; it saves them the time and effort needed to try to assess the group's interests.

The person leading the hearing has responsibilities both to the committee and to those being questioned. The committee must be led through a planning process if it is to work. Each member should have a good overview of the issue being investigated and an understanding of the process to be followed. Although questioning cannot be preplanned in detail, the committee can think through trends of investigation and responsibilities of individual members. It is also the leader's responsibility to see that the expert's qualifications are established so that members know the reliability of opinions presented. Thought also needs to be given to allowing the witness to function effectively. This often calls for a prestatement by the expert before questioning begins. Because of the pressure that can be exerted by group questioning, means of providing support during the hearing such as pauses to summarize or clarify should be considered also.

Adapting Committee Hearings. To compensate for lack of expertise on the part of committee members or to give order to the investigation, assign the lead-in questioning to an expert. Committee members are then allowed limited time to follow up on the expert's questions or on issues of special interest to them. A teacher concerned about the adequacy of questions directed to a classroom guest might assume such a role in the questioning—perhaps after the committee of students has asked its questions.

The interaction of a committee hearing, especially on complex issues, benefits from a period of synthesis or summary. This can be done by devoting time at the end of the hearing for committee members to discuss the insights they have developed. The instructional leader or someone assigned could also perform this task.

CHAPTER SIX

Evaluating Teaching Strategies

*A*ngie Javor sat in her office and pondered her next move. As assistant director for continuing education at Valley View Community College, she had enjoyed her experiences in developing educational programs for adults during the past five months and she looked forward to new challenges. When the director indicated the need for a system for evaluating teachers in the program, Angie accepted his request. She felt that her years of public school teaching experience would help and she just knew that the adult education literature would be filled with suggestions and advice about how to evaluate teachers. However, after three weeks of reviewing books, journals, and research reports and conducting various searches through the ERIC literature, she was virtually empty-handed. Much had been written about program *evaluation in adult education but little about* teacher *evaluation. There were references to faculty evaluation in colleges and universities and to teacher evaluation in the elementary and secondary schools, but would the same principles and concepts apply to adult education? There were many models discussed, but they too were for evaluating programs. Where could she get some useful information for evaluating adult education teachers? she pondered . . .*

Where indeed? As Angie indicated, adult education literature contains much information about program evaluation, but little about teacher evaluation. Why? Perhaps evaluating others in their teaching roles creates a negative connotation in the minds of educators. When one realizes the effects that negative evaluation may have on individuals' teaching efforts or even upon their careers, the task appears difficult, even frightening. Perhaps, teachers are too accustomed to considering the classroom their private bailiwick to think positively of the benefits that could be derived from outside evaluation. More likely though, in traditional evaluations of teaching almost total responsibility for the success or failure of the teaching/learning transaction has been placed on the teacher. The question has even been asked, perhaps facetiously, "If no one has learned, has anyone really taught?" The theme of this book is that good teaching is a combination of teachers, learners, content, and situations. Any evaluation of teaching should take all four areas into consideration.

What Is Evaluation?

Evaluation is difficult to define. One reason is that educators disagree about what evaluation is and what it should do. We could blame differences in educational philosophy for this lack of agreement, but much of it is because evaluation has received limited attention by educators until recently. As Worthen and Sanders (1973, p. 20) have pointed out, measurement specialists tend to equate evaluation with measurement, while those concerned with accreditation of formal educational programs tend to equate it with professional judgment on the value of a program. At the

147

same time, those enamored of behavioral objectives use evaluation as a tool to define how well those objectives are being met. Today these three different rationales are still being promoted in definitions of education evaluation. However, in the late 1960s and especially in the 1970s, when funding sources began to require that all proposals include descriptions of evaluation procedures, a more comprehensive role was proposed for evaluation, and definitions began to appear that spoke of evaluation as a process in which information is gathered to assist decision makers. This approach offers the most value for evaluators of the teaching/learning transaction.

The working definition of evaluation used in this book is as follows: *Evaluation is the gathering of information that will assist in the making of decisions, which will lead to the improvement of the teaching/learning transaction*. This identifies three essential elements of effective evaluations: (a) the gathering of relevant data, (b) the concern for the decisional process, and (c) the ultimate purpose of the process, that is, the improvement of education.

It has been pointed out (Conti & Fellenz, 1987) that different stances on the purpose of evaluation have led to two basic approaches to educational evaluation, one emphasizing measurement, the other discovery. Realizing the varied assumptions that underlie these two approaches can help educators design more effective evaluations. At least three such distinctions can be made.

The purpose of an evaluation can be either summative or formative. In general, educators have been more familiar with summative approaches; that is, with evaluations conducted near the end or even after a program has been completed that attempt to *summarize* how effective various elements of the program were. Grades, certificates, and final reports are examples of this approach.

Formative evaluations, on the other hand, can be conducted at various points in the educational process. Because the purpose is not to make an assessment of value but to suggest ways of *improving* the educational process, such evaluations are usually done while the program is in progress. Assessments of student needs and supervisory assistance to teachers are two examples of formative evaluation.

A second distinction useful in understanding evaluation involves the focus of the evaluation. Guba and Lincoln (1981) described the difference between focusing on merit or on worth. *Merit* relates to intrinsic qualities of the individual or program such as intelligence, competencies, or facilities. *Worth* refers to extrinsic factors such as the competencies required in a specific training program or the specialized skills of a teacher. *Merit* considerations tend to be long-term concerns, while *worth* pertains to an immediate situation.

Evaluation designs can be predetermined or developmental in nature. The predetermined design concentrates on set objectives and attempts to be as objective as possible in measuring variables. Reports and recommendations are carefully prepared and submitted formally to decision makers. Developmental approaches are flexible and responsive to situations. Evaluators immerse themselves in the evaluation process and frequently adjust information-gathering devices to the emerging needs discovered. Information is shared and discussed with policy makers as well as with others involved in the teaching/learning process in an attempt to involve everyone in the decision process.

Successful evaluations of teaching, therefore, require careful planning. The ultimate goal, improving the teaching/learning transaction, must be the foremost consideration. What are the decisions that need to be made to improve teaching and learning? Who needs to make them? Once this is determined, information essential to making valid decisions can be determined. It is only then that one is in a position to select methods to be used for gathering information.

Frequently such decisions are not as simple as they seem at first glance. Putting one's finger on the precise aspect of the teaching/learning transaction that needs improvement calls for insight into the adult-learning process and the relation of the instructional agent to the learner. As is suggested throughout this book, the interaction of content and situation with the teacher and learner must also be understood. Because measurement is an important aspect of evaluation, the validity, reliability, and efficiency of various methods of gathering information is another important consideration. To use a survey, for example, to try to gather information that can only be appreciated through observation is a waste of time. But similarly, placing responsibility for decisions regarding curricular matters on students or teachers without enabling them to garner the necessary information for making those decisions intelligently is a serious omission by the evaluation designer. Good evaluators are constantly searching for feedback on their designs so that they can make appropriate decisions essential to good evaluation of teaching.

Why Evaluate?

Educational philosophers from Plato to Freire have been insisting that teaching is not a neutral process; it leads either to the liberation or to the control of men and women. Not all educators want to accept such a philosophy of education for it is disturbing to constantly ask oneself whether one's teaching is helping or hindering people. It is much simpler to accept teaching as a helping pro-

fession and presume that everything done in education's name is for the good of society. Regardless of a person's stance on the neutrality of education, it is impossible to label the teaching/learning process as anything less than one of the loftiest enterprises open to a human being. Efforts to improve the process through evaluation should automatically be of interest to all teachers.

However, evaluation takes time and effort. Adult learners and their teachers are often goal directed. Time is valuable, and the temptation is to dedicate it all to the teaching/learning process rather than "waste" any of it on evaluation. Thus, it may be valuable to review the literature of adult education to see how authors in the field have proven that evaluation will enable teachers to improve their teaching. That seems to be the reason given most often for evaluating instructional activities. A review of literature (Draves, 1984; Grotelueschen, Gooler, & Knox, 1976; Knappes, Geiss, Pascal, & Shore, 1977; Luke, 1971; R. I. Miller, 1972; Verduin et al., 1977) identified the following reasons as the most important for evaluating teaching:

1. *Improve the instruction.* Most writers indicated that improving instruction is the most important reason for evaluating teaching. The most effective method for this is *formative* evaluation, which involves data collected continuously throughout the learning experience for the purpose of improving the teaching/learning transaction. These data are used to see if the learners are progressing well or if changes in the instructional strategies are needed. If no other reasons are indicated for evaluating, this one alone is sufficient to justify the expenditures of time, energy, and finances needed for quality evaluation. Adult students

deserve the best teaching that can be offered, and formative evaluation can help determine when and how to improve strategies.

2. *Promote individual growth and self-evaluation.* Self-evaluation was deemed important by various authors, and some written forms were even recommended for this purpose. Teachers as well as students in adult education have the opportunity to learn. Because adults will usually let a teacher know when progress is not occurring, teachers can learn about teaching by constantly assessing the reactions of their students to their teaching strategies. Absences, nonresponsiveness in class, glares or looks of puzzlement, and poor performance are all indicators that changes may be needed. Teachers can also learn much about life in general from the experiences of their students and can use this knowledge when appropriate to foster learning by others.

3. *Assess the degree of demonstrable achievement attained by the teacher.* The evaluation used for this purpose is often called *summative* and involves obtaining information at the end of the learning activity by means of one or more methods to be discussed later in this chapter. Summative evaluation may be more formal in nature, and these data, often collected annually in the case of full-time teachers, can be used to compare achievement, or lack of it, during any specific period of time. The data are often used in a *performance appraisal review* conducted by or with the teacher's supervisor. Areas of strength should be indicated, and areas needing improvement should be presented in a supportive

manner with specific recommendations about how to achieve such improvements.

4. *Diagnose future learning needs.* All professionals must strive to keep up with the latest developments in their fields of endeavor. Teachers of adults are no different. With increasing research in learning styles, the teacher should determine if further study is needed in that area. Any further learning that would enhance one's teaching ability or use of strategies should be a must. Teachers of adults should perceive themselves as lifelong learners just like their students.

5. *Enhance one's own sense of merit or worth.* The learning environment is a good place for both teachers and learners to improve their self-concepts. Each positive experience or comment about their teaching can be accepted graciously but also as a challenge to do even better. Results from a positive learning experience can boost learners' feelings about work, peer relationships, ability to perform well, and the value of education. Discovering both that they can learn and learn how to learn, as evaluations may show, can do much for their self-concepts.

6. *Identify and/or clarify desired behaviors.* To develop acceptable performance standards, desired behaviors must be attained and reinforced, while undesirable behaviors must be minimized or eliminated. For example, what kinds of behaviors do good teachers exhibit? The writings of several authors (Draves, 1984; Eble, 1976; Fellenz, Conti, & Seaman, 1982; Good, Biddle, & Brophy, 1975; Grotelueschen et al., 1976; R. I. Miller,

1972; Verduin et al., 1977) suggest that good teachers exhibit the following behaviors:

☐ Encourage students to become active in their learning efforts

☐ Motivate students to learn

☐ Encourage discussion of points of view other than their own

☐ Be knowledgeable in the subject being taught

☐ Be well prepared to facilitate learning

☐ Be well organized

☐ Be enthusiastic, dynamic, and energetic

☐ Be committed to teaching as a career

☐ Have interactive styles of presentation

☐ Explain clearly, often repeating important material

Although all readers may not agree with all of these characteristics, evaluation of a number of good teachers can provide standards or benchmarks for future comparison. Even though the ideal teacher may be impossible to identify, certain desirable characteristics can be determined. However, one must be aware that "Most researchers argue that effective teaching is situation-specific. The acts of teaching . . . and learning are influenced by a myriad of factors which seldom interact in precisely the same way at different times or in different settings" (Grotelueschen et al., 1976, p. 207).

Evaluation of Teaching

In keeping with the theme of this book, this section will examine methods for evaluating the four major elements of the teaching/learning interaction, that is, the learner, the teacher, the content, and the situation.

Several techniques will be proposed for evaluating each of these elements. However, it is not the technique itself but how it is used that makes it useful or nonuseful in evaluating the teaching of adults. Methods are but tools to gather information that can help decision makers improve the instructional process.

Evaluation of the Adult Learner

Passages on the evaluation of the learner usually start with discussions of test construction and grading practices. In adult education they frequently center on satisfaction indices or certification practices. These are valuable evaluation techniques, but they are usually used in a summative manner, that is, applied after the teaching transaction has been completed in order to assess how good a job has been done. When discussing the improvement of teaching, it is more productive to begin with formative approaches such as assessment of learning styles, learner needs or interests, or learner self-evaluation. Thus, this section will examine several formative evaluation strategies before turning to summative approaches.

Assessment of Learning Needs. Assessing the needs of adult learners has been a dictum so broadly advocated in adult education circles that its universal practice is presumed. This presumption, like many others, is dangerous to make.

One of us once took a Conversational Spanish class with a dozen other adults, many of whom were friends or neighbors. The teacher had excellent skills in teaching Spanish; however, at the end of the first class, I made a bet with the person next to me that less than one-half of the class would continue to the end of the eight-week course. In spite of the fact that another five people joined the group in the following weeks, there were only six people present for the last class. Why? From listening to fellow students, I knew that some had a very good grasp of the Spanish language and were seeking an opportunity to brush up their skills before taking a trip to a Spanish speaking country. Others knew not a single word of Spanish. Moreover, some had had poor training in language arts and could not differentiate between nouns and verbs. Rather than assess needs, the teacher began with the first page of the book and never realized why most of the students left before the end of the course.

Need assessments can be done in many ways. Learners can be asked about their needs and interests orally or through some written assessment, or they can be led to demonstrate their abilities. Because adults may be reluctant to admit their weaknesses to a stranger at first encounter, experienced teachers often seek to establish rapport with the learners and give them some initial learning success before entering into any formal needs assessment. However, formal tests, informal or teacher-made assessments, interviews, observations, problem-posing strategies, and surveys of various kinds all can be profitably used to gain insight into the needs and interests of adult learners.

Because techniques for assessing the needs of adult learners have been treated extensively in the literature of the field, they will not be examined in depth here. There are several sources on the specific treatment of needs assessment. Malcolm Knowles's suggestions in *The Modern Practice of Adult Education* (1970) have been followed for decades, while Stephen Brookfield (1986) provides updated insights in *Understanding and Facilitating Adult Learning*. Alan Knox in *Helping Adults Learn* (1987) raises some excellent questions about the feasibility of evaluations and offers practical suggestions for conducting program assessments. Others

such as Beatty (1981) and Sork (1986) have tried to get adult educators to examine philosophical bases for the use of need assessments.

Identification of Learning Styles. The same drive to individualize instruction for adults that promoted the use of traditional needs assessment techniques more recently has led to interest in evaluating the learning style of individuals. Teachers of adults, especially ones working in basic education programs, have long advocated the value of discovering how the student learns most effectively. In some cases such information has enabled people who have had trouble coping with formal learning environments to become enthusiastic nontraditional learners. Such successes have led others to wonder whether adapting learning environments to learning styles might help many adults to be more efficient learners. Developments in cognitive psychology and brain science have encouraged further studies in learning style.

Keefe (1982) defines learning style as "cognitive, affective, and physiological traits that serve as relatively stable indicators of how learners perceive, interact with, and respond to the learning environment." This may be a broader approach to defining style than some prefer, but it does allow for a holistic approach to the discussion of individual learning traits. Cognitive aspects include such characteristics as perceptual or sensory modality strengths, field dependence/independence, hemisphere dominance, perceptual techniques, and information-processing habits. Although it is not always clear to what degree these traits are inherited or learned, research is clearly establishing that they do affect how well adults learn under various circumstances (Hoffer, 1986). Affective traits are more difficult to characterize but include such preferences as desire for structure in the learning environment, interaction with teachers or peer learners, autonomy in one's learning, and approaches to dealing with content as well as subject matter to be studied. Such preferences are not easily distinguished from physiological traits such as time of day and environmental factors, which appear to affect learning efficiency. The important fact is that all seem to influence how effectively adults learn.

While learning styles do influence how adults learn, it is not easy to tell teachers how learning styles should influence their teaching. Attempts to match students with certain learning style characteristics with teachers of similar characteristics have not always resulted in improved learning. Perhaps this is because we have not yet clearly identified all the important learning style traits; perhaps it is due to faulty methods of measurement or teaching. However, it does seem that knowledge of learning characteristics and guidance from an instructional leader on how to use this information can help students take a more effective approach to their own learning (Belisle, 1987). Thus, assessment of learning styles can be important to an informative evaluation of a teaching/learning situation.

There is no single, comprehensive instrument for the measurement of learning style. The following are offered as means for gaining insight into various learning style traits. The Embedded Figures Test (Witkin et al., 1954) has been used extensively, both in its individual and group forms, to identify the extent to which an individual is field dependent or independent. This provides insight into the global or analytic style the individual uses in information processing. Anthony Gregorc's (1979) Style Delineator and David Kolb's (1976) Learning Style Inventory examine information processing according to the degree of abstract versus concrete processing in which the individual engages. The Canfield Learning Styles Inventory (Canfield, 1977) has been used to assess preferences for learning. Dunn, Dunn, and Price (1979) have provided a similar measurement of affective traits of adults in their Productivity Environmental Preference Scale. Instruments developed for different purposes such as the Myers-Briggs Type Indicator (Myers, 1962) and Rotter's I/E Scale (Rotter, 1954) also have been used to gain insight into individual learning differences. However, Hoffer (1986) has been one of the few to use actual learning activities to assess style differences and their affect on adult learning.

Teacher Observation of Learners. Many consider teacher observation of learner progress such an integral part of teaching that they never think of it as part of an evaluation system. However, identifying it as an element in the formative evaluation process has the advantage of giving such observation formal status and, hopefully, formalizing such observation. This may seem insignificant to some, but the very fact that teachers pause to check their particular manner of observing and recording student progress can lend more power to that process. It might also encourage teachers who pay little attention to the learning events of their adult students to adopt a more learner-centered approach.

Questions similar to the following might be asked to strengthen teacher observations. When checking student work for mistakes, do you try to determine *why* errors were made and not just count the number of inadequate responses? These *whys* can provide excellent feedback on the teaching/learning process. Teaching habits are easily formed, so observers might ask, Am I looking at many elements in the learning process or concentrating on only a few? Adults bring a vast amount of experience and many outside responsibilities to the classroom, and these often affect their learning progress. Sharing observation findings with adult learners is another excellent way of perfecting one's techniques. This can help both the teacher and the learner develop their understanding of the learning process.

Insight into a teacher's observational skills can also be gained from the questions students ask and the type of responses given to student questions. In a recent study of adult learners in Montana's Tribally Controlled Colleges, students repeatedly pointed to teachers' responses to questions as the most significant indicator of the instructor's ability to understand and relate to students. They needed only two or three classes to determine how open the teacher was to their learning needs and how much feedback it was safe to give that teacher.

Learner Self-Evaluation. No other element of evaluation holds as much promise for the improvement of the teaching/learning interaction as does self-evaluation by the adult learner. Done thoughtfully, it can lead to a better understanding of the learning process and of individual learning traits. The better we understand a process, the more likely we are to do a good job at it. Self-evaluation can also help students recognize blocks to their learning, be they physiological, attitudinal, or experiential. Learning impediments that cause much frustration and self-belittling are much easier to accept and diminish once recognized. For those who profess the personal development of the adult learner as the ultimate goal of adult education, self-evaluation should be a most valued tool. The learner doing an insightful job of self-evaluation is a learner well on the way to taking charge of his or her own learning and growth.

The issue is not so much whether to evaluate one's learning as how to do it. Adults are constantly evaluating the learning process. If they find it wanting, they move on to something else. Often they are not sure what was wrong; it just did not seem to be worth their time and effort. Such situations provide excellent opportunities for gaining insight into oneself and the learning process. What an opportunity missed if no teacher ever helps them learn how to evaluate their own learning!

At least four aspects of the teaching/learning transaction can readily be evaluated by the adult learner (Fellenz, 1976). Cognitive psychology (Glass & Holyoak, 1986; McKeachie, Pintrich, Lin, & Smith, 1986) has provided ample evidence that giving *order* to subject matter makes it easier for the learner to remember. The adult who reflects upon a learning interlude and personally puts order into what was learned should have much better use of that knowledge. This relates to a second aspect of cognitive processing that could be strengthened through self-evaluation, namely, *level of processing*. Thinking about content at a level beyond mere acceptance ensures better retention. Thus, simple reflection upon potential use of newly acquired knowledge or its relationship to other information can reinforce learning. Such reflection can also stimulate *motivation* to acquire additional knowledge in related areas. Finally, *process elements* and their impact on learning can also be recognized and affected through an evaluation process. For example, self-evaluation can lead one to see that emotions can color the interpretation given to certain information and result in a more honest judgment of reality.

Figure 6.1 shows a simple form that has been used on several occasions to help adult learners practice their self-evaluation skills. It presents open-ended questions designed to promote learner thinking in the areas discussed previously. Users of the form are encouraged to adapt it to their situations and, when feasible, to spend time discussing with adult learners the processes involved.

The purpose of this form is to assist the adult learner in evaluating the outcome of a learning situation. The questions posed are essential to effective learning.

1. What was the most important thing I learned?

2. Does what I learned relate to something else I know?

3. Where can I apply what I learned?

4. What prevented me from learning more?

5. What else do I want to know about this subject?

Figure 6.1
Aid in Self-Evaluation

There are many other ways to encourage self-evaluation of learning and to promote the development of skills useful in that process. Open-ended questions in group situations initiate discussion of elements of the learning process. "I learn best when . . . " or "Another way this knowledge can be used is . . . " are examples of such discussion starters. The teacher who has developed rapport with adult learners can occasionally open discussions on the learning process with questions such as "What prevented us from learning more tonight?" or "What could I (or you) have done to improve the learning situation?" Although this is not exactly self-evaluation, it does expose learners to methods they could use to evaluate their learning experiences. R. M. Smith (1982) has suggested many ways to

help adults learn how to learn, and such procedures could also be used to facilitate self-evaluation. He suggests, for example, developing and analyzing plans for learning projects, talking to peers about good and bad learning experiences, and writing papers about what one learned about one's own learning.

Summative Evaluation of Adult Learners. Summative evaluation is described by Skager (1978) as "assessing and recording what the learners have accomplished." As such it has many uses, for example, to credential or certify, to justify a program, to announce accomplishments, to provide satisfaction to learners and teachers. However, as with so many aspects of evaluation, summative evaluation of students is laden with negative connotations. Usually it is spoken of in terms of testing and grading—thus raising the spectre of potential failure, at least in the minds of some. Mistakes are highlighted; weaknesses revealed. How much more profitable it would be to conceive of summative evaluations of adult learners as celebrations, that is, as opportunities to recognize the worth of a person or occasion and to do so publicly and with joy. To see summative evaluations of learners as occasions for saying "It is good to be a learner!" would fulfill certifying and crediting functions and instill enthusiasm for lifelong learning. The following sections will discuss some methods for evaluating learner performance, competency, and satisfaction.

Evaluating Learner Performance. Many analysts would suggest that the ultimate evaluation of the teaching/learning transaction lies in improved learner performance. "An individual who undertakes a program of self-improvement is expected, on its completion, to be able to understand and do things that were not possible before" (Houle, 1981, p. 248). This, of course, seems most logical.

The problems arise when discussion turns to methods for measuring improved performance. The difficulty multiplies if we take a holistic approach, for then another of Houle's admonitions must be borne in mind. "The evaluation of a professional's learning must be broader and more significant than the measurement of competence and performance achieved in any single educational program or sequence of programs" (1981, p. 252). At this point in time, the challenge to develop ways to assess improvement in practice is more obvious than methods for doing so.

Two complex issues are involved in the assigning of cause for improved performance. Ability to perform a task is not a positive indication that the task will be carried out in the prescribed manner. Many trained in cardiopulmonary resuscitation (CPR), for example, have confessed that they are not sure they could perform adequately in a life-or-death situation. Similarly, an unmotivated practitioner might not perform according to level of training or ability. Prior experience often has as great an effect on improved performance as does a specific training activity. Distinguishing between the credit due training and the credit due experience is often impossible, as is understanding the reason for not implementing newly learned skills. An important conclusion, therefore, is that assessment of performance will usually manifest much subjectivity. With that in mind various methods of evaluating performance can be noted.

Peer appraisal of performance has been suggested by Houle (1981) as one method for evaluating change in performance. At the same time, it allows one to take a broader look at professional practice as the result of more than a single training event. Such an approach fits the belief that professionals are responsible for the control and advancement of their profession and places content-

knowledgeable people in charge of the assessment. However, competitive environments can destroy peer trust and cooperation. In any case, it is important that standards describing desired performance and a system for gathering data on individual performance be developed in detail and be agreed upon by all. Such systems should be open in the sense that all know how they are being evaluated and what conclusions are being reached. Any system should reflect the way the reward system of the organization actually works and should promote professional cooperation rather than competition.

Another approach to performance appraisal involves the use of an in-house evaluator. This person's role could vary somewhat according to the needs of the organization, but a major responsibility would be the improvement of professional performance. Responsibility for training would extend from the assessment of needs to the evaluation of performance. Such a comprehensive assignment together with involvement in the overall goal of the organization would provide a base for assessing individual performance. Outside experts might also be used for this purpose; however, it would be difficult to envision them doing so except in a very subjective manner. A series of well-planned interviews and observations could lead to insight into change in performance and perceived causes for such change.

Evaluating Learner Competency. It is useful here to distinguish between the crediting, certifying, and selecting functions of summative evaluations of learner competency (Skager, 1978). The teacher or institution enters into a crediting mode when publicly recognizing that an individual has gone through an educational program. It surprises some to realize how valued such certificates of completion are to many adults; as symbols of learning success they can definitely encourage continued learning. Certification provides additional recognition of competency achieved. Such recognition is useful not only to the learner but also to various societal agents such as employers or guardians of the public good. The third function, that of selecting, makes comparisons among learners and notes those who have done very well academically. Grading is the common form of this type of evaluation.

There have been many calls to move from a deficit model to a positive approach in the crediting, certifying, and selecting functions of evaluating adult learner competency. The traditional mode of doing this has been some version of the graduation celebration. Such celebrations have been incorporated into basic education and other programs with great success. Teachers have built classes toward some concluding project, programmers have used media, and agencies have given salary increases to recognize learning accomplishments. If such approaches reduce fear of failure so prevalent in programs that rely on the threat of diplomas withheld or grades of "D" or "F," they might even improve learning. Recent research (Conti & Fellenz, 1986; McKeachie et al., 1986) indicates that student expectancy of success in an academic task is a powerful motivator and frequent predictor of success. Moreover, positive approaches to crediting, certifying, and selecting could give learners a stronger sense of control over academic success—another motivating factor.

Despite these cautions, testing of students, *when done properly,* can be an acceptable measure of the quality of the education they have received. Eble (1976) indicates that the teacher must first determine the answers to these questions: "Why am I testing?", "How am I testing?", and "What results am I getting?" (p. 102). Eble suggests

the use of testing to help motivate students to learn. How? By developing testing procedures that enable students at all levels to succeed. He cites an individual who, as a regular practice, develops some tests on which slow, or lower-level, students will do well. "They need to win once in a while," the teacher rationalizes, and we concur. This concept is crucial in adult basic education, where students have experienced more than their share of failure in the past. Seeing even small progress on a regular basis can be stimulating to adults who have not experienced such success in their lives. McKeachie et al. (1986) use somewhat different logic but agree that testing can be motivational in that, "Tests provide an operational definition of goals that is very compelling for students" (p. 76). Tests help students realize what is important and thus guide their study efforts. If the purpose of testing is motivational and not indicative of "the more common desire to separate sheep from goats, establish the curve, or to get the lazy bastards who never show up for class and don't respond to the teacher's brilliance when they do" (Eble, 1976, p. 103), then testing can be useful in evaluation of teaching.

How one tests, particularly in adult education, is also extremely important. Draves (1984) suggests that there are good practices to follow in testing adults. These include using tests which are not only practical but also cover material that is important for the adult students to know. Roussos and Seaman (1972) stress the importance of informing the adults of *why* they are to be tested and of giving them sample test items so they will become familiar with the wording and marking procedures. Many adults have never used a scoresheet, and they can become apprehensive and confused the first time they see one. Practice tests not only aid in the learning process but also improve an adult's ability to perform realistically on the actual test.

Similar to testing, grading is an object of scorn for many teachers of adults. This is due partly to feelings of inadequacy on the part of teachers; that is, no grade seems to express adequately and reliably what an adult student knows. But it is also due partly to the inadequacy of grading systems in the eyes of many adult learners. Thus, a number of alternative practices have been suggested (Marshall, 1987) and adopted. One frequently used is contract evaluation. The student and instructional leader enter into a simple learning contract that specifies beforehand the objectives, activities, and evaluation procedures to be used in the learning activity. Descriptive records have been used by others to replace letter or numeric grades. Some employers prefer this approach since it gives them better insight into the learning that occurred. One version of this approach simply lists the objectives mastered by the learner. Pass/fail systems and multiple grades are adaptations of the traditional grading system and attempt to remove some of the inadequacy of the single grade by simplifying distinctions among students or supplying a variety of indicators upon which each learner can be rated. Still other approaches attempt to incorporate peer learner or self-evaluation into the grading system.

Evaluating Learner Satisfaction. The adult learner's degree of satisfaction with the learning environment is frequently very important information for the instructional leader. Dissatisfaction not only interferes with the learning process but frequently leads adults to remove themselves from the learning situation. Because dissatisfaction can occur even when progress is being made on course objectives and because adults seldom display their displeasure openly, measures of assessing learner satisfaction can be useful.

A system devised by Kropp and Verner (1957) provides an interesting model for attitude assessment. By listing many of the common evaluative expressions used by participants at the end of meetings or conferences and by having a jury of experienced educators rate each descriptive expression from highly positive to extremely negative, they selected the twenty that best describe the range of satisfaction possible. Attendees simply check the statements on the list that represent their feelings at the end of the meeting, and the leader has a quick but fairly accurate indication of how people feel. It would be simple to put together such a list for local use.

One approach we have used frequently in both formal and informal settings requires a small, blank sheet of paper for each participant. These are distributed at a session midway through a series with the encouragement to "say something about how the course is going—either positive or negative." Usually, there is much cooperation as the small size of the paper (three by five or four by six inches) seldom inhibits participation, and the open-ended approach invites expressions of feelings on issues important to the learners that may never have occurred to instructors.

Feedback, of course, can also be gained through nonwritten means. Interviews with selected participants or the use of advisory committee members to sample participant satisfaction have identified sources of positive and negative feelings. Training staff to record both favorable and nonfavorable comments—anonymously—can also provide input.

Evaluation of the Teacher of Adults

As already indicated, educational decisions to be made should determine the emphasis given to any aspect of an evaluation system.

Decisions regarding teaching can vary from what is good teaching and what type of teaching style is most effective in a particular environment to how effective a teaching job a person did on a specific teaching task or what training needs a particular staff has. Similarly, the basic stance taken in an evaluation of teaching can be formative (How can the on-going teaching process be improved?) or summative (What measurement of teaching effectiveness is being sought?) Each variation influences the appropriateness of the source from which information is best obtained and the effectiveness of the method for gathering such data. These distinctions should influence the selection of strategies for the evaluation of teachers of adults.

Identification of Teaching Style. Just as understanding student learning styles can help those involved in the teaching/learning transaction design more effective strategies for learning, so can an understanding of the elements involved in good teaching assist in instructional design. But what is it that makes a teacher great? Certainly knowledge of the topic being taught and of effective strategies for designing learning activities are vital, but these vary with the situation. Flanders (1970) has suggested that the most important element is the relationship between teacher and learner. His famous interaction scale to assess teacher/student interaction is based on this premise. Much of the literature on the teaching of adults advocates an approach that treats the adult learner as an adult, not a child. Learners are to be recognized as mature, independent individuals with specific needs and interests and with many other responsibilities in life. Thus, a learner-centered style is the suggested approach.

A recently developed approach to the identification and assessment of elements involved in teaching *style* and to the evaluation

of the effect that such traits have on student learning has been led by Conti. "Style," he writes, "is a pervasive quality that persists even though the content that is being taught may change" (1985, p. 7). In his Principles of Adult Learning Scale (PALS), he incorporates elements of the learner-centered approach to teaching, which has been advocated as more effective when working with adults. PALS has been used to assess the effect of teaching style on the learning ability of many different adult audiences. Conti's conclusion is, "As with several previous studies, teaching style as measured with PALS does make a difference in student achievement" (p. 53).

Teacher Self-Evaluation. Most teachers of adults do some kind of self-assessment, perhaps on a haphazard yet continuous basis. All teachers think about what they are doing at least some of the time. However, systematic, planned self-evaluation is rare and as R. I. Miller (1972) indicates, "Some contend that teacher self-evaluation is a waste of time—an excessive introspection when the emphasis should be external, on the student. Furthermore, they contend that any use of such ratings in performance evaluation will show the results upward" (p. 35).

Nevertheless, the use of self-evaluation in adult education has been encouraged in the literature, and several ways of conducting such evaluation have been suggested. Robinson (1979) advocates "habitual but unorganized introspection," which means simply stopping for a time and examining mentally the final outcome of one's teaching. Too often teachers plod along doing the same things they have always done before without considering whether they might be harming students rather than helping them. Robinson also suggests that the teacher develop a list of questions to guide this type of evaluation. Dutton and Seaman (1975) support that suggestion and offer the following questions for the teacher's use in that regard:

1. Have the adults shown any change of interest in their participation?

2. Have they contributed to class activities through asking questions or making pertinent comments during class discussions?

3. Do the adults ask for assistance when needed, or do they hesitate to "bother" the teacher? (p. 266)

Answers to questions like these should help teachers assess how well they are assisting their students in their learning endeavors. They should also foster change, if warranted, in the teacher's activities or teaching strategies. In this way, self-evaluation becomes a process of formative evaluation, which should result in the improvement of the class, workshop, training, or whatever method is used to promote learning.

As Dutton and Seaman (1975) have indicated, different kinds of forms or checklists for the use of teachers or facilitators can be developed. The one illustrated in Figure 6.2 is simple to use, but the questions are very important for teachers of adults. A "yes-no" response produces only minimal data, but it should at least stimulate them to consider their performance and how they can improve. Modifications of this instrument, self-rating scales, or other types of written self-appraisal sheets can be utilized effectively by the truly concerned facilitator of adult learning.

Another way for teachers to evaluate their teaching is by examining student records. Data recorded about participation can be helpful to the teacher. For example, did student attendance decrease during the course? Did any patterns of leaving or absences emerge? Did attendance or participa-

tion patterns vary by age, gender, ethnicity, or other factors? Were there other signs of interest or discouragement during the sessions?

Videotape is also useful for teacher self-assessment. Centra (1979) indicates that video equipment is being used more readily in teacher self-assessment, although many teachers still view it as disruptive or threatening. They are more likely to use the video playback when it can be viewed privately, with nobody to assess their behaviors and actions. However, Centra indicates that, "a change in teaching behavior is much more likely when a peer or teaching counselor analyzes or 'focuses' the playback" (p. 55). Viewing the videotape with someone who understands what to look for in good teacher performance gives the teacher some data for comparison. In any case, the playback should be used in a nonthreatening manner.

Student Evaluation of Teachers. Both oral and written evaluations by students can be meaningful and helpful for improving teacher effectiveness. As Johnson (1976) indicates:

> It is often the individual student who knows best whether or not he is learning. It is the student who knows best when he cannot understand or already knows what is being discussed. It is the student who knows a course is stimulating him to learn more about a subject or whether it is boring him to death. It is the student who can best formulate those fundamental and personal questions so bothering him that he cannot proceed to other academic matters. It is the student who can best evaluate when he is beginning to integrate the process of learning with the problems he continually confronts in life (pp. 289–290).

Almost all of the learning in which adults engage is related to some problem, issue, or need they face in life. Therefore, the adult learner can judge whether the teacher or

Do you:

1. Know the names of your students?
   _____ Yes   _____ No
2. Arrive at class early?
   _____ Yes   _____ No
3. Dress neatly for each class?
   _____ Yes   _____ No
4. Smile and project a warm and inviting atmosphere?
   _____ Yes   _____ No
5. Speak clearly and distinctly?
   _____ Yes   _____ No
6. Keep your classroom neat and attractive?
   _____ Yes   _____ No
7. Prepare a lesson plan for each class?
   _____ Yes   _____ No
8. Know something about the background of each student?
   _____ Yes   _____ No
9. Speak clearly and slowly so that all can understand?
   _____ Yes   _____ No
10. Feel that you project that learning is exciting?
    _____ Yes   _____ No
11. Spend some time in the room after class so that the adult students may pursue matters that are not clear to them?
    _____ Yes   _____ No
12. Use many different techniques in your teaching procedure?
    _____ Yes   _____ No
13. Use various teaching aids and devices?
    _____ Yes   _____ No
14. Treat your students as adults?
    _____ Yes   _____ No
15. Encourage three-way communication— teacher-student, student-teacher, and student-student?
    _____ Yes   _____ No
16. Talk to your students instead of to the blackboard?
    _____ Yes   _____ No
17. Admit it if you do not know the answer to a question but promise to search for it before the next session?
    _____ Yes   _____ No
18. Praise the adults when they make progress, no matter how small?
    _____ Yes   _____ No
19. Make every effort to make the classroom as physically comfortable as possible?
    _____ Yes   _____ No
20. Involve the adult students in determining their needs?
    _____ Yes   _____ No
21. Involve the adult students in planning learning experiences that will meet their needs?
    _____ Yes   _____ No
22. Inquire as to why students are absent?
    _____ Yes   _____ No
23. Follow up absentees?
    _____ Yes   _____ No
24. Know why students have dropped out?
    _____ Yes   _____ No
25. Use a wide variety of relevant materials rather than depending on a basic textbook for instructional purposes?
    _____ Yes   _____ No

Figure 6.2
Teacher's Self-Appraisal (Reprinted with permission from Klevins Publications.)

learning facilitator is being a help or a hindrance in the learning activity. Since adults are often voluntary consumers of learning activities (whether they pay *fees* is irrelevant since they pay in terms of time, energy, effort, and convenience), they can evaluate the worth of the activity from their points of view and from their immediate needs and corresponding costs.

Obtaining evaluations from adult students does not require elaborate end-of-class instruments or sophisticated questionnaires. Simple forms will do. Regardless of whether the teacher seeks formative input for improvement during the learning activity or summative information at the end of the activity, student feedback is important. Examples of forms for both purposes are shown in Figures 6.3 and 6.4. They are relatively simple in construction and easy to administer. The teacher can encourage objective input by requesting that no names be put on the questionnaire and can even have one of the class members summarize the responses and report only the summarizations to the teacher. To carry this one step further, the

Figure 6.3
Class Mid-Point Evaluation Form

MID-POINT EVALUATION

In regard to this course:

1. Are your learning objectives being met?

    _____ yes   _____ no   _____ somewhat

    If no, or somewhat, please indicate what changes can be made to better meet your objectives.

    _____

    _____

    _____

2. Is the instructor following the stated or agreed-upon objectives as you understand them?

    _____ yes   _____ no   _____ somewhat

    If no, or somewhat, please indicate which objectives are not being followed or met.

    _____

    _____

    _____

3. To this point in time, what are the strengths of the class?

    _____

    _____

    _____

4. Also, what are the weaknesses of the class?

    _____

    _____

    _____

WORKSHOP EVALUATION

Rate 1 to 5 with 1 being highly positive and 5 highly negative. Add any comments you might wish beneath the questions.

1. Would you recommend this workshop to someone who works in adult literacy or a related field?   1 2 3 4 5

2. Do you feel better prepared to work in adult literacy from your experiences in this workshop?   1 2 3 4 5

3. Was there adequate opportunity for participation as a workshop participation?   1 2 3 4 5

4. Were the workshop objectives followed adequately?   1 2 3 4 5

5. Were the teaching methods varied enough to maintain motivation?   1 2 3 4 5

6. Were the mannerisms and teaching style of the leaders and presenters conducive to learning?   1 2 3 4 5

7. Have you benefited from the shared experiences of other workshop participants?   1 2 3 4 5

8. Which discussion or presentation did you enjoy or benefit from the most (if any) and why?   1 2 3 4 5

9. Which class presentation or discussion did you least enjoy or benefit from (if any) and why?   1 2 3 4 5

Figure 6.4
Workshop Evaluation Form

class or group can conduct an oral summary if deemed appropriate, and one student can report this summary to the teacher or leader. The teacher must believe that a few assertive students will not have undue influence over the others before this kind of evaluation will be effective.

Oral conversations with mature students before or after class or during a break can often provide important feedback about how students feel about the course. Indirect questions to elicit general impressions or feelings may be appropriate to ascertain if changes are needed. However, with special groups such as adult basic education classes, certain precautions should be taken as Grotelues-

chen et al. (1976) suggest. Traditional procedures will not work with students who have low levels of education because of their poor reading abilities. Some students who do not understand the nature of adult education fear they may be asked to leave the program if they report negative reactions about the teacher. In addition, those who see adult basic education as their last chance to improve their lives and their social or economic status are reluctant to say or do anything which may threaten the existence of the classes or their opportunity to participate.

Student input into teacher evaluation is important, but the data must be obtained objectively and carefully. The students must feel that their feedback will be considered or used in some way, and they must not feel threatened in any way for their input. It is always advisable to balance student input with information obtained in other ways.

Peer Evaluation and Professional Growth. One way that teachers of adults may be helped to improve their instructional strategies is for a colleague to observe them in their regular activities during a learning process that has several sessions or meetings. By observing at different times one can avoid biasing the results when the teacher's strategy or the content of the lesson had special significance for the observer or it was an unusual day for teacher, learners, or observer. A review of selected literature indicates that the use of observation in evaluating a teacher should include the following aspects:

1. An observation sheet, which guides the observer in the recording activities, must be developed and used carefully. It should be easy to follow and not so complicated or difficult that the observer has no time to observe and record information other than that found on the observation sheet. There is considerable variety in instruments used for this purpose. Simon and Boyer (1970) identified seventy-nine different observation systems (including guides or tally sheets) used mostly in public schools; some could be adapted for adult education learning activities. However, Grotelueschen et al. (1976) point out that, "Many classroom observation techniques are very complicated to use and interpret. As a result, few of them are used by teachers" (p. 217). They also caution, "In simplifying any technique, there is a danger that its

crucial elements might be misused" (p. 217), and they offer for consideration the Classroom Observation Technique (see Figure 6.5) for use by adult education teachers. Even though considerable time and effort may be required, observation and feedback to teachers can be useful in their struggles to make their teaching more effective and meaningful.

2. Observers must be trained in the process of evaluating teaching through observation, and they must be aware of important criteria to be considered. Some writers suggest that simply asking a colleague to sit in on an activity and then give some suggestions is sufficient. However, without proper training, many errors in judgment could be made, and the observer's perceptions about what is important may differ from those of the person being observed. "Care must be taken that the observer does not screen the teacher's performance too much through his own selective perceptions of what constitutes good teaching" (R. I. Miller, 1972, p. 31). One way to train observers is to select or identify several people who will assume this role, have them evaluate a teacher's performance in a group by means of videotape, and let them share their scoring with each other under the guidance of a trained leader. This process should be repeated until group members attain acceptable, consistent score-ratings on the same instrument they will be using in their observation activities. Then they are ready to observe and evaluate teaching. Of course, feedback to the teacher should be immediate or as soon as possible after the observation is completed.

CLASSROOM OBSERVATION TECHNIQUE

Teacher _____   Observer _____

Length of period or lesson _____   Date _____

| | Frequency of Occurrence | | | |
Category	Period/ Lesson 1	Period/ Lesson 2	Period/ Lesson 3	Period/ Lesson 4
Information Dispensing				
1. Lecturing	_____	_____	_____	_____
2. Reading from text	_____	_____	_____	_____
3. Conversation	_____	_____	_____	_____
Teacher Questions: To Whom?				
4. Individual	_____	_____	_____	_____
5. Group	_____	_____	_____	_____
Teacher Questions: What Kind?				
6. Recognition	_____	_____	_____	_____
7. Meaning	_____	_____	_____	_____
8. Application	_____	_____	_____	_____
9. Evaluation	_____	_____	_____	_____
Teacher Responses				
10. Supportive	_____	_____	_____	_____
11. Nonsupportive	_____	_____	_____	_____

Figure 6.5
Classroom Observation Technique (Reprinted with permission
from the Interstate Printers and Publishers, Inc.)

3. The observation notations should be made within a specified time period. These notations range from three-second intervals to thirty-minute (or longer) intervals. Although there is not much agreement in regard to the best time period, both the observer and the teacher should be in agreement about the time frame selected for a specific observation.

Peer input into professional evaluation and growth, however, should not stop with classroom visitation. Both Houle (1981) and R. M. Smith (1982) have made us more aware that much professional learning and growth occur in collaborative, practice situations. Professionals working together and providing feedback to one another on performance and on topics of mutual interest are a natural evaluation system, for this is a most effective way of improving educational decisions. Whether such interaction occurs in formal staff meetings or structured retreats or whether it grows out of mutual concern and takes place during coffee breaks or informal brainstorming sessions, it fits well the definition of evaluation as "the gathering of information for the purpose of making better educational decisions." (See beginning of this chapter.)

Supervision and Staff Development. The evaluation of teaching by people in supervisory positions is complicated by the fact that such personnel often have a voice in the retention and promotion of the teacher. This can be such a serious impediment to open and honest evaluation and continued development of the teacher that generally suggested practice calls for the separation of supervisory duties from those of staff development—even to the extent that they *not* be done by the same person. Theoretically, however, many of the same strategies that can be used in a formative sense to discover training needs of teachers can also be used in a summative manner to grade a teacher's performance.

Observation is the typical strategy used in supervisory evaluation. Much of what was said earlier about peer observation and evaluation of teachers applies also to supervisory evaluation. Because of the implied relationship of manager to practitioner, it is especially important that the teacher and supervisor meet beforehand to clarify what aspects of teaching will be under close scrutiny. The teacher should know exactly

what to expect, and the supervisor should look for strengths as well as areas in need of development. After the planned classroom observation has occurred, the meeting of the people involved should balance an analysis of what was observed with planning for the instructor's future development. Fulfillment of staff development duties implies consensus on needs for training, mutual setting of goals, and supervisory input on resources suited to future development as well as strategies and support for their use.

The supervisor is often in a strong position to promote other strategies for teacher evaluation that will lead to staff development. For example, the person in charge of development can set an atmosphere conducive to self-evaluation and peer evaluation strategies already mentioned. Materials supportive of such strategies, positive attitudes toward development, and support for further training are important in promoting such an atmosphere.

Evaluating Teaching by Its Results. The evaluation of teachers by measuring the progress of their students is definitely a controversial issue at any level of education, but especially in adult education. For example, in a number of situations achievement scores on some standardized test have been used to justify or extol one teacher or a certain program over others without any consideration of other variables such as entry level of students. Similarly, some have used academic credentials or grade point average as the measure of success even though such measures do not correlate with stated program goals such as student development or professional training. Yet testing of results by one means or another is used, and teachers are often judged by such criteria. One reason is the concept of accountability described by Grotelueschen et al. (1976) as follows:

> Accountability has become a critical issue in teacher education; some have advanced the

notion that accountability means teachers will be held responsible for what learners under their direction do or do not learn. Teacher evaluations are then seen as attempts by administrators to gather information about the extent to which learners learned and, by extrapolation, how well teachers taught. (p. 228)

Clark (1979) feels that student achievement is a fundamental indicator of teacher performance. However, he also cautions, "Teacher evaluation through student achievement testing seems to be straightforward, but in close examination of its theoretical and practical implications several problems appear which must be resolved before it can be used in instructional assessment" (p. 93). Authors such as Grotelueschen et al. (1976) support this by explaining:

Two problems present themselves in this conception of accountability: the selection of measures or indicators used to determine what one has learned and the difficulty of attributing what someone learns to a particular source. (p. 227)

Therefore, while the evaluating of teaching by its results may be a laudable goal, special care must be given to such assessment practices. The question of what outcome measure will be used is vital. Measuring teaching according to standards that were not the actual goals of the teachers or the learners makes the whole process invalid. Unreliable results are obtained when attributing total responsibility to teaching without controlling for other variables. Doing so in a haphazard way simply to justify a teaching approach or program destroys all significance of the evaluation.

Evaluation of the Teaching Situation

Because the situation in which the teaching/learning transaction occurs can have a tremendous impact on the effectiveness of the instruction, situational factors should not be ignored in evaluation systems. The sponsoring organization with its philosophy, public image, support for the program, and policies and procedures has perhaps the most significant positive or negative affect on teaching. However, the physical facilities, social environment, and support materials are other important situational factors. Often overlooked are the influence on teaching of the supporting staff, recruitment and follow-up procedures, and the timing of course offerings. Admittedly, many of these factors are under the control of administrators or programmers rather than instructors. Nevertheless, they are of concern to the effective teacher, and when they begin to affect instruction, the professional educator does whatever is necessary to alleviate their negative impact or to utilize their potential aid.

Several of the strategies described earlier in this chapter can also be used to evaluate situational factors. For example, evaluations of learner satisfaction with instruction can readily uncover attitudes toward situational factors—provided that the approach used is broad enough to include such elements. Peer evaluations of teaching allow opportunities to take a holistic look at the instructional situation. Described next are a few specific strategies for evaluating the teaching situation.

Evaluating the Sponsoring Organization. A distinctive trait of adult education is the fact that many, perhaps even the majority, of the instructional offerings are supported by agencies whose primary purpose is other than education. It is not surprising then that the philosophy and goals of the organization can at times be at odds with good instructional practice. Businesses, correctional institutions, churches, and military posts, for example, may logically place a higher priority on profit, security, dogma, or loyalty than on learning. But then schools and colleges may act similarly, prizing public image and reputation above learning. The dilemma is obvious. As an employee, the teacher is expected to be supportive of the goals of the organization; however, as an instructional leader, the teacher's professional duty is to build effective learning environments.

Instructional leaders have used advisory committees to recognize and deal with the effect that the organization is having on the instructional program. This approach is especially useful if the members of the committee are indeed representative of the instructional clientele and if they are adept at communicating with those holding power within the organization. The role of the evaluator here would be to pose appropriate questions for the consideration of the committee and to assist in the gathering of appropriate information. In other situations an educator might be able to use the model of the *quality circle* to accomplish this purpose. This approach calls for involving small groups of program participants in discussion of the educational program for the purpose of improving teaching and learning. For this strategy to be effective, leaders within the organization must make apparent their approval of such an approach.

The outside evaluator or evaluation team is another approach to assessing the impact of the organization on teaching. The role of the instructional leader in this case is to convince organizational leadership that evaluation is important and then to work with the outside evaluator to establish goals and procedures for the evaluation and effective ways of reporting findings.

Evaluating the Physical Environment. Those who have worked with adults in noncaptive learning situations have long known that the physical setting of the learning activity can have a great influence on who attends a program. Today, increased thought is being

given to how physical factors actually influence the amount of learning that occurs in a particular situation. Weinstein (1979) listed specific variables such as room size, acoustics, lighting, heating, crowding, and privacy, which researchers believe determine the amount of learning that occurs. Adult educators have often mentioned others such as seating arrangements and comfortable furniture, formality or informality of the setting, and clues that speak of schooling rather than learning. With the advent of computer-assisted instruction, more and more attention has been given to the *ergonomics* of the learning situation, that is, how well the physical setting is suited to the learning task. However, Weinstein (1979) also reminds us that it is important to look beyond individual variables to the *ecology* of the learning situation. How natural a setting for learning is this? How is the total situation perceived by the learner?

Granted that such physical factors can contribute to or interfere with the learning task, how do instructors acquire appropriate information about such environmental factors? Two considerations might guide their choice. Many of the physical factors mentioned affect individuals differently, and it is easier to measure their effect on satisfaction than on achievement. Thoughtfully designed interviews or surveys of the learners themselves are appropriate in this situation. In addition, the advice of outside experts can be helpful. Architects, instructional designers, and experienced adult educators could make insightful evaluations of the learning setting.

Evaluating Material Resources. Formerly, evaluation of material resources was based almost exclusively on the accuracy of the content and the clarity of presentation in such resources. Educators working with adults have frequently added one other consideration: Are the materials adult oriented or do they appear to have been designed for children? With the advance of cognitive science, however, we are beginning to see that the types of materials used in the learning situation can significantly determine the level of information processing or manner in which the brain stores the new knowledge (Chang, Crombag, vander Drift, & Moonen, 1983). Written instruction tends to present knowledge in an abstract, symbolic form while instructional TV does so in a concrete, episodic manner. Computer-assisted instruction can be used as an expensive way of transmitting knowledge, or it can be used in situations where controlled drill and practice under varying situations is essential to the learning task. We have come to realize that not everyone learns in the same manner; some learn more efficiently when using print materials, but others need audio or tactile-kinesthetic approaches to do so.

Evaluating the Social Environment. Several situational factors can be grouped under this variable. The rapport between teachers and learners, the attitude of learners toward one another, the interaction of support staff with students, and even methods used to recruit and retain learners affect the social environment. When the totality as perceived by participants is threatening, hostile, or negative, both the internal and external processes of learning are impaired. Internally, maintenance of the self becomes more important than growth or learning; externally, physical avoidance of the learning situation becomes the choice of many adults.

Several strategies have been used to assess the social environment. Darkenwald and Valentine (1986) describe the development and testing of the Adult Classroom Environment Scale based on the following dimensions:

Affiliation, defined as student interaction and cohesion; Teacher Support, defined as sen-

sitivity and encouragement; Task Orientation, defined as focus and accomplishment; Personal Goal Attainment, defined as relevance and flexibility; Organization and Clarity, defined simply as organization and clarity; Student Influence, defined as collaborative planning and participation and satisfaction. (p. 78)

Three forms of this scale report *student ideal, teacher real,* and *student real* perceptions of the environment.

Measurement of social interaction or communication patterns have also been used to gain insight into the atmosphere of the learning situation. This is perhaps best accomplished through the use of trained observers, who diagram the communication exchanges within the classroom or among support staff and participants. Shirk (1983) carried this analysis a step further by developing sociographs depicting the learning resources used by adults in self-directed learning activities.

Attendance records can be indicators of difficulties in the social environment. Adults tend to drop out of unpleasant situations rather quickly. Large numbers of such program leavers can indicate a perceived hostile environment or disillusionment with the reality of the program in comparison with expectations. Informal surveys or spot interviews may be sufficient to identify the problem.

Evaluation of the Content Taught

Decisions about content in a teaching/learning transaction are not limited to selecting teaching strategies appropriate to the subject. Exactly what content is to be covered? Appropriate objectives directed to the learners' level of needs are vital if progress and satisfaction are to result from the learning experience. The order in which the various aspects of the subject are presented can also affect the learning process. This is especially true when trying to deal with varied entry levels of knowledge and experience as teachers so frequently must do when working with a group of adults. Finally, the instructional leader must know when the job has been done; there must be some level of mastery or competency that indicates satisfactory completion of the learning task.

Some interesting conclusions are being made today regarding the interaction of what we learn and the strategy by which we learn it. Chang et al. (1983), for example, insist that "Information is always acquired through one activity or another, symbolic or actual, and stored in a form shaped or conditioned by the activity in question" (p. 8). If true, this means that the same information learned in a lecture, in a discussion, or in a laboratory is remembered differently dependent upon the strategy used to learn.

The tremendous advances being made in knowledge today have led others to conclude:

> Why is meaningful organization so important? The answer lies in a superordinate goal: *Students should continue to learn and to use their learning in more effective problem solving for the rest of their lives.* When one takes life-long learning and thinking as a major goal of education, knowledge becomes a means rather than an end, and other formerly implicit goals become more explicit. Surely one of the most important determinants of continued learning is interest in behavior and experience. A course that dulls the students' curiosity and interest must be a failure no matter how solid the content. (McKeachie et al., 1986, p. 1)

Various factors influence the selection of appropriate strategies for teaching content. Expectations of the learners are an important but often forgotten variable. Adults studying history expect lectures from the instructor; they expect demonstrations and lab work in science classes; and they expect interactive

strategies in communications courses. Adult learners also expect teachers to "start at the beginning and take them to the end." The problem in group situations is that the beginning and the end are seldom the same for all adult participants.

But perhaps even more important than expectations are the objectives of the learning situation. While the techniques described in the chapter on presentation strategies may be very effective in lessons aimed at having learners comprehend factual knowledge, they are seldom as effective when trying to teach skills or higher cognitive abilities such as application or synthesis. Bloom's (1956) long accepted taxonomy of educational objectives is still a guide worth keeping in mind when evaluating the level of objectives in any teaching situation.

In addition to learner expectations and instructional objectives, the order in which the content is to be presented must also be considered. Research has not conclusively shown that we always learn in an orderly manner (McKeachie, 1974), but it does seem most logical that a teacher should present concepts in an order that builds one concept upon another until the level of competency or mastery expected in the situation is reached. If expectations are that the participants in the learning activity will continue to improve their knowledge or skill after the learning experience is concluded, then the ground work for continuing education, that is, the attitudes and skills essential to such continued development, must also be laid during the course of instruction.

Five strategies for evaluating content taught will be examined next: subject matter tests, learner participation in the setting of objectives, task or job analyses, the use of subject-matter specialists, and follow-up studies. In some situations other strategies, discussed earlier in this chapter, would also be effective.

Subject Matter Tests. The testing of adult learners has been discussed earlier in this chapter as a strategy for evaluating the teacher. When thus used to gather information about the teacher, a testing strategy usually leads to rather general conclusions; for example, the teacher is doing very well, or the teacher is doing something wrong. When used as a device for gathering information on the teaching of content, a test can provide much more specific insight. However, it is vital that before selecting or constructing a subject matter test, the instructor decide exactly what information is sought regarding the teaching of content.

How well were certain concepts learned or specific processes taught? Much useful information can be obtained by analyzing where most mistakes were made on an examination. However, this presumes two things; first, the test examined accurately the learners' knowledge of vital concepts and processes, and second, the teacher is interested not only in *what* errors were made but also in *why* such errors occurred. A complicating factor is that mature learners will often use their own resources to develop skills or insights in a certain area even though the teacher did not do a good job of teaching. Nevertheless, mistakes on tests are indications that information was not processed and retained. Such information can be useful both for group analysis (Why were so many not able to solve this problem?) and for individual follow-up (Do Jose and Sally not have the prerequisite experience to master this?).

The selection of testing devices to assess the teaching of content implies clarity regarding the type and level of objectives that are to be acquired by the learners. To direct instruction to higher-order cognitive objectives or to the formation of attitudes and then test for factual information provides little information on the attainment of objectives. In

fact, McKeachie et al. (1986) believe such testing can have a negative effect.

> If teachers say that they are concerned about developing skills and strategies for further learning and problem solving and that they hope to help students develop cognitive structures that will form a foundation for continued learning and then give tests that require memory of individual facts, definitions, and isolated information, students will memorize the facts, definitions, and information on which they expect to be tested. In so doing they will use memorization, repetition, and other learning strategies unlikely to be useful for achieving the higher-order cognitive objectives we have proclaimed. (p. 76)

Learner Participation in the Setting of Objectives. Adults frequently approach learning activities with definite learning objectives. Teachers frequently approach teaching assignments with definite instructional objectives. Unless there is an awareness of the potential diversity of objectives and some attempt to reconcile expectations, the teaching/learning interaction can degenerate in frustration. The teacher who is aware of the objectives of learners can adjust preplanned course goals, or individualize instruction, or reach some agreement with group members about content to be taught. When such interaction is impossible, the instructional leader can at least make certain that the description of course content and objectives is clearly stated in publicized information on the course. This is true of informal conference presentations as well as multisession course offerings.

Strategies for gathering information on learner objectives vary greatly according to the instructional setting. Teachers may feel there is little they can do with large groups of participants of varied backgrounds meeting for a single session. In some situations a clear statement of instructional objectives and provision of some personalizing opportunity, such as small-group discussions or a question-and-answer period, are all that can be done. However, a planning committee of representative participants might be brought together beforehand to discuss appropriate instructional objectives. In addition, programs with well-designed evaluation systems might have summative evaluations on file of previous offerings that were similar in nature. Such evaluations could provide insight into objectives of typical participants. Knox (1987) suggests these two approaches as well as four additional strategies for reconciling teacher and learner objectives: the use of (a) learning contracts, (b) subgroup recommendations, (c) presentations of examples of effective performance or course outcomes, and (d) the nominal group technique.

The nominal group approach has advantages in reconciling objectives, for it was designed not only to uncover participants' goals and objectives but also to bring some consensus to a group (Delbecq et al., 1975). This strategy was described earlier in this book as a version of brainstorming. When used as an evaluation strategy to assess learner objectives, the general procedures would be as follows:

1. Participants (and perhaps the teacher) list their objectives individually.

2. Each person rank orders his or her own objectives.

3. The group generates a master list of objectives by allowing members in turn to contribute the top priority from their own lists. If a similar objective is mentioned by another member, all others cross it off their list. This process continues until everyone has had an opportunity to contribute any objective desired for inclusion in the master list.

4. A group discussion occurs in which all participants have an opportunity to clarify, amplify, or combine objectives—provided all members agree.

5. Each participant privately selects the five objectives considered the most important and lists them in rank order.

6. The leader assigns points according to the rankings of the group members and informs the group of the final rankings of the objectives.

Both the instructional leader and the participants are now aware of the goals of all participants and of the total group preference. It becomes a much simpler task for the leader to indicate which objectives will be given greater or lesser emphasis and which objectives will have to be pursued individually by the members who consider them important.

Task or Job Analyses. Especially useful when instruction is directed to job preparation or the performance of a specific exercise is a task analysis approach to the clarification of teaching objectives. This strategy calls for the careful analysis of the actual performance of that exercise or job. This is usually done by a group of trained observers or by using a system such as the Comprehensive Occupational Data Analysis Program (CODAP) developed by the Air Force (Morsh & Archer, 1967). However, a teacher or group of teachers could take this task upon themselves—if they were willing to plan their analysis carefully.

A typical procedure for doing a task analysis is to begin with a general description of the duties or skills that must be performed if the exercise is to be performed adequately. These general duties are then divided into specific tasks involved in actual performance. Although printed material, such as training manuals or curriculum guides, can be helpful in doing this, it is usually advisable to check such job descriptions with people experienced at performing that skill or exercise. When a satisfactory listing of all tasks associated with the job or exercise has been developed, the list can be taken to people in the field, that is, people actually performing the exercise, to have them indicate which tasks they do perform. Additional information regarding the tasks can be picked up, such as relative amount of time spent on the various tasks, importance of that task to the overall job or exercise, or difficulty of learning each task, depending upon the information sought by the teacher or instructional leader. The compilation of results gives a picture of what is actually done in performing that job or exercise.

The idea behind such a task analysis is that the content and skills taught in a class should reflect the content and skills used in the performance of the job or exercise. Proponents of task analysis believe instructors should not waste time teaching content that is not used to do the job. While there is some truth in that, teachers might also look at tasks not frequently performed to determine whether performance would improve if they were done. Perhaps teaching needs to be adjusted to instill positive attitudes toward the use of that task or to provide more effective practice in its use.

Subject Matter Specialist. Each content area has certain principles and processes that are special to that area. Each has a unique vocabulary. People knowledgeable in the area become adept at the use of these principles, processes, and vocabulary; novices in the area have difficulty even identifying them. Thus, subject matter specialists can be useful

in identifying, clarifying, and ordering the content to be taught.

Subject matter specialists can be employed as outside evaluators. As such, they can examine the content being taught and respond to questions such as the following:

1. Is the content being taught accurate, and is the instructional leader up-to-date?

2. What are the essential principles and processes to be emphasized, and what is the best order for their presentation?

3. How can the goals of the teacher and the participants best be reached within the limitations of the program?

4. What are the criterion or mastery levels that should be reached within the confines of this instructional program?

5. What resources are available for the improvement of instruction within this content area?

It is vital, though, that the instructional leader consider the kind of information that would be most useful. Specialists know their area; they do not know the concerns and aspirations of local personnel. Unplanned use of specialists can be a waste of time and money.

The insights of specialists can also be garnered from the literature of the content area. Therefore, another approach to the evaluation of content taught involves the formation of a curriculum committee to search the literature for insights into teaching in that area. Curriculum guides, texts, and instructional manuals are sources for such information. In place of committees formally appointed by some administrator, groups of teachers can voluntarily gather together as curriculum assessors. In this way they add their own expertise as teachers to that of the subject matter specialists.

Follow-Up Studies. Contact with former students can be beneficial in numerous ways, but the information that such studies provide about the manner in which the content was taught can be especially significant. Former students can now view course content and teaching from the perspective of adults who have tried to put that learning into practice. They have also moved away from the immediate relationship of teacher/student to an independent stance from which they may supply more objective opinions. Details about presentation of the content may have escaped them, but they can reflect upon major issues relating to the teaching experience.

Strategies for getting the information from former students can vary from comprehensive surveys to informal interviews, depending on the purpose of the evaluation and the resources available. However, accepted principles regarding valid and reliable means of gathering information should be observed. In general this means that the survey instrument or interview schedule will be clear, unambiguous, and directed to the purpose of the evaluation. The students questioned will be a representative sample who have experienced the teaching under consideration and who are not selected in a prejudiced manner. Anonymity of response usually relieves much of the pressure to respond in a socially acceptable manner, but some acknowledgment of participants' contributions to program improvement builds good public relations. Finally, the manner in which the information is compiled and analyzed must be impartial and directed toward the goals of the evaluation.

Long-range planning of follow-up studies makes it possible to do things in conjunction with a teaching interlude that make such

evaluations even more productive. Knox (1987) emphasizes that program participants could be encouraged to formulate the objectives they hope to implement as a result of their learning experience and leave them with the teacher. Some time later the teacher would follow up to discover the degree to which such objectives have been implemented and the relative strength or limitations of the instruction in this regard. Similar activities could be preplanned by enterprising teachers. However, if any type of follow-up studies are to occur, someone in the organization must have the foresight to develop a record system that will expedite the contacting of former students. The development of a mailing list or telephone directory after students have left a learning situation is difficult.

Reporting Evaluation Findings

Evaluation of teaching is the gathering of information that will assist in the making of decisions that will lead to the improvement of the teaching/learning transaction. Because the selection of appropriate teaching strategies is dependent upon learner, teacher, situational, and content factors, information regarding these four areas is important in adopting effective instructional strategies. Such information can be gathered in a number of ways, as suggested in earlier sections of this chapter. The purpose of the evaluation and the specific aspect of the teaching/learning transaction to be examined guide the selection of the specific evaluation strategy to be used.

Evaluations, however, are not simply the collection of relevant information. No evaluation is complete until the data have been analyzed and compiled in such a manner that they can be readily communicated to the decision maker(s). In some evaluations this will be a very simple task; the information will practically speak for itself. In other instances, the gathering of appropriate data may be a simple task in comparison to the challenge of interpreting what this information means or compiling it in a manner easily understood by decision makers.

When the teacher or instructional leader is both the director of the evaluation and the decision maker, the process is usually quite simple. The teacher may want to consult with others to confirm that the interpretation given to the evaluation results is accurate or to determine the best way to deal with problems that have been unearthed. However, if the adult learner is the decision maker or a vital partner with the teacher in the effort to improve the teaching/learning transaction, the teacher may need to give considerable thought as to how best to present the information to the learner. A primary concern should always be to check the learner's interpretation of the facts. Was the information gathered correct and was the teacher's interpretation of it accurate? Moreover, the fact that learning is natural to humans does not mean that all adults are adept at all aspects of the learning process. People often need help in clarifying their learning needs, in identifying appropriate resources, in estimating the appropriateness of progress being made, and in various other aspects of the learning process. Self-concepts are often vulnerable in a change situation. Providing evaluative information calling for change is more effectively done by a supportive teacher than by an impersonal, demanding method.

In instances in which the evaluation has concentrated on situational or content aspects of the teaching/learning transaction, the effective decision makers may not be immediately involved in the instructional process. In such cases the evaluator or the instructional leader may need to plan carefully the presentation of the results of the evaluation to the decision makers. The teacher is usually the expert on the teaching situation. No one else is in a position to understand as well the interaction of the teacher, learner, situational, and content factors. But the teacher does not always have the authority to change situational factors and, as a result, may have to educate appropriate decision makers both as to the significance of evaluation findings and as to effective educational approaches. The same may be true of content-related issues, although it is more likely that in such instances the teacher will be approaching subject matter specialists who need the local teaching situation interpreted for them. Again, the way the information gathered through the evaluation strategy is presented to the decision maker will affect the decisions made.

The continued learning of adults is important to the growth of the individual and vital to the well-being of a democracy. The selection of effective strategies for teaching adults enables this process to proceed effectively. But it is the evaluation process that can be the oil that ensures the smooth running of the teaching/learning transaction.

REFERENCES

Apps, J. W. (1978). *Study skills for those adults returning to school.* New York: McGraw-Hill.

Beal, G. M., Bohlen, J. M., & Raudabaugh, J. N. (1962). *Leadership and dynamic group action.* Ames: Iowa State University Press.

Beatty, P. T. (1981). The concept of need: Proposal for a working definition. *Journal of the Community Development Society, 12,* 39–46.

Belisle, M. L. (1987). *The effects of disclosure of learning style, information on learning strategies, and counseling on learning resources on academic achievement and course satisfaction in United States Air Force security police courses.* Unpublished doctoral dissertation, Texas A&M University.

Bergevin, P. E. (1967). *A philosophy for adult education.* New York: Seabury Press.

Bergevin, P. E., & McKinley, J. (1965). *Participation training for adult education.* St. Louis: Bethany Press.

Bergevin, P. E., Morris, D., & Smith, R. (1963). *Adult education procedures: A handbook of tested patterns for effective participation.* New York: Seabury Press.

Bloom, B. (Ed.). (1956). *Taxonomy of educational objectives: The classification of educational goals.* New York: David McKay.

Bormann, E. G. (1975). *Discussion and group methods: Theory and practice* (2nd ed.). New York: Harper and Row.

Boyd, J. (1984). Language and dialogue construction in ESL. *Adult Literacy and Basic Education, 8,* 88–89.

Boyd, R. D., Apps, J. W. (Eds.), & Associates. (1980). *Redefining the discipline of adult education.* San Francisco: Jossey-Bass.

Boyle, P. G. (1980). Adult educators and community analysis. In R. D. Boyd & J. W. Apps (Eds.), *Redefining the discipline of adult education* (pp. 89–98). San Francisco: Jossey-Bass.

Bradford, L. P., Gibb, J. R., & Benne, K. D. (1964). *T-Group theory and laboratory method.* New York: John Wiley and Sons.

Bredemeier, M. E., & Greenblat, C. S. (1981). The educational effectiveness of simulation games. *Simulation and Games, 22*(3), 307–332.

Brilhart, J. K. (1982). *Effective group discussion* (4th ed.). Dubuque, IA: William C. Brown.

Brookfield, S. D. (1984). *Adult learners, adult education, and the community.* New York: Teachers College Press.

Brookfield, S. D. (1986). *Understanding and facilitating adult learning.* San Francisco: Jossey-Bass.

Bruner, J. (1963). *The process of education.* New York: Vintage Books.

Bunyan, J. A., Crimmins, J. C., & Watson, N. K. (1978). *Practical video: The manager's guide to applications.* White Plains, NY: Knowledge Industry Publications.

Bureau of Educational Research and Service. (1972). *Individualized instruction at the college level.* Knoxville, TN: College of Education, University of Tennessee.

Buskey, J. H. (1984). Using technology to enhance learning. In T. J. Sork (Ed.), *Designing and implementing effective workshops* (pp. 69–84). San Francisco: Jossey-Bass.

Cabot, H., & Kahl, J. A. (1953). *Human relations, concept, and cases in concrete social science.* Cambridge: Harvard University Press.

177

Cameron, C. (1982). *The case method as an instructional strategy in adult and continuing education.* Unpublished manuscript.

Campbell, M. D. (1980). Community education for group growth. In R. D. Boyd & J. W. Apps (Eds.), *Redefining the discipline of adult education* (pp. 140–154). San Francisco: Jossey-Bass.

Canfield, A. A. (1977). *Learning styles inventory.* Ann Arbor, MI: Humanics.

Carp, H., Peterson, R., & Roelfs, P. (1974). Adult learning interests and experiences. In K. P. Cross, J. Valley, & Associates (Eds.), *Planning nontraditional programs: An analysis of the issues for post-secondary education* (pp. 11–53). San Francisco: Jossey-Bass.

Carpenter, W. (1967). *Twenty-four group methods and techniques in adult education.* Tallahassee, FL: Adult Education Research Information Processing Center, Florida State University.

Cass, A. (no date). *Basic education for adults.* New York: Association Press.

Cawley, W. V., Miller, S. A., & Milligan, J. N. (1976). Cognitive styles and the adult learner. *Adult Education, 26,* 101–116.

Centra, J. A. (1979). *Determining faculty effectiveness.* San Francisco: Jossey-Bass.

Chamberlain, V., & Kelly, J. (1981). *Creative home economics instruction.* New York: McGraw-Hill.

Chang, T. M., Crombag, H. F., vander Drift, K. D. J. M., & Moonen, J. M. (1983). *Distance learning: On the design of an open university.* Boston: Kluwer-Nijhoff Publishing.

Chartier, M. R. (1981). Facilitating simulation games. In J. E. Jones & S. W. Pfeiffer (Eds.), *The 1981 annual handbook for group facilitators* (pp. 247–258). San Diego: University Associates.

Clark, J. L. D. (1979). Measures of student learning. In J. A. Centra (Ed.), *Determining faculty effectiveness.* San Francisco: Jossey-Bass.

Coggins, C. C. (1980). Individual growth through community problem solving. In R. D. Boyd & J. W. Apps (Eds.), *Redefining the discipline of adult education* (pp. 155–171). San Francisco: Jossey-Bass.

Cohen, R. (1969). Conceptual styles, culture and conflict, and non-verbal tests of intelligence, *American Anthropologist, 7,* 828–856.

Conti, G. J. (1985). Assessing teaching style in adult education: How and why. *Lifelong Learning, 8,* 7–11, 28.

Conti, G. J., & Fellenz, R. A. (1986). Reassessing the Canfield Learning Style Inventory. *Proceedings of the Twenty-Seventh Annual Adult Education Research Conference* (pp. 72–76). Syracuse, NY: Syracuse University.

Conti, G. J., & Fellenz, R. A. (1987). Evaluation: Measurement and discovery. In C. Klevins (Ed.), *Materials and methods in adult and continuing education.* Los Angeles: Klevens Publishing.

Cross, K. P. (1982). *Adults as learners.* San Francisco: Jossey-Bass.

Cross, K. P., Valley, J., & Associates. (1974). *Planning non-traditional programs: An analysis of the issues for post-secondary education.* San Francisco: Jossey-Bass.

Cunningham, J. B. (1984). Assumptions underlying the use of different types of simulations. *Simulation & Games, 15*(2), 213–234.

Darkenwald, G., & Merriam, S. (1982). *Adult education: Foundations of practice.* San Francisco: Jossey-Bass.

Darkenwald, G., & Valentine, T. (1986). Measuring the social environment of adult education classrooms. *Proceedings for the Twenty-Seventh Annual Adult Education Research Conference* (pp. 77–81). Syracuse, NY: Syracuse University.

Delbecq, A. L., Van de Ven, A. H., & Gustafson, D. H. (1975). *Group techniques for program planning.* Glenview, IL: Scott, Foresman.

Dooley, A., & Skinner, W. (no date). *Casing Case Methods* (a monograph from Harvard Business School Series). Cambridge: Harvard University Press.

Draves, W. A. (1984). *How to teach adults.* Manhattan, KS: Learning Resource Network.

Dunn, R. S., Dunn, K. J., & Price, G. E. (1979). Identifying individual learning styles. In J. W. Keefe (Ed.), *Student learning styles: Diagnos-*

ing and prescribing (pp. 39–54). Reston, VA: National Association of Secondary School Principals.

Dutton, M. D., & Seaman, D. F. (1975). Self-evaluation. In C. Klevins (Ed.), *Methods and materials in adult education.* Los Angeles: Klevens.

Eble, K. E. (1976). *The craft of teaching.* San Francisco: Jossey-Bass.

Egan, G. (1970). Encounter: *Group processes for interpersonal growth.* Belmont, CA: Brooks/Cole Publishing.

Fellenz, R. A. (1974). How to teach what you know. In P. Langerman (Ed.), *You can be a successful teacher of adults.* Washington, DC: National Association for Public Continuing Adult Education.

Fellenz, R. A. (1976). Self-evaluation—the student. In C. Klevins (Ed.), *Materials and methods in continuing education.* Los Angeles: Klevens.

Fellenz, R. A., Conti, G. J., & Seaman, D. F. (1982). Evaluate: Students, staff, program. In C. Klevins (Ed.), *Materials and methods in adult and continuing education.* Los Angeles: Klevens.

Flanders, N. A. (1970). *Analyzing teaching behavior.* Reading, MA: Addison Wesley.

Frederick, P. J. (1986). The lively lecture—8 variations. *College Teaching, 34,* 43–50.

Freire, P. (1970). The adult literacy process as cultural action for freedom. *Harvard Educational Review, 40* (2).

Friedman, L., & Knight, D. (1970). *Handbook for teachers of reading in adult basic education.* Jackson, MS: Mississippi State Department of Education.

Gagne, R. M. (1965). *The conditions of learning.* New York: Holt, Rinehart, and Winston.

Gayeski, D. M. (1983). *Corporate and intellectual video: Design and production.* Englewood Cliffs, NJ: Prentice-Hall.

Glass, A. L., & Holyoak, K. J. (1986). *Cognition* (2nd ed.). New York: Random House.

Good, T. L., Biddle, B. J., & Brophy, J. G. (1975).

Teachers make a difference. New York: Holt, Rinehart, and Winston

Gregorc, A. F. (1979). Learning/teaching styles: Potent forces behind them. *Educational Leaderships, 36,* 234–236.

Grotelueschen, A. D., Gooler, D. D., & Knox, A. B. (1976). *Evaluation in adult basic education: How and why.* Danville, IL: Interstate.

Guba, E.G., & Lincoln, Y. S. (1981). *Effective evaluation.* San Francisco: Jossey-Bass.

Guetzkow, H., Schultz, R. L., & Sullivan, E. M. (1972). In Guetzkow, H., Kotler, P., & Schultz, R. L. (Eds.), *Simulation in social and administrative science.* Englewood Cliffs, NJ: Prentice-Hall.

Gulley, H. E. (1968). *Discussion, conference, and group process* (2nd ed.). New York: Holt, Rinehart, and Winston.

Hand, S. E., & Puder, W. (1967). *A preliminary overview of methods and techniques in adult literacy and adult basic education.* Tallahassee, FL: Florida State University.

Harrington, F. H. (1977). *The future of adult education.* San Francisco: Jossey-Bass.

Heinich, R., Molenda, M., & Russell, J. (1982). *Instructional media and the new technologies of instruction.* New York: John Wiley and Sons.

Hensley, B. (1972). *In-service in reading in adult basic education.* Jackson, MS: Mississippi State Department of Education.

Hiemstra, R. (1976). *Lifelong learning.* Lincoln, NE: Professional Educators.

Hoffer, S. M. (1986). *Adult learning styles: Auditory, visual, and tactual-kinesthetic sensory modalities.* Unpublished doctoral dissertation, Texas A&M University, College Station, TX.

Houle, C. O. (1972). *The design of education.* San Francisco: Jossey-Bass.

Houle, C. O. (1981). *Continuing learning in the professions.* San Francisco: Jossey-Bass.

Hyman, R. T. (1978). *Simulation gaming for values education: The prisoner's dilemma.* New Brunswick, NJ: The University Press of America.

Johnson, J. A. (1967). Instruction: From the consumer's view. In C. B. T. Lee (Ed.), *Improving college teaching* (pp. 288–292). Washington, DC: American Council on Education.

Johnstone, J. W. C., & Rivera, R. (1965). *Volunteers for learning*. Chicago, IL: Aldine Press.

Kahler, A. A., Morgan, B., Holmes, G. E., & Bundy, C. E. (1985). *Methods in adult education* (4th ed.). Danville, IL: Interstate.

Keefe, J. W. (1982). *Learning style profile: Examiner's manual*. Reston, VA: National Association of Secondary School Principals.

Kemp, J. E., & Dayton, D. K. (1985). *Planning and producing instructional media*. New York: Harper and Row.

Kidd, J. R. (1973). *How adults learn*. New York: Association Press.

Klevins, C. (Ed.). (1972). *Materials and methods in adult education*. Los Angeles: Klevens.

Knappes, C. K., Geiss, G. L., Pascal, C. E., & Shore, B. M. (1977). *If teaching is important. . . .* Ottawa, Canada: Clarke, Icwin, and Company.

Knowles, M. (Ed.). (1960). *Handbook of adult education in the United States*. Washington, DC: Adult Education Association of the U.S.A.

Knowles, M. (1970). *The modern practice of adult education*. New York: Association Press.

Knowles, M. (1973). *The adult learner: A neglected species*. Houston, TX: Gulf Publishing Company.

Knowles, M. (1975). *Self-directed learning*. New York: Association Press.

Knowles, M. (1980). The growth and development of adult education. In J. Peters (Ed.), *Building an effective adult education enterprise* (pp. 12–40). San Francisco: Jossey-Bass.

Knox, A. B. (1977). *Adult development and learning: A handbook on individual growth and competence in the adult years for education and helping professions*. San Francisco: Jossey-Bass.

Knox, A. B. (1987). *Helping adults learn*. San Francisco: Jossey-Bass.

Kolb, D. A. (1976). *Learning style inventory technical manual*. Boston: McBer and Company.

Kropp, R. B., & Verner, C. (1957). An attitude scale technique for evaluating meetings. *Adult Education, 7* (4).

Legge, D. (1974). The use of the talk in adult classes. In M. D. Stephens & G. W. Roderick (Eds.). *Teaching techniques in adult education*. London: David and Charles.

Lewin, K. (1951). *Field theory in social science*. New York: Harper & Row.

Lorge, D. (1947). *Effective methods in adult education*. (Report of the southern regional workshop for agricultural extension specialists). Raleigh, NC: North Carolina State.

Luce, R. D., & Raiffa, H. (1957). *Games and decisions*. New York: John Wiley and Sons.

Luke, R. A. (1971). *How to train teachers to train adults*. Englewood Cliffs, NJ: Prentice-Hall.

Mager, R. F. (1968). *Developing attitudes towards learning*. Palo Alto, CA: Fearon.

Maier, N. R. F., Solem, A. R., & Maier, A. A. (1975). *The role play technique: A handbook for management and leadership practice*. La Jolla, CA: University Associates.

Maier, N. R. F., & Verser, G. C. (1982). *Psychology in industrial organizations* (5th ed.). Boston: Houghton Mifflin.

Marshall, J. C. (1987). *Student evaluation: Strategies for effective teaching*. Manuscript submitted for publication.

Mattran, K. (1976). *Teaching adults English as a second language*. Atlanta: Avatar Press.

McCullough, K. (1980). Analyzing the evolving structure of adult education. In J. Peters (Ed.), *Building an effective adult education enterprise* (pp. 158–163). San Francisco: Jossey-Bass.

McInnes, J. (1980). *Video in education and training*. New York: Focal Press.

McKeachie, W. J. (1974). Instructional psychology. *Annual Review of Psychology, 25,* 161–193.

McKeachie, W. J., Pintrich, P. R., Lin, Y., & Smith, D. A. F. (1986). *Teaching and learning in the college classroom: A review of the research literature*. Ann Arbor, MI: National Center for Research to Improve Post-Secondary Teaching and Learning, University of Michigan.

Mezirow, J., Darkenwald, G., & Knox, A. (1969).

Last gamble on education. Washington, DC: Adult Education Association of the U.S.A.

Miller, H. L. (1964). *Teaching and learning in adult education.* New York: Macmillan.

Miller, R. I. (1972). *Evaluating faculty performance.* San Francisco: Jossey-Bass.

Mitchell, H., & Corby, L. (1984). Teaching techniques. In D. J. Blackburn (Ed.), *Extension handbook* (pp. 79–92). Guelph, Ontario, Canada: University of Guelph.

Morgan, B., Holmes, G. E., and Bundy, C. E. (1960). *Methods in adult education.* Danville, IL: Interstate.

Morgan, B., Holmes, G. E., and Bundy, C. E. (1963). *Methods in adult education.* Danville, IL: Interstate.

Morgan, B., Holmes, G., & Bundy, C. (1976). *Methods in adult education.* Danville, IL: Interstate.

Morsh, J. W., & Archer, W. B. (1967). Procedural guide for conducting occupational surveys in the United States Air Force (PRI-TR-67-IIM; AD-664-036). Lackland AFB, TX: Personnel Research Laboratory, Aerospace Medical Division.

Myers, I. B. (1962). *Manual: The Meyers-Briggs Type Indicator.* Princeton, NJ: Educational Testing Service.

National Association for Public Continuing Education. (1974). *You can be a successful teacher of adults.* Washington, DC: National Association for Public Continuing Education.

Niemi, J., & Gooler, D. (Eds.). (1987). *Technologies for learning outside the classroom.* San Francisco: Jossey-Bass.

Penland, P. (1979). Self-initiated learning. *Adult Education, 29,* 170–179.

Reiser, R. A., & Gerlach, V. S. (1977). Research on simulation games in education: A critical analysis. *Educational Technology,* December, 13–18.

Renner, P. F. (1983). *The instructor's survival kit.* (2nd ed.). Vancouver: Training Associates Ltd.

Robinson, R. D. (1979). *Helping adults learn and change.* Milwaukee, WI: Omnibook.

Robinson, R. D. (1980). Group transactional mode and community client focus. In R. D. Boyd & J. W. Apps (Eds.), *Redefining the discipline of adult education* (pp. 55–67). San Francisco: Jossey-Bass.

Rotter, J. B. (1954). *Social learning and clinical psychology.* Englewood Cliffs, NJ: Prentice-Hall.

Roussos, P., & Seaman, D. F. (1972). Testing and evaluating in adult basic education. In M. L. Morrison (Ed.), *A handbook for adult basic education* (pp. 145–148). Montgomery, AL: Alabama State Department of Education.

Schultz, R. L., & Sullivan, E. M. (1972). Development in simulation in social and administrative science. In H. Guetzkow, P. Kotler, & R. L. Schultz (Eds.), *Simulation in social and administrative science* (pp. 3–47). Englewood Cliffs, NJ: Prentice-Hall.

Seaman, D. F. (1977). *Adult education teaching techniques.* Columbus, OH: Clearinghouse on Career Education.

Shaw, M. E., Corsini, R., Blake, R. R., & Mouton, J. S. (1980). *Role playing: A practical manual for group facilitators.* San Diego, CA: University Associates.

Shirk, J. C. (1983). *Relevance attributed to urban public libraries by adult learners: A case study and content analysis of eighty-one interviews.* Unpublished doctoral dissertation, Texas A&M University, College Station, TX.

Simon, A., & Boyer, E. G. (1970). *Mirrors for behavior.* Philadelphia: Classroom Interaction Newsletter.

Skager, R. (1978). *Lifelong education and evaluation practice.* New York: UNESCO Institute for Education.

Smith, E. (1970). *Literacy education for adolescents and adults.* San Francisco: Boyd and Fraser.

Smith, R., Aker, G., & Kidd, R. (Eds.). (1970). *Handbook of adult education.* New York: Macmillan.

Smith, R. M. (1982). *Learning how to learn.* Chicago: Follet.

Snyder, R. (1971). *Decision-making in the planning and implementation of instruction in adult basic education.* Tallahassee, FL: Adult Education Research Information Processing Center, Florida State University.

Snyder, R. (1972). *Guide to teaching techniques in adult education.* Englewood Cliffs, NJ: Prentice-Hall.

Sork, T. J. (1986). Yellow brick road or great dismal swamp: Pathways to objectives in program planning. *Proceedings for the Twenty-Seventh Annual Adult Education Research Conference* (pp. 261–266). Syracuse, NY: Syracuse University.

Stephens, M. D., & Roderick, G. W. (1974). *Teaching techniques in adult education.* London: David and Charles.

Takemoto, P. A. (1987). Exploring the educational potential of audio. In J. A. Niemi & D. D. Gooler (Eds.), *Technologies for learning outside the classroom* (pp. 19–28). San Francisco: Jossey-Bass.

Tough, A. (1971). *The adult's learning projects: A fresh approach to theory and practice in adult learning.* Toronto, Canada: Ontario Institute for Studies in Education.

Tough, A. (1978a). *The adult learner: Current issues in higher education.* Washington, DC: American Association for Higher Education.

Tough, A. (1978b). Major learning efforts: Recent research and future directions. *Adult Education, 28* (4), 250–265.

U.S. Department of Education. (1986). *Participation in adult education.* Washington, DC: Center for Statistics, Office of Educational Research and Improvement.

Udvari, S. (1972). Insights into the nature of the culturally unique. In C. Klevins (Ed.), *Materials and methods in adult education* (pp. 103–118). Los Angeles: Klevens.

Ulmer, C. (1972). *Teaching the disadvantaged adult.* Washington, DC: National Association for Public Continuing Adult Education.

Verduin, J. R., Jr., Miller, H. G., & Greer, C. C. (1977). *Adults teaching adults.* Austin, TX: Learning Concepts.

Verner, C. (1962). *A conceptual scheme for the identification and classification of processes.* Washington, DC: Adult Education Association of the U.S.A.

Verner, C., & Dickenson, G. (1967). The lecture: An analysis and review of research. *Adult Education, 17* (2), 85–100.

Wagner, R. H., & Arnold, C. C. (1965). *Handbook of group discussion.* Boston: Houghton Mifflin.

Weinstein, C. S. (1979). The physical environment of the school: A review of the research. *Review of Educational Research, 49* (4), 577–610.

Wiesner, P. (1987). Utilizing television. In J. A. Niemi & D. D. Gooler (Eds.), *Technologies for learning outside the classroom* (pp. 9–18). San Francisco: Jossey-Bass.

Witkin, H. A., Lewis, H. B., Hertzman, M., Machover, K., Meissner, P. B., & Wapner, S. (1954). *Personality through perception.* New York: Harper and Brothers.

Worthen, B. R., & Sanders, J. R. (1973). *Educational evaluation: Theory and practice.* Worthington, OH: C. A. Jones Publishing Company.

Wright, J. W. (1980). Community learning: A frontier for adult education. In R. D. Boyd & J. W. Apps (Eds.), *Redefining the discipline of adult education* (pp. 99–125). San Francisco: Jossey-Bass.

Zoll, A. A. (1969). *Dynamic management education* (2nd ed.). Reading, MS: Addison-Wesley.

SUBJECT INDEX